Dust Inside

DUST INSIDE

Fighting and Living with Asbestos-Related Disasters in Brazil

Agata Mazzeo

berghahn
NEW YORK • OXFORD
www.berghahnbooks.com

First published in 2021 by
Berghahn Books
www.berghahnbooks.com

Library of Congress Cataloging-in-Publication Data

Names: Mazzeo, Agata, author.
Title: Dust inside : fighting and living with asbestos-related disasters in Brazil / Agata Mazzeo.
Description: New York : Berghahn Books, 2021. | Includes bibliographical references and index.
Identifiers: LCCN 2020026202 (print) | LCCN 2020026203 (ebook) | ISBN 9781789209310 (hardback) | ISBN 9781789209327 (ebook)
Subjects: LCSH: Asbestos industry—Health aspects—Brazil. | Asbestos—Health aspects—Brazil. | Asbestosis—Brazil.
Classification: LCC HD9585.A66 B74 2021 (print) | LCC HD9585.A66 (ebook) | DDC 363.17—dc23
LC record available at https://lccn.loc.gov/2020026202
LC ebook record available at https://lccn.loc.gov/2020026203

British Library Cataloguing in Publication Data

A catalogue record for this book is available from the British Library

ISBN 978-1-78920-931-0 hardback
ISBN 978-1-78920-932-7 ebook

For my parents Bettina and Salvatore Mazzeo

For Mariuccia

Contents

List of Illustrations viii
Acknowledgements ix
Note on Translation xii
List of Abbreviations xiii

Introduction My Path into the Dust 1
Chapter 1 The Toxic Market of Asbestos and Global Health Disasters 26
Chapter 2 Osasco: City, Work and Struggles 49
Chapter 3 Suffering and Embodied Disasters 74
Chapter 4 The Politics of Anti-asbestos Activism 107
Chapter 5 Engaging Global Health, Anti-asbestos Activism and Ethnography 135
Conclusion 157

Glossary 162
References 163
Index 181

Illustrations

1.1 Map of the Eternit plant in Osasco (demolished in 1993), drawn by a study participant. Osasco, São Paulo, Brazil, 2015. 37

2.1 City seal drawn in a graffiti. Osasco, São Paulo, Brazil, 2015. 51

3.1 Absence–presence of an anti-asbestos activist who died of lung cancer in 2013. Osasco, São Paulo, Brazil, 2015. 79

3.2 Absence–presence of an anti-asbestos activist who died of malignant mesothelioma in 2009. Osasco, São Paulo, Brazil, 2015. 83

3.3 Eternit plant in Rio de Janeiro, Brazil, 2015. 85

3.4 Aquilino dos Santos – Vítima do Amianto [Asbestos Victim] Square. Osasco, São Paulo, Brazil, 2015. 103

4.1 Membership cards of anti-asbestos activists. Osasco, São Paulo, Brazil, 2015. 117

5.1 Osasco, São Paulo, Brazil, 2015. 155

Acknowledgements

> *Talvez seja uma das experiências humanas e animais mais importantes. A de pedir socorro e, por pura bondade e compreensão de outro o socorro ser dado. Talvez valha a pena ter nascido para que um dia mudamente se implore e mudamente se receba.*
>
> [Perhaps it is one of the most important human and animal experiences. That of asking for help and, just because of simple goodness and understanding of the other, the help is given. Perhaps it is worth being born just for a day silently imploring and silently receiving.]
>
> —Clarice Lispector, *A Descoberta do Mundo*

This book has been written through months of solitary work, and I am the only person responsible for its contents and any limitations in its results. However, I would never have been able to design, carry out and conclude the research that this book is based on without the anti-asbestos activists I met across Italy and Brazil. Over the years, my encounters with them have marked my private and academic life. Their struggle provides a constant inspiration for me; from them I have learnt a lot, especially the importance of not giving up on something you believe in, despite the numerous problems you may have to face on the path towards your objective.

Also, this book would never have been finished without the love of those who are crucial presences in my life – my family and friends. Their encouragement and support have been essential during the most difficult moments of writing under the pressures and duties of a precarious occupational life conducted inside and outside academia.

I thank the Associação Brasileira dos Expostos ao Amianto (ABREA) [Brazilian Association of Persons Exposed to Asbestos] in Osasco, São Paulo, Brazil. This book is rooted in the stories of the lives, suffering and activism of its members. I thank all the men and women who participated in my study and welcomed me with patience, smiles and kindness. I am grateful to them for having shared with me a piece of their struggle, conducted on a daily basis with dignity, passion, commitment and dedication.

I thank the current ABREA president, Mr Eliezer João de Souza, and Ms Fernanda Giannasi for introducing me to the field and for exchanging opinions and conversations with me that were fundamental for my understanding of the anti-asbestos movement in Brazil.

I do not mention the names of the majority of my interlocutors in the field, nor their affiliations, in order to safeguard their anonymity. However, I wish to thank all the Brazilian professionals, researchers, anti-asbestos activists and members of non-governmental organizations who welcomed me in São Paulo (Osasco, São Caetano, Santo André), Rio de Janeiro (Cabo Frio, Rio de Janeiro), Goiás (Goiânia), Bahia (Salvador, Simões Filho, Poções, Bom Jesus da Serra), Paraná (Londrina) and Santa Catarina (Florianópolis).

I am grateful to the professionals and activists from the public health institutions, associations and trade unions operating in Osasco, São Paulo and Rio de Janeiro. They helped me to situate anti-asbestos activism in the local and national contexts.

In Italy, I thank the Associazione Familiari e Vittime Amianto (AFeVA) [Asbestos Victims and Relatives Association] in Bari and Casale Monferrato. My engagement with the study of the suffering and activism experiences related to the tragedies provoked by the global market of asbestos began with my encounter with their members. I am also grateful to the AFeVA Emilia Romagna (based in Bologna) for its support in disseminating my research findings, and for the enthusiasm with which its members have welcomed me in setting up new projects together based on ethnographic research on the local anti-asbestos mobilization.

In the international context of the movement for the global prohibition of asbestos, I thank the Asbestos Disease Awareness Organization (ADAO) in the United States, and the International Ban Asbestos Secretariat (IBAS) in the United Kingdom.

I thank all the researchers who have helped me to further my understanding of asbestos-related suffering and activism with their insights. Among them, particular thanks go to Benedetto Terracini, Arthur Frank, Pietro Comba, Daniela Marsili, Roberto Pasetto, Eduardo Algranti, Hermano Albuquerque de Castro, Vilma Santana, Ubiratan de Paula Santos, Jefferson Benedito Pires de Freitas, Vanda D'Acri, Cyro Haddad Novello and Juan Pablo Ramos-Bonilla.

I thank the professors and colleagues from the universities of Bologna, São Paulo and Amsterdam, where I studied and nurtured my passion for medical anthropology. In particular, I thank Ivo Quaranta (University of Bologna) for his precious advice and supervision from the beginning of my study on asbestos-related experiences of suffering and activism; Rubens de Camargo Ferreira Adorno (University of São Paulo) for his advice and interest in my research in Brazil; and Cristiana Natali (University of Bologna) for her encouragement.

A special thank you is addressed to Stuart Blume (Emeritus Professor, University of Amsterdam) for his mentorship. Without his wise advice, sense of humour, encouragement and trust I would probably never even have conceived of, let alone written, this book.

I thank my Brazilian friends for their emotional and practical support during my fieldwork, and for their insightful opinions on Brazilian literature, music, history and politics, all of which enriched my understanding of the field.

I also thank the women who have encouraged me and filled my life with love, grace and daily examples of strength; they are always with me despite the distances and irreversible losses: my grandmother Agata, my mother Bettina, my sister Raffaella, my niece Giorgia, and my friends Elisabetta, Julia, Marta, Silvia, Silke, Selma, Nuria, Noemi, Ilaria, Maria, Suzanne, Paola, Miriam, Loredana, Alice, Claudia and Arianna. Moreover, my research gave me the precious gift of the friendship of two women who dedicated their efforts and energy to the struggle for an asbestos-free world: Romana Blasotti Pavesi and Maria Ottone (Mariuccia), both from Casale Monferrato (Italy).

I thank Stefano/Noise for enriching my life with love, smiles and music. Together we are learning to take care of each other – and that is a wonderful journey.

Last, but not least, I thank my parents for their unconditional love and support. Knowing that I could always count on them has been an irreplaceable source of strength for me.

This book is dedicated to the memory of my mother, who, in the hardest moments of our lives, silently taught me the beauty of life, the preciousness of friendship and the magic of care.

Bologna, February 2020

Note on Translation

All translations from Portuguese and Italian are by the author.

Abbreviations

ABREA	Associação Brasileira dos Expostos ao Amianto [Brazilian Association of Persons Exposed to Asbestos]
AC	Asbestos-Cement
ACP(s)	Asbestos-Containing Products
ADAO	Asbestos Disease Awareness Organization
ADI	Ações Diretas de Incostitucionalidade [Direct Actions of Unconstitutionality]
AFeVA	Associazione Familiari e Vittime Amianto [Asbestos Victims and Relatives Association]
AIEA	Associazione Italiana Esposti Amianto [Italian Association of Persons Exposed to Asbestos]
ANPT	Associação Nacional dos Procuradores do Trabalho [National Association of Labour Attorneys]
AR	Asbestos-Related
ARCE	Associação Recreativa dos Colaboradores Eternit [Recreational Association of Eternit Collaborators]
ARD(s)	Asbestos-Related Disease(s)
BEC(s)	Base Ecclesial Communities
CEREST	Centro de Referência em Saúde do Trabalhador [Reference Centre for Occupational Health]
CGT	Confederação Geral do Trabalho [General Labour Confederation]

CNTI	Confederação Nacional dos Trabalhadores na Indústria [National Confederation of Industrial Workers]
CUT	Central Única dos Trabalhadores [General Confederation of Workers]
DNPM	Departamento Nacional de Produção Mineral [National Department of Mineral Production]
FIOCRUZ	Fundação Oswaldo Cruz [Oswaldo Cruz Foundation]
FUNDACENTRO	Fundação Jorge Duprat Figueiredo de Segurança e Medicina do Trabalho [Jorge Duprat Figueiredo Foundation of Safety and Occupational Health]
GIETEA	Grupo Interinstitucional de Estudo de Trabalhadores Expostos ao Asbesto [Inter-institutional Study Group of Asbestos-Exposed Workers]
IARC	International Agency for Research on Cancer
IBAS	International Ban Asbestos Secretariat
IBGE	Instituto Brasileiro de Geografia e Estatística [Brazilian Institute of Geography and Statistics]
ISS	Istituto Superiore di Sanità [Superior Health Institute]
LT	Liberation Theology
MM	Malignant Mesothelioma
MPT	Ministério Público do Trabalho [Public Ministry of Labour]
NGO	Non-Governmental Organization
PT	Partido dos Trabalhadores [Workers' Party]
SAIAC	Societé Associé d'Industries Amianteciment [Associated Society of Asbestos-Cement Industries]
STF	Supremo Tribunal Federal [Federal Supreme Court]
TACS	Termos de Ajustamento de Conduta [Agreements of Conduct Adjustments]
WHO	World Health Organization

Introduction

My Path into the Dust

May 2009, early one afternoon. Outside, a blue sky, a fresh breeze from the sea, and warm light embracing everything. I am in Bari in Southern Italy, my home town.

I am sitting at a kitchen table, having a conversation. The woman I am talking to is Angela, diagnosed four years earlier with malignant mesothelioma (MM), the cancer provoked by the inhalation of the carcinogenic fibres of asbestos minerals. She developed MM following environmental exposure to asbestos while living near an asbestos-cement factory in Bari.

As one lung was removed in the attempt to treat her cancer surgically, Angela can only breathe with an oxygen tank. Her face is swollen owing to the side effects of chemotherapy. Several pauses interrupt our conversation. Physical pain makes speaking difficult for her. More than once, I tell her that we can stop whenever she wants. She replies that it is fine. She says that she wants to tell her story and that she just needs time and patience, as she can only speak slowly....

Angela died a few months later, in October 2009, aged 55.

This book is based on ethnographic fieldwork conducted in Osasco (São Paulo, Brazil), where I researched local experiences of asbestos-related (AR) disasters and health-based grassroots activism. However, the journey that led me in Osasco in 2014 began in Italy, and more precisely in my home town, Bari, in 2009. Angela was the first person with MM that I ever talked to.

Between then and my fieldwork in Brazil, I conducted research with people with MM, their relatives, exposed men and women with a diagnosis of other asbestos-related diseases (ARDs) affecting their respiratory system and thus living with the risk of developing MM, in Bari and two other Italian locations: Casale Monferrato, in Piedmont, and Bologna, where I now live.

Indignation and passion are the two feelings that triggered and continue to motivate my decision to explore from an anthropological perspective the processes of AR disasters, and how they are contested by communities living and working in contaminated sites. The first time I felt indignation in relation to AR disasters and their impact on public health was in 2009. Watching a journalistic inquiry into the scale of asbestos contamination in Italy, I perceived the silence regarding a large, contaminated and, by that time, highly polluting site – the former 'Fibronit site' in Bari – as an unjust lack of recognition of an important issue affecting the lives of a number of my fellow citizens, who, in the programme's narration, simply did not exist. As a citizen of Bari, I knew about the presence of an abandoned factory where asbestos had been processed for decades, and which had provoked diseases and deaths among workers and residents living nearby. However, my knowledge was vague and my understanding of the health dangers of asbestos was very low. It is only through my intellectual and ethical engagement in the anthropological study of AR disasters that I have developed the awareness of my own condition of being an environmentally exposed citizen who had grown up in a neighbourhood bordering the so-called 'red zone' of the former 'Fibronit site' (Musti et al. 2009).

Watching the journalistic inquiry, I felt a sudden need to know more about an issue that I was starting to consider as something personal, even though at that time I had no direct involvement in the suffering related to asbestos exposure. Only later would I painfully experience the sorrow of losing a relative to MM provoked by domestic exposure to asbestos.

The indignation I felt then combined with the passion that the classes I was taking as a graduate anthropology student at the University of Bologna were nurturing in me in relation to medical anthropology and the anthropological consideration of the body in socio-cultural, political and economic processes. Therefore, thanks to the positive response I received from the Associazione Familiari e Vittime Amianto (AFeVA) [Asbestos Victims and Relatives Association], a non-governmental organization (NGO) founded in Bari by sufferers from ARDs, I started walking my own personal 'path into the dust' – a journey that, after Bari, led me to Casale Monferrato, a town of 35,000 inhabitants in the Piedmont region.

In Casale Monferrato the largest asbestos-cement (AC) plant owned by the Eternit firm in Italy had been in operation for eighty years, from 1907 to 1986 (Altopiedi 2011). Starting from the early 1980s, the increasing number of people in Casale Monferrato diagnosed with, and dying from, ARDs triggered a workers' and civil mobilization that led to the promulgation in 1987 of the first law prohibiting asbestos-containing products (ACPs) in Italy (Mossano 2010). Over the years, the anti-asbestos movement in Casale Monferrato has reached other important achievements with an impact at local, national and international level. Among their achievements, there is the organization of the first trial – the so-called 'Eternit trial' – of an AC corporation accused of environmental disaster manslaughter. In 2009, more than 2,800 injured parties, including individuals, NGOs and public institutions (Rossi 2012: 19), brought the Eternit corporation to trial. Although in the end the Italian Supreme Court did not uphold the decision of the lower courts, the 'Eternit trial' became a strategy replicated by others in countries affected by the health effects of the toxic market of asbestos, such as Brazil (see Altopiedi 2011; Rossi 2012; Altopiedi and Panelli 2012; Allen and Kazan-Allen 2012).[1]

The significance of the narratives presented and discussed in this book can only be grasped if we situate them within the historical processes and the socio-economic dynamics at play in the global context in which we all act our roles. Understanding the connections between local practices and transnational processes presented a theoretical and methodological challenge that I navigated by following the trajectories connecting Italy and Brazil – and, in particular, Casale Monferrato and Osasco. The connections linking the AR grassroots activism and disaster processes in Casale Monferrato and Osasco led me to choose the latter, a city in the state of São Paulo, as the third context of a 'multi-sited ethnography' (Marcus 1995), which began in Italy in 2009. The first connection concerns the history of the Brazilian city and the Italian migratory flow towards Latin America in the nineteenth century. According to the official historiography, the founder of Osasco was Antonio Agù, who had emigrated to Brazil from Osasco in Piedmont (hence the name of the Brazilian municipality) at the end of the nineteenth century. The Italian emigrant, who left from a rural village situated not far from Casale Monferrato, takes on the traits of a legendary character in the historiographical documents emphasizing his promotion of Osasco's capitalistic and urban development (see Collino de Oliveira and Marquetti Rocha Negrelli 1992; Sanazar 2000; Marquetti Rocha Negrelli and Collino de Oliveira 2003). The second connection concerns the global economics of asbestos. Casale Monferrato (Italy) and Osasco (Brazil) had the largest AC Eternit plants in Europe and Latin America respectively. In Osasco the plant owned by the Eternit do Brasil Cimento e Amianto S.A. began production in 1941 and closed in 1993 (Giannasi 2012). Both the plants were eventually demolished, the one in Osasco in 1995 and the one in Casale Monferrato in 2007. In both urban contexts, the impact of the asbestos industry on the health of workers and residents living nearby has been profound (see Magnani et al. 1987; Algranti et al. 2001). Moreover, during the socio-economic crisis affecting post-Second World War Europe, workers who were originally employed at the Eternit plant in Casale Monferrato emigrated to Brazil to work at recently opened AC plants, where a specialized workforce was needed and the chance to earn a decent salary was guaranteed. During my fieldwork, I interviewed a couple of people who had emigrated from Casale Monferrato to Rio de Janeiro in the 1940s, together with their families. A similar phenomenon is illustrative of the management of the workforce and plants based on economic strategies transnationally planned by the multinational firm, thus confirming the intertwined nature of the processes of both the disasters and the grassroots activism in the two countries. With a high number of citizens employed at the local Eternit plants, it is not by chance that in both Casale Monferrato and Osasco exposed workers and citizens initiated a grassroots movement and mobilized anti-asbestos efforts. The two NGOs with whom I conducted research in Casale Monferrato and Osasco are the Associazione Familiari e Vittime Amianto – AFeVA [Asbestos Victims and Relatives Association], and the Associação Brasileira dos Expostos ao Amianto – ABREA [Brazilian Association of Persons Exposed to Asbestos] respectively. The two NGOs are engaged in a constant dialogue, and have supported each other since the early 2000s.

In 2011, in Casale Monferrato on the occasion of an international conference organized through the 'Eternit trial', I made my first contact with the Brazilian anti-asbestos activists who would later introduce me to the field in Osasco. Three years later, on the 19 November 2014, I was in Rome when the Supreme Court pronounced the final verdict at the end of the 'Eternit trial'. I was there with activists I knew from Italy and Brazil, together with other anti-asbestos activists, public health officers, administrators, journalists and lawyers from Japan, the United Kingdom, Switzerland, Belgium, France, Spain, Argentina and the United States. Social actors from various contexts had followed the Italian lawsuit, thanks to the actions promoted by anti-asbestos NGOs, journalists, writers, video-makers and photographers, whose writings and visual documents had been circulating through social networks, blogs, mailing lists and online magazines, thus making the 'Eternit trial' resonate far beyond the local context.

Dr Luciano Lima Leivas, at that time prosecutor at the Brazilian Ministério Publico do Trabalho – MPT [Public Ministry of Labour], together with a delegation of Brazilian anti-asbestos activists in Rome, attended the verdict. Soon afterwards, I talked to Dr Lima Leivas, who commented on the verdict with these words:

> This final sentence was expected to be a pedagogical mark pointing out that asbestos is a well-known carcinogenic substance that has killed and continues to kill many people who are or have been exposed, especially among workers. Although the physical person representing the corporation's leadership responsible for asbestos use in Italy has been acquitted tonight, asbestos was not acquitted. The trial has clearly shown that thousands of people in Italy have died because of asbestos, and the leadership was only acquitted according to an exclusively technical and legal expedient. This is a crucial aspect to be considered and clarified in Brazil: the absolution of Stephan Schmidheiny [an Eternit manager in Casale Monferrato] does not mean the absolution of asbestos.

Asbestos had not been absolved, and such an end to the lawsuit profoundly and painfully marked Italian and international grassroots activism for the global prohibition of such carcinogenic minerals.

I attended the Supreme Court's pronunciation as, at one and the same time, a researcher, a supporter of the anti-asbestos movement, a friend of some of the activists I had met through my research, and an Italian citizen. Surrounded by activists and victims from a number of countries, I could almost physically feel the strength of the global dimension of the toxic market of asbestos and of the grassroots movement organized by those affected by its impact on health. We, the witnesses and the survivors, took the judicial failure to acknowledge an AR disaster in Casale Monferrato as a further act of violence and injustice perpetrated against all of us.

AR health disasters are paradigmatic of the political and economic dynamics in action in our globalized, interconnected world characterized by increasing inequality and double standard management of risk and health hazards (Castleman 1983, 2016). In a similar global context, the above-mentioned connections represented the trajectories that I decided to follow on my personal 'path into the dust' and that made me choose Osasco in Brazil as the third context of my research. In this book, I reflect on the practices by which social actors locally experience, conceive, oppose and divert the transnational trajectories producing global health disasters. In particular, I focus on how these trajectories are diverted and resisted. My main research objective has been to explore a case of health-based activism from an anthropological perspective centred on the bodily experience of disasters and activism.

What motivates a sufferer to become an activist? Which processes and contingencies can favour a person's sociopolitical engagement in a grassroots movement? How does one perform activism in daily life, and what are the meanings attributed to it? To what extent can the practices undertaken by sufferers facing the impact of asbestos contamination on their lives change the sociopolitical and moral context in which they act and live? While I consider AR disasters to be processes occurring beyond national borders, time and geographical distances, I would like to draw attention to the connections linking the practices of anti-asbestos activism occurring in multiple contexts by defining them as part of a transnational movement aimed at the global prohibition of asbestos and at social justice.[2] By following the traces of my personal 'path into the dust' across Italy and into Brazil, this book shows how a global dimension does not characterize just the processes of AR disasters, but also the mobilization of those suffering from those very same processes.

Osasco, Brazil

Osasco is a city of 700,000 inhabitants, bordering the western area of the megalopolis of São Paulo. Osasco was the industrial neighbourhood of São Paulo until 1962, when it became a separate municipality in a referendum promoted by '*os autonomistas*', a political movement advocating administrative and political autonomy from the government of São Paulo (Sanazar 2000). According to the list of the richest Brazilian municipalities published in 2013 by the Instituto Brasileiro de Geografia e Estatística – IBGE [Brazilian Institute of Geography and Statistics], Osasco is the ninth richest district in Brazil.[3] Up until the 1990s, Osasco's economics had been based on the industrial sector; the glorious past of industrial development can still be perceived in the city. Examples include the importance of the metallurgic union in the local sociopolitical context, and personalities such as Antonio Agù celebrated by local historiography, as well as the evidence present in the number of bodies of men and women who have contracted occupational diseases or suffered accidents while working in the numerous factories operating in the city. During my fieldwork this last aspect was particularly visible to me, as the majority of the study participants were involved in or were in contact with NGOs, unions or political parties addressing occupational health issues (e.g. hazards, diseases and injuries).

In Osasco, industrial, economic and demographic development boomed in the 1940s. Thanks to a massive flow of immigration, the population had increased from 15,000 to 41,000 by the end of the 1940s (ACEO 2003/2006). In the same period, large plants including the Eternit do Brasil Cimento e Amianto S.A. and the railway industry Cobrasma were set up there, as well as the Indústria Eléctrica Brown Boveri S.A. and the Indústria de Artefatos de Ferro Cimaf, producing electrical and iron products respectively (ibid.). These plants were located where industrial development had begun a couple of decades earlier with the setting-up of factories dedicated to various sectors of industrial production (e.g. ceramic, textile, automotive and chemical). Furthermore, by the end of the 1950s, when the Brazilian government was encouraging international firms to establish factories in the country, several multinational corporations including Osram and Ford had moved to Osasco (ibid.).

Considering the crucial role of industrial development in Osasco's growth as a municipality, it is not surprising that Osasco is still associated with the words *cidade* (city) and *trabalho* (work) in its official emblem, graphically represented by two cogs and two hammers.

As the industrial sector grew, Osasco became an attractive destination for families looking for better life conditions. It provided an escape from poverty and starvation in the rural and marginal areas of São Paulo State and in the economically depressed regions of Europe and Japan, especially after the Second World War. Together with the influx of foreign capital, people from a variety of cultural and geographical backgrounds arrived in Osasco, where they contributed to a cultural *mistura* (mixture) that still pervades every aspect of Brazilian society. Along with the fervent movement of money and people, ideas, values and religious beliefs were also circulating, and these deeply influenced the city's cultural, political and moral context. In particular, the socio-political relevance of discourses and practices of the trade unions and militant groups active in Osasco during the period of military dictatorship (1964–84) was an important founding background for Brazilian anti-asbestos activism, which started in Osasco in the mid-1990s.

Inspired by the principles and methods of Freire's 'pedagogy of the oppressed' (Freire 1967, 1970, 1980, 2005), Liberation Theology (LT) (Gutiérrez 1972, 2007; Rowland 2007) and the political thought behind the European working-class struggles of the 1960s (Giannotti 2007), militants in Osasco organized actions that represented exceptional cases of overt resistance to the military regime at the time (Bauer 2010). Militants found legitimation in Freire's pedagogy and LT, which promoted the active role of oppressed groups in the world in the development of critical thinking to emancipate themselves from processes of subordination and exploitation. In a similar cultural context, on 17 July 1968, and organized by the metallurgic union (Antunes and Ridenti 2007), the workers in the city's largest factories mobilized after months of 'hard work of social turmoil and hectic political propaganda to denounce bad working conditions, the lowering of wages and the high cost of living' (Bauer 2010). Together with the student movement and the most radical and left-wing currents of a Catholic political movement, *guerrilha* actions were organized in Osasco against the dictatorial regime. These actions were in clear opposition to the populist strategies promoted by the State's union organization (ibid.), whose representatives were considered *pelegos*, a Portuguese adjective to indicate unionists who defend the State and companies' interests instead of workers' rights (Antunes and Ridenti 2007: 81).

The novelty of the strikes in Osasco at the end of 1960s lay in the central role of workers in the resistance at a political, economic and social level. Examples include the management of the political struggle, occupation of factories, taking control of production processes (Bauer 2010) and assiduous campaigns of *conscientização* (the elaboration of critical thinking) (Freire 1980) organized among the population, especially the poor, marginalized and exploited. The military regime's repression was harsh, and included the murder, kidnapping, arbitrary detention or torture of any workers or students who had dared to express dissent to the dictatorship (Bauer 2010).

The practices and strategies of anti-asbestos activism discussed in this book are rooted in Osasco's historical, socio-cultural, political and economic processes and dynamics. In fact, it is from the abovementioned scenario of the hectic movement of bodies, capital, ideas and struggles that the practices and actions of the Brazilian anti-asbestos activism emerged in the mid-1990s. By that time, a group of former workers who had found themselves contaminated with ARD symptoms had founded ABREA and begun to mobilize against the asbestos companies who had never alerted the workers or the local citizens to the dangers of asbestos. The majority of my interlocutors in the field were ABREA members and supporters.

ABREA activists operate in a local and national context that is characterized by increasing and profound inequalities. These socioeconomic inequalities seem to not only be self-reproducing but also functional for a model of accelerated economic growth, with no concern for the devastation it causes in terms of environmental and social disasters. These inequalities mould the practices and processes through which the vulnerable and marginalized groups experience, counteract, claim and negotiate their citizenship. In this regard, Brazilian anti-asbestos activism has opened paths of active and critical citizenship claiming social rights and recognition for invisible disasters – paths that I followed in the company of the anti-asbestos activists I encountered during my fieldwork.

Disasters

According to the most recent registered data, 107,000 women and men die every year because of ARDs (Prüss Ustün et al. 2011); however, an increase is expected in the coming years as 125 million people are still exposed to asbestos in workplaces (WHO 2018). On the basis of similar evidence and the knowledge acquired throughout my decennial research into asbestos-contaminated sites, I refer to the impact of the toxic market of asbestos on local communities of exposed workers and residents in terms of global public health disasters. By using the plural 'disasters', I want to highlight the multiplicity of the impact of asbestos pollution (on the environment, public health and society at large), and the complexity of transnationally intertwined dynamics lived and conceived of through a variety of practices and discourses rooted in the specificity of each sociocultural context where affected individual and collective social actors play their role in various parts of the world.

The decision to talk about the health impact of the asbestos market in terms of disasters stems from anthropological literature on disasters and the trajectory of my personal 'path into the dust'. It was during my fieldwork in Casale Monferrato, Italy, that I began to use the term 'disaster' to define the asbestos-contaminated sites of my fieldwork. In Casale Monferrato, the narratives of my interlocutors pivoted around the disaster as a category to make sense of the effects of exposure to asbestos on their community. I was immersed in an environment where collective and individual suffering were being framed and conceived of in terms of a disaster by the local residents, who had appropriated the narratives emerging from the first trial against a corporation profiting from asbestos and accused of environmental disaster manslaughter, and which the local anti-asbestos NGO was frantically disseminating through awareness campaigns.

From an anthropological perspective, a disaster is a process in which multiple aspects (e.g. cultural, political, economic and social) are at play

(Das 1995; Fortun 2001; Da Silva Camargo 2001, 2010; Ligi 2009, 2011a, 2011b; Benadusi, Brambilla and Riccio 2011). The Italian anthropologist Gianluca Ligi, who researched the impact of the Chernobyl disaster on the Sami populations (2009), referred to the definition of disaster proposed by one of the most influential voices in the anthropological debate about disasters, Oliver-Smith. From this perspective, a disaster 'can be described as a combination of potentially disruptive agents deriving from a technological or natural environment which has an impact on a human community held in a condition of vulnerability that is socially or technologically produced' (Hoffman and Oliver-Smith 2002; also cited in Ligi 2011a: 126). Accordingly, the catastrophic event, such as the visible effects of an earthquake, flood or epidemic, represents just a phase of a complex process that in certain circumstances can be very slow and remain unperceived for decades, while the condition of vulnerability to specific hazards is being determined. I found the above-mentioned definition of disaster to be theoretically and ethically appropriate in analysing the experiences of disaster and the practices of activism in the light of a similar anthropological understanding.

Asbestos-related health and social disasters consist of silent and slow processes that escape recognition in most countries where they continue to occur (Pasetto et al. 2014; Petrillo 2015), and the vulnerability characterizing asbestos-contaminated communities resides in what the anthropologist Linda Waldman calls the 'elusiveness of asbestos' (Waldman 2011: 6), while Braun and Kisting (2006) speak of a 'social production of an invisible epidemic'. Based on research conducted in South Africa (which before asbestos prohibition was among the major asbestos exporters in the world), Braun and Kisting reflect on the invisibility of the epidemic revealed in the onset of ARDs and deaths among workers and residents of an asbestos mining village (Braun and Kisting 2006). In Italy, a team of researchers conducted a qualitative study on the effects of the legal/illegal recovery of railway carriages containing asbestos at the Isochimica plant in Avellino (in the region of Campania, southern Italy), and reflected on the 'silence' surrounding AR disaster processes (Petrillo 2015).

In my analysis, I refer to the impact of the asbestos market on the exposed communities and the environment in terms of 'invisible disasters' (Mazzeo 2017a). The invisibility of AR disasters resides in a variety of processes and elements. Firstly, it is related to the microscopic dimension of asbestos fibres and their invisible nestling in a person's lungs for decades. Moreover, the invisibility of AR disasters resides in the workers' lack of means to recognize a dusty environment as a potential source of fatal danger. Similar ignorance was utilized in specific strategies designed by asbestos lobbies to minimize and deny the health hazards related to asbestos exposure. These efforts have contributed to delays in the perception of AR disasters in numerous and widespread contexts, and extended by decades the suffering of exposed communities hidden by a veil of invisibility. To the above-mentioned dynamics producing the invisibility of AR disasters, I would add the uncertainties about the cause–effect relationship between asbestos exposure and the onset of ARDs, as is supported by certain biomedical discourses, and the lack of epidemiological evidence, especially in those countries where asbestos is still legal (Pasetto et al. 2014; Marsili et al. 2016; Algranti et al. 2019).

Moreover, I situate the invisibility characterizing AR disasters within the processes through which risk categories and scientific knowledge about the effects of asbestos exposure on health are elaborated and communicated. These categories and forms of knowledge are neither objective nor neutral descriptions of the reality (Lupton 1999), but rather represent the results of negotiation processes in which various social actors and forces are involved (cf. Ciccozzi 2013).

Systems of power create their own categories of risk, and approach the situations of danger that they themselves produce by elaborating various definitions and strategies (Douglas, Thompson and Verweij 2003). Throughout the twentieth century, the concept of risk assumed a negative connotation and came to be identified with danger: 'now the word risk means danger, great risk means too much danger' (Douglas and Wildavsky 1982). However, in the past, the concept of risk had a neutral if not positive meaning, and taking a risk could lead to the improvement of a life situation (Boholm 2003). This positive meaning can be found in the etymology of the word 'risk', about whose origins various hypotheses have been advanced. For some scholars, the etymology of risk is the Latin word *risicum*, derived from the ancient Spanish 'rock', referring to a source of danger for ships. Others believe that the etymology can be found in the Greek word *rizicon*, with reference to the concept of destiny. Still other scholars relate the etymology of risk to the Arabic word *rizq*, meaning 'what comes from God', or to the Latin word *resecar* alluding to 'cutting the waves', dangerously and courageously (Ligi 2009: 135–36).

Therefore, in this book, particularly influenced by the contributions of scholars who operate within a global 'risk and anxiety society' (Beck 1992) where 'risk' seems to coincide exclusively with 'danger', the term 'risk' assumes connotations that are mainly negative.

Body

I will discuss anti-asbestos activism from a perspective focused on the centrality of the body in the elaboration of new meanings and practices (Scheper-Hughes and Lock 1987; Csordas 1990; Lock 1993; Quaranta 2012a). This approach requires the consideration of the dynamics that define negotiations and practices by which biomedical knowledge and epidemiological data are elaborated (Good 1994; Kleinman 1980, 1995; Scheper-Hughes 1997; Krieger 2003), and suffering is experienced (Scarry 1985; Kleinman and Kleinman 1991; Kleinman 1997, 1999, 2006, 2009; Quaranta 1999, 2006a, 2006b, 2006c; Pizza 2007; Cappelletto 2009). I will take into account issues related to disease, death, grieving and memory, as they emerged as crucial elements in the observed experiences of the activists' suffering and struggle.

As stated by Hoffman and Oliver-Smith, the heart of the social-anthropological approach to extreme events is that disaster is a phenomenon that occurs at the point of connection between society, technology and the environment, and can be interpreted as an extremely exceptional effect caused by the in-depth interaction of these three elements (Hoffman and Oliver-Smith 2002). However, in anthropology,

> this critical point of connection between society, technology and environment is not studied in an abstract way. For the anthropologist, the critical point suddenly emerges in people's lives – as a fracture, as a singularity in the fabric of the daily experience of those involved – people who, one by one, face to face, he/she meets in the field. (Ligi 2011b: 63–64)

In AR disasters, the 'critical point of connection' primarily concerns and resides in the body of the exposed person. The fracture in the relationship with the surrounding world is lived in the flesh and is provoked by the experience of serious, disabling diseases such as asbestosis and malignant mesothelioma (MM). The latter, as a life-threatening cancer, can on its own represent a catastrophe that destroys 'our sense that we are in control of our fate' (Kleinman 2006: 4).

Anti-asbestos activists from Osasco were living in a context of disaster in which the catastrophic event became manifest in the sick, decaying and dying bodies of those exposed to asbestos.

In the experience of both AR disasters and activism, the body then assumes a crucial role and, at the same time, represents an effective lens through which to interpret the sociocultural and political phenomena considered as sets of bodily practices (Csordas 1990). Starting from this theoretical premise, and adopting a phenomenological approach to the analysis of the dynamics characterizing the global context of the toxic market of asbestos and its effects on public health, I will focus on the experiences of illness, risk and grief related to environmental and occupational exposure to asbestos. I consider these experiences as ones of disasters lived and occurring primarily through the contaminated, suffering and decaying body of the exposed person, which becomes the site of a catastrophic event (Ligi 2011a) and represents the crucial fragment of a scattered disaster.

Experiences of illness (especially those related to a disabling or fatal disease such as MM) impose an awareness that the body can no longer be taken for granted; the body 'is no longer the subject of an unconscious assumption, but becomes the object of a conscious thought' (Good 1999: 191). The suffering body is conscious and, by unveiling hidden wounds, urges action. The afflicted body then becomes a tool of resistance and triggers changes in the sociopolitical context. I draw attention to Frankenberg's words about the body as 'fertile soil' for new practices and meanings:

> The body is not merely ... a symbolic field to mirror or reproduce dominant values and concepts; it is also a site for resistance to, and transformations of, imposed meanings. ... Cultural meanings are not only shared and given, they are fragmented and contested. Social life is divisive as well as cohesive. The body makes, and is made by, a fractured social world. (Frankenberg 1992: xvii, and cited in Quaranta 2006b: 275)

The suffering body, experiencing the interstitial and pervasive disasters caused by asbestos, becomes the site from which new practices and meanings are elaborated. In this regard, by offering their body to be scrutinized, asbestos-contaminated men and women enter the processes by which biomedical knowledge and epidemiological evidence are elaborated.

By sharing disaster experiences, anti-asbestos activists mobilize and partake in a grassroots movement that could be included among the 'embodied health social movements' (Brown et al. 2004; Brown and Zavestosky 2004). In the name of social justice and by sharing a 'biosocial condition' (Rabinow 1992; Petryna 2002; Fassin and Rechtman 2009), they undertake sociopolitical actions, and mobilize to see their suffering recognized (Fraser 1968; Hobson 2003). In so doing, they enter the processes through which citizenship and rights to health are negotiated, achieved and established (Hofrichter 1993, 2003a; Petryna 2002; Rose 2007; Nguyen et al. 2007). In similar practices of grassroots activism, emotions and affects play a crucial role in determining one's decision to become sociopolitically engaged and persist in such activism (cf. Jasper 1998; Polletta 1998a, 1998b; Polletta and Jasper 2001; Goodwin, Jasper and Polletta 2000, 2001; Klawiter 2004, 2008; Gould 2009).

In my fieldwork, in the attempt to grasp the affective dimension of the practices of activism, I focused on affect as potential when I reflected on the potentialities of the (suffering) body and its capacity to affect and be affected (Deleuze 1988). I approached the Spinozian concept of affect and the philosophy of Deleuze through the contributions offered by Massumi (2002), Gregg and Seigworth (2010), Biehl and Locke (2010), Athanasiu, Hantzaroula and Yannakopoulos (2008), Negri and Hardt (1999), and Shouse (2005). 'Movements of feelings' (Massumi 2002) and the 'passage of intensities from body to body' (Gregg and Seigworth 2010: 3) characterized the daily experiences of activism and circulated among anti-asbestos activists, as well as between them and me. These movements influenced my fieldwork experience. I did not ignore them, adopting a phenomenological approach to them in both data collection and analysis, as I will later discuss.

To sum up, the practices of anti-asbestos activism pivot around the centrality of the body suffering, feeling and acting in a local context linked to a global world crossed by unpredictable movements of people, capital, struggles, passions and disasters. In this context, those affected by AR disasters play a crucial role as activists, and use their body, or evoke the defeated body of their relatives, friends and comrades who have died from ARDs, as a tool (Mauss 1973) of political action to tear the veil of invisibility hiding their suffering.

Memory, Care and Activism

Memory played a crucial role in my fieldwork, as it was subtly and deeply linked to practices and discourses of the body, and the body is a 'site of memory' (Fassin 2011). Memories moulded the narratives and the practices elaborated by study participants during our encounters. In their bodily struggle their memories became militant, as recalling the past represented an act of resistance to the injustices that the disaster survivors continued to suffer in the present (Mazzeo 2017b). The activists' sociopolitical engagement could not be understood without reference to the memory of past experiences that they or their loved ones who had died had lived through.

Remembered and 'remembering bodies' (Fassin 2007) represented the main tools of political action in the areas of AR disasters where I did fieldwork, both in Italy (my earlier work) and Brazil (this book). Memory appeared to be fundamental in legitimizing the disaster survivors' struggle in the name of justice and recognition for their suffering. On a private level, the social actors felt the 'urgency of doing something' for those who had already died from ARDs, as a study participant once told me. They wanted to preserve the memory of their loved ones' life stories; this implied an emotional engagement with the past and with comrades who shared similar experiences of disaster (Halbwachs 1987; Assmann 2002). On a sociopolitical level, past experiences of mobilization in the local context seemed to empower and legitimize the activism in the present. It was not by chance that the anti-asbestos activism I investigated in Osasco (Brazil) emerged from a socio-political and cultural context significantly marked by the struggles undertaken by workers and citizens' organizations, such as unions and civil committees, in the previous decades. In Osasco, AR sufferers found favourable conditions to experience their suffering socially and form a community. The new knowledge and meanings they were elaborating were revealed to be the results of an ongoing dialogue between their imagined future, charged with aspirations for change, and the past, representing the sediment for their struggles in the present (Appadurai 2013).

Our memories compose the indefinite puzzle of our present and forge our future. We are living history, and our past breathes through our body and beats under our skin. Anti-asbestos activism emerges as a grassroots movement triggered by social and bodily experiences of suffering, and from the attempts to care for it. As Bourdieu and Wacquant (1992) argue, the embodiment of the structures of power that influence our actions leaves room for margins of indeterminacy. Although 'everything is pre-determined, not everything is determined', since there is a possibility for social actors to act and not just reproduce the structures ruling their individual and social existences (ibid.: 18). The interstices left free by such indeterminacy are the places where the practices of activism and care relate to the creative power that accompanies the crisis provoked by a suffering experience. Embracing the crisis provoked by the catastrophe in their lives, anti-asbestos activists invent a new role for themselves in the power relations ruling the social fields where their actions take place. Engagement with activism gives them the space to perform their victimhood 'as agents … who are socially constituted as active and acting in the field under consideration by the fact that they possess the necessary properties to be effective, to produce effects, in this field' (ibid.: 107).

In line with Bourdieu, I consider the crises triggered by the disaster experiences as events that can make individuals call into question their preconceived knowledge and promote change (Bourdieu 1991: 131; and cited in Grenfell and Lebaron 2014: 55). Anti-asbestos activism's strength resides in the appropriation of such potential critique by providing the tools and words to 'uncover the social at the heart of the individual, the impersonal beneath the intimate, the universal buried deep within the most particular' (Bourdieu and Wacquant 1992: 44).

The experiences of AR disasters are permeated by the dynamics that define social suffering as a condition deriving from 'what political, economic and institutional power does to people, and, reciprocally, from how these forms of power themselves influence responses to social problems' (Kleinman, Das and Lock 1997: ix). At the same time, experiences such as health threats and diseases (e.g. those provoked by the contamination of one's body from asbestos) affect the most intimate spheres of one's existence and are related to the individual suffering lived by AR disasters survivors. Simultaneously, the experience of a catastrophic event, such as a serious and debilitating disease, concerns not only the body – and the world – of the contaminated subject, but also the entire social context in which he/she acts, lives and dies (Gordon 1991).

Suffering is as private as it is social. The traces of asbestos contamination in the bodies of exposed women and men, and their experiences of suffering, which destroy much of their world, do not only represent a private tragedy caused by an unlucky fate. Rather their bodies reflect violence and injustices through their embodiment of socio-cultural, political and economic processes (Csordas 1990; Quaranta 2006b, 2012b). The usurped body preserves the proof of 'corporate crimes' (Altopiedi 2011). In anti-asbestos activism, the body then becomes the site where the evidence of disaster is sought and acknowledged (Fassin 2011: 284), the 'human rights arena in which many forces struggle for control' (Mack 2011: xviii).

My use of the concept of violence refers to the definitions proposed by Bourdieu (Bourdieu and Wacquant 1992) and has been particularly influenced by the reflections of Farmer (1996) and Fassin (2007). According to the definition proposed by Farmer, structural violence is

> 'structured' by historically given (and often economically driven) processes and forces that conspire – whether through routine, ritual, or, as is more commonly the case, the hard surfaces of life – to constrain agency. For many choices, both large and small, are limited by racism, sexism, political violence and grinding poverty. (Farmer 2005: 40)

Fassin, reflecting on the concept, argues that structural violence is

> a relatively abstract and elusive concept. It concerns the way historically constituted social structures interfere with people's needs, capabilities and aspirations. In various ways, it combines economic inequality, social injustice, racial discrimination and diverse forms of denial of human and citizens' rights. It is more difficult to apprehend than political vio-

> lence ... Its imprint on the body is more profound but less tangible. It has no immediate visibility, but there are also more interests at stake in keeping it invisible, since *its systematic unveiling could have unexpected consequences on the social order* [my emphasis]. (Fassin 2011: 293–94)

I focus on the 'unexpected consequences on the social order' that occur when the veil of invisibility hiding AR disasters is torn by the sufferers who engage with activism.

We live in a 'world of flows' (Appadurai 1996) which cross each other along unpredictable trajectories defined by 'different speeds, axes, points of origin and termination, and varied relationships to institutional structures in different regions, nations or societies' (Appadurai 2000: 5). However, in such a world-in-motion, barriers and walls still exist and continue to be erected, and the freedom of movement for all is more than a utopia (Scheper-Hughes 1995). When the trajectories intersect, fundamental 'problems of livelihood, equity, suffering, justice and governance' may derive from the resulting 'relations of disjuncture' (Appadurai 2000: 5) or 'frictions' (Tsing 2005). I interpreted the movement for the global prohibition of asbestos by gathering multiple and various examples of anti-asbestos activism(s) performed locally. They are creative, militant responses emerging from the intersection of those trajectories, determining the conditions not just for inequalities, suffering and misunderstanding, but also for the empowerment of the struggles of distinct social actors mobilizing together, despite the differences between them (Tsing 2005).

The investigated anti-asbestos activism can be situated in the broader scene of social movements in contemporary Latin America (Negri and Cocco 2006; Holston 2008), transnational grassroots activism (Della Porta et al. 2006), and contemporary social movements at large (Koensler and Rossi 2012).

Methods

> Every practical choice has a theoretical root. (Bourdieu and Wacquant 1992: 35)

In the ethnographic encounters I had in Osasco, São Paulo, Brazil, being there both physically and with my background, while approaching and sharing affects with my interlocutors, I had the opportunity to grasp the nuances of non-institutionalized political fields as they were experienced and performed in daily life by the activists. The majority of the study participants were activists, despite being sick, elderly men. They embodied something subversive that I read as a resistance to the dominating moral values concerning ageing, the body and life in contemporary Brazil. I reflected on, and then analysed, this embodied resistance enacted through gestures and postures that I considered to be bodily signs of struggle since, 'as their voices were silenced, it was their bodies that spoke' (Fassin 2011: 288).

The methodological choices I made were based on my aim of deepening my knowledge of precisely the processes of disaster and activism that my interlocutors embodied and carried forward.

The peculiarity of ethnographic research resides in the 'thickness' (Geertz 1973) characterizing the data produced by the encounter between the researcher and her collaborators in the field. My interlocutors were mostly activists in the anti-asbestos movement in Osasco and other Brazilian cities. The majority of them were former workers (employees and miners who had been exposed to asbestos) and family members (especially widows and children of workers who had died of ARDs). To broaden my understanding of AR suffering and activism and to get distinct perspectives on them as processes of disaster and health-based grassroots mobilization, I conducted interviews with professionals in the field of public health (biomedical doctors, epidemiologists and lung specialists), lawyers, trade unionists and members of NGOs and associations of workers who had been exposed to other toxic substances, such as mercury.

Aiming to collocate the activism occurring in Osasco within the local and national sociopolitical context, I visited and participated with ABREA members at events and in awareness campaigns in various Brazilian settings impacted by the toxic market of asbestos. My field trips took place in the states of São Paulo (São Caetano, Santo André and São Paulo), Rio de Janeiro (Rio de Janeiro), Bahia (Salvador, Poções and Bom Jesus da Serra), Santa Catarina (Florianópolis), Goiás (Goiânia) and Paraná (Londrina). However, the main site of my fieldwork was Osasco, and the majority of the participants in my study were ABREA members living in Osasco, where I conducted twenty-six in-depth interviews with nineteen men and seven women involved in AR disasters and activism.

This book is grounded in ten months of ethnographic fieldwork, conducted in two phases. During the first phase (August to October 2014), I established my contacts with ABREA activists, especially with those who later became my gatekeepers. Together we evaluated the research project's feasibility by considering the willingness of ABREA members to take part in the project. These first two months spent in Brazil allowed me to start my own slow, and sometimes emotionally difficult, process of becoming more familiar with a context I was encountering for the first time. It was challenging not to become lost in São Paulo and Osasco, with their 13 million inhabitants, a language spoken with so many local accents, and a sense of time and space that was so different from what I was accustomed to while living in Europe.

The second phase of the fieldwork (February to October 2015) was crucial for the research project's development. It was during this phase that the encounters emerged from which the majority of the narratives presented in this book took place. I conducted participant observation, semi-structured in-depth interviews (recorded after receiving formal consent) and focus groups. Data collection began with participant observation and informal conversations with ABREA activists. The definition of participant observation proposed by Pigg (2013: 132–33) gives an accurate description of the theoretical background informing my attitude as 'participant observer':

> We might rename as *mindfulness* [my emphasis] the sensibility that was once invoked as participant observation. It is a mindfulness of being-in-place (context); mindfulness of voice and tone (socially differentiated points of view); mindfulness of pattern, contradiction and complexity (social structure); mindfulness of temporality and unfolding (practice); mindfulness of self and other (accountability and intersubjectivity); and mindfulness of shape and process (theoretical propositions). Ethnographic sitting, and the mindful perception and listening it fosters, is part of anthropological practice. Ethnography is both a mode of attentiveness and an openness to being taken off course. The capacity to be surprised is the motor that moves ethnography forward into a potential usefulness in the debating of public problems. Ethnography is an intellectual, imaginative and affective disposition that deliberately holds open a space between research questions (formed in anticipation of categories for empirical discovery) and the interactions that alert the researcher to the assumptions and limitations embodied in those very questions.

During the first months of fieldwork, I preferred not to plan formal interviews, but rather to just spend time with ABREA members and start the process of our mutual acquaintance. For this reason, I attended all the events the ABREA activists were organizing or attending in Osasco, São Paulo, and other Brazilian cities. I tried not to miss any occasion to observe and, at the same time, to be observed. I decided to use the first months of fieldwork in this way because I wanted to be confident about my communication skills in Portuguese (a third language for me) before starting with formal interviews. Later I was able to conduct the interviews in Portuguese alone without the help of an interpreter. This was a fundamental goal, as I did not want to rely on a third person who would inevitably have interfered during the encounters with study participants whose life stories and narratives

I wanted to understand directly, with all their nuances. I developed the ability to conduct and transcribe formal interviews and have informal conversations in Portuguese during my daily life and study in Brazil. The delicate issue of language, writing and translation has been widely investigated and discussed in the literature (cf. Clifford and Marcus 1986). I found that being able to communicate in Portuguese favoured my research experience and facilitated my theoretical and emotional understanding of the context.

Moreover, I thought that we – my interlocutors and I – all needed some time in the beginning to get used to each other. In fact, I was aware that I represented a markedly visible 'otherness' in relation to them. I was afraid that an (ethnographic) encounter could have been seriously compromised by the fact that we embodied completely distinct life stories and distant socio-cultural and economic backgrounds. In the field, I had to consider my gender (female), my age (33 years in 2015), my professional life (almost exclusively characterized by intellectual activities) and my own environmental exposure to asbestos as inexorable dimensions of my being the principal research instrument. On the contrary, the majority of my collaborators were former workers, male[4] (age range 65–85), with at least one ARD diagnosis, embodying a strong masculine culture, with knowledge acquired by manual professional experience. I believed it was both necessary and prudent not to ignore our differences, but rather to invent strategies to make the otherness we embodied in our relationship a possibility of encounter, rather than a clash. From a methodological point of view, spending several months participating in ABREA activities before scheduling interviews and entering the intimate space of activists' daily lives turned out to be an effective strategy to favour mutual knowledge and to establish the empathic communication that is essential for anthropological research (cf. Wikan 1992; Piasere 2002). Therefore, in addition to scheduled meetings and interviews, the narratives in this book emerged from informal conversations during lunches, nightly travels by bus across Brazil, walks through Osasco, conferences, political events and ABREA monthly meetings.

In Osasco, I tried not to plan more than one scheduled interview per day. I soon noticed that after my first interviews, those that followed had a similar pattern. Generally, I proposed to meet at 10 AM at my interlocutor's home. During this fieldwork, I lived in São Paulo, in a neighbourhood bordering Osasco. I usually left my home soon after 8 AM, travelling by public transport (bus and train), which took at least one hour to arrive at Osasco's train station. From there I reached my interlocutor's home on foot or by bus. Most study participants lived in neighbourhoods close to the area where the Eternit plant had been situated before being demolished, so most homes were reachable on foot from the train station. However, some interviews took place in the most peripheral of Osasco's neighbourhoods, which were also the poorest ones, and then I needed to take a bus. On average, the interviews lasted two hours, but they were usually followed by an invitation to lunch, which I always accepted (except once). For this reason, the whole meeting, arranged on the pretext of the interview, could last five or six hours. As an anthropologist inspired by serendipity as a fruitful attitude to experience the field, and by the importance of empathy in the encounters in the field – always defined by the relationships occurring in it (Bourdieu and Wacquant 1992) – those extra unplanned hours spent with my research partners were highly valuable. In fact, with the recorder off, and free from the emotional and practical constraints linked to the interview, I could take notice of more nuances in my interlocutors' lives. Thus, I was able to situate the stories I heard during the interviews within a world closer to the daily lives of the narrators. I soon realized that my research partners probably felt honoured by the visit of an Italian researcher to their home, as they often invited other family members to meet me for lunch or for a *cafezinho*, a cup of coffee. On those occasions, I could gain other perspectives on the experiences of AR disasters and activism, as lived within the family's context.

In order to stimulate the narratives from study participants, I opened the interviews with 'grand tour questions' (Spradley 1979). Because I was interested in listening to the trajectories, contingencies and life experiences that determined the narrator's involvement in AR suffering and activism, my interlocutors often showed me old documents and photographs of their work at the plant, medical examinations, judicial actions against the firm, and experiences of activism. Sometimes I asked for these documents, yet at other times they showed them to me on their own initiative. During the narratives, their work at the plant, as well as their engagement in anti-asbestos activism, was described with constant references to significant episodes in their lives (e.g. migration, marriage, birth of children, illness experience, and death of a loved one due to an ARD).

I formally interviewed my gatekeepers and a few other study participants more than once, and I accompanied one of them (diagnosed with asbestosis and pleural plaques) to two of his periodical lung examinations at the hospital.

In addition to oral data, collected through formal interviews and informal conversations, this book is based on visual and written data from the ABREA archives and website, as well as my studies at Osasco's public library, research institutes and museums, where I consulted newspaper articles and traced Osasco's history through old pictures and objects of material culture.

The narration taking shape through the pages of this book is grounded in my field experience, and in my own feelings, perceptions and emotions that I felt during the encounters with those I met. In the phases of data collection and analysis, I considered the contingencies and shared affects that made each encounter unique, not just as possible sources of bias but as unavoidable and precious aspects of ethnographic research. This consists of encounters in which the emotions of both the researcher and her interlocutor(s) matter; reflecting on them is essential in analysing the relational (emotional) knowledge produced by those encounters (Rosaldo 1984; Lutz and White 1986; Kleinman and Copp 1993; Leavitt 1996; Pussetti 2005; Ligi 2011b). I tried to save and transpose in words the evanescent but incisive presence of those feelings in my fieldnotes written in Italian, my mother tongue. Driven by a sort of urgency not to forget, I usually wrote my notes soon after any interview, informal conversation or meeting. I used to write down my notes (depending on how crowded the bus or train was) during my daily two-hour journey from Osasco back to São Paulo, or between my home and the Faculty of Public Health of the University of São Paulo, to which I was affiliated as a visiting PhD student during my stay in Brazil. Night-time was also favourable for elaborating my notes and writing my diary when I came back to the place that was my home during the fieldwork, and where I could isolate and protect myself from the urban jungle I had faced during the day. In fact, my constant feeling while I was living in São Paulo was of being immersed in a vibrating flux of restless movement through bodies, cars, buildings and lights. While this made me feel alive and excited, at the same time it made me feel incredibly tired and sometimes overwhelmed by the pulsating enormity of the life around me.

In addition to my fieldnotes, photographs played a fundamental and unexpectedly important role in the development of my research, in both my personal experiments of data collection and my interlocutors' narration of their stories. I refer to contributions from studies on photography (Sontag 1990; Bourdieu and Bourdieu 2004), visual anthropology (Chiozzi 1993) and those implementing a phenomenological approach in both data collection and analysis (Grenfell and Lebaron 2014), as photography was another method to collect and record what I had perceived in the field, but which could not be expressed or heard in words.

On the one hand, basing my research on the centrality of the body in the disaster and activism experiences, I tried to capture the traces of asbestos contamination inscribed in the bodies of the 'sufferer-activists'[5] (Mazzeo 2017b) I met through a camera. On the other hand, while sharing their life stories, my interlocutors often showed me pictures of their youth, marriages and children to elaborate their narrative, and in doing so, they facilitated my entrance into a world that I otherwise could only access through their memories. Moreover, photographs, especially portraits of relatives and friends who had already died from ARDs, were used as instruments of struggle during awareness campaigns, denunciations and protests. ABREA activists strategically used the potentiality of critique of the 'suffering body', even in the physical absence of the victim who was remembered and indeed present in the practices of activism, which were at the same time practices of struggle, memory and care (Mazzeo 2017b, 2018c, 2019).

Managing a constantly evoked past and the daily remarked-upon absence of a loved one proved to be one of the more emotionally and challenging aspects of my research. I include a few of the photographs I took in Brazil in this book, which is rooted in the life stories of the men and women I encountered throughout my fieldwork, while following the transnational trajectories of disaster and grassroots activism connecting Casale Monferrato (the site of my previous research in Italy) and Osasco in Brazil.

In conclusion, I wish to draw attention to a relevant ethical issue that I had to consider while writing this book: it concerns the study participants' anonymity. Throughout this ethnography, I use pseudonyms to refer to the majority of my interlocutors in the field, even though I agree with Fonseca (2010), who states that anonymity does not necessarily mean being respectful of researchers' interlocutors. While researching practices of anti-asbestos activism, I often encountered social actors who considered their participation in my study as a political act, and who explicitly told me that they would be honoured for their names to appear in a publication about their struggle. This wish is understandable, especially if we consider the kind of social movement – revolving around recognition (Hobson 2003) – in which the participants in my study were engaged. However, in order to safeguard my research partners, I decided to preserve the anonymity of nearly all of them. I only explicitly mention study participants' real names when keeping them anonymous would represent a lack of respect for the true authorship of narratives and original insights that had made essential contributions to the knowledge that my interlocutors and I co-produced in the course of our encounters.

Structure of the Book

This book is a polyphonic historically rooted ethnography revolving around the life stories of those suffering from the impact of the toxic market of asbestos on their existences, and who decided to engage in grassroots health-based activism. My understanding is grounded in the practices and meanings performed and elaborated locally by the anti-asbestos activists I met, and my aim is to save the bodily, dynamic and concrete dimension of the processes of AR health disasters (which often persist in invisibility) in the textual transposition of my research experience and data interpretation.

The chapters that follow aim to acknowledge and understand the role of the social actors who embody, contest and divert those same processes affecting their lives. To this end, ample space is given to the sufferers' and activists' narratives, which are extensively quoted throughout the book. Besides scientific purposes, the decision to include extensive quotations from the interviews conducted during fieldwork was taken upon the ethical commitment to listening to the too-often-silenced voices of those primarily affected by invisible disasters, and who promote change from below in the name of social justice. Beyond the particular/universal, local/global, individual/collective and private/social dichotomies, the life stories recalled in this book represent the sap of intricate transnational processes, and allow us to sense the fleshly, daily-life dimension of dynamics that would otherwise remain evocated as invisible forces.

Chapter 1 retraces the historical processes and economic dynamics moulding the global market of asbestos, and focuses on the impact of asbestos exposure on global public health. Chapter 2 delves into the historical and sociocultural context of the Brazilian city of Osasco, where the practices and strategies of anti-asbestos activism discussed in the book emerged. Chapter 3 moves further into everyday experiences of AR disasters; sufferers' narratives and memories accompany the reader through the unpredictable and painful trajectories of illness, contamination and grief experiences. Chapter 4 focuses on the practices and strategies of anti-asbestos activism observed in Osasco during my fieldwork with the ABREA members. Lastly, Chapter 5 expands its scope to reconnect the meanings and practices of this anti-asbestos activism with the global context of the health movement, which is global public health (Farmer et al. 2013). It discusses the moral commitments behind health-based activism and research, and shows the contribution that anthropology might offer to a transdisciplinary understanding and tackling of global public health issues.

Notes

1. The so-called 'Eternit trial' started in 2009 and ended in November 2014. Stephan Schmidheiny and Louis de Cartier de Marchienne (deceased in 2013) were the parties accused of the crimes of environmental disaster, manslaughter and voluntary omission of accident prevention precautions in relation to their responsibilities in the management of the Eternit plants in Italy at Casale Monferrato, Cavagnolo, Bagnoli and Rubiera. Ultimately, in November 2014, the Supreme Court did not recognize the crimes, declaring them to be prescribed, contrary to what had been established by the previous judgments pronounced in First and Second Degree by the Court of Turin. Afterwards, a second judicial action, the so-called 'Eternit bis', started. This time, Stephan Schmidheiny is the only party accused of voluntary homicide for the deaths of 258 exposed workers and residents who had died from MM between 1989 and 2014. The first hearing will take place in November 2020.
2. Throughout the book, I use the expression 'social justice' (Rawls 1971) in line with Hofrichter's reflections on social justice and global public health (Hofrichter 2003b). According to Hofrichter (ibid.: 12), 'social justice is not a thing but rather an ongoing series of relationships that permeate everyday life. Social justice concerns the systematic treatment of people as members of a definable group'. For a deeper understanding of social movements in the name of social and environmental justice, compare with Cable and Benson 1993 and Nixon 2011; for a focus on the Brazilian context, compare with Acselrad, Herculano and Pádua 2004; Souza Bravo, D'Acri and Bilate Martins 2010; Milanez et al. 2013; and Porto Pacheco and Leroy 2013.
3. Data available online at www.ibge.gov.br (last accessed 21 March 2017).
4. I interpret the low number of women actively participating in ABREA as the consequence of the low number of women working at the Eternit plant in Osasco, where the majority of ABREA members had worked and where only a few women were employed in the administrative sector. Other Brazilian anti-asbestos NGOs with workers from factories where the female presence was higher than at the Eternit in Osasco had more female members (see D'Acri, Marques dos Santos and de Souza 2010).
5. I consider the complex subjectivities of study participants whose lives suffer from the impact of AR disasters, and who, at the same time, are activists mobilizing in the name of social justice. Inspired by the seminal reflections on intersectionality by Crenshaw (1989), I often refer to anti-asbestos activists by the intersectional term 'sufferer-activists' (see also Mazzeo 2017b, 2018a, 2018c).

1

The Toxic Market of Asbestos and Global Health Disasters

Rome, 19 November 2014, ten past nine in the evening, and most had already left for home, as news had circulated that the judgment would not be pronounced that day. However, in the end, the sentence was pronounced late that evening, with just a few of us remaining, including the anti-asbestos activists from Casale Monferrato (Italy) and the foreign delegations, among which the Brazilians were the most numerous.

It took just one minute to destroy the expectations of justice built through decades of mobilization, including meetings, demonstrations and rituals of collective and individual mourning, involving the elderly men and women from Casale Monferrato who had attended all the hearings at the Court of Turin for more than two years. As an activist once told me, by their physical presence, the disaster survivors had shown the lawyers of the accused that they knew exactly the causes and names of those responsible for the suffering and deaths of their loved ones.

I wrote down the following sentences: 'In the name of the Italian people, the Supreme Court … annuls the contested judgment without indictment … the accused Stephan Schmidheiny is acquitted from the crime defined by Article 434 of the penal code'. I felt a sense of vertigo, the words blurred. I remembered the speech made by the prosecutor, F.M. Iacoviello, in the afternoon. His statement, 'justice and law do not coincide, and in case of doubt, the judge has to opt for the law', echoed in my mind; the doubt concerned interpretative issues about the appropriateness of defining and consequently judging the crime as manslaughter by disaster. 'The unnamed disaster is a disaster without typicality; therefore, it finds its typicality only if it presents the same characteristics as named disasters. Accordingly, it must have the same characteristics as a building collapse: instantaneousness and violence on things provoking danger for people', the Prosecutor had said. He continued by saying that the 'violence' could be found in the introduction of asbestos fibres into the air, thus provoking a change in the environment and representing a danger for people, but it was hard to talk about 'instantaneousness' for disasters that remain silent for decades. By the following words, he stated that an epidemic disaster is not a disaster.

> What is an epidemic? It is a relevant number of deaths and diseases … but a disaster-event does not coincide with a disease or death event … The epidemic cannot be considered as an additional event to the massive (and violent) introduction of fibres into the environment, [but] is instead a characteristic of that event. The epidemic represents an aspect of a disaster event, not the disaster itself.

Accordingly, if a disaster occurred, it occurred in concomitance with the leaking of fibres, and therefore ceased when production ceased in Casale Monferrato in the 1980s. 'The crime is extinguished because the prescription occurred before the first judgment had been pronounced … The public hearing is concluded'. Shouts and whistles arose from the public in attendance, who had listened to every single word in a very disciplined way until that moment. 'Shame on you! Shame on you! Your conscience is black and you cannot wash it anymore! You have killed justice tonight!'

I was speechless and incredulous. An activist, aged about 80, with whom I had become friends over the years, came to me and talked as if she wanted to give me solace. I felt as though I did not have the same right as she did to feel outraged and offended – but still, I was. She had made a six-hour journey by bus from Casale Monferrato to Rome to honour the memory of her brother and sister-in-law. They had died from malignant mesothelioma (MM) and, in a moment of deep sadness and frustration, she was taking care of me! 'We already knew', she said in a disillusioned tone of voice; 'The TV and radio had already spread the news at 8 P.M.' 'How was it possible that journalists knew the judgment before it had been pronounced?' I asked. 'It always works that way, we're always the last to know', she answered. A younger activist passing by us looked into my teary eyes. I felt outraged and embarrassed about the suffering and further violence perpetrated against the sufferers whose struggle I had been accompanying since 2009. I felt as if they were being physically beaten in front of my eyes, and I could not do anything. 'Why this reaction? Did you still believe in justice?' the younger activist asked. My elderly friend answered before I could utter anything, 'No, I never believed in it'.

In this chapter, I will propose a reflection on the processes of health, environmental and social disasters related to the toxic market of asbestos. I will focus on the disaster experiences lived by anti-asbestos activists in Osasco, and situate them in the transnational dynamics at play in the processes of global health disasters. I will refer to the anthropological literature on disasters and present my interlocutors' narratives, showing how the disaster processes occur and which practices have exacerbated the impact of asbestos exposure on their lives. In particular, I will draw attention to the connections I found by following the trajectories linking the experiences of asbestos-related (AR) activism and suffering in Casale Monferrato (Italy) and Osasco (Brazil).

I will consider the practices of risk denial adopted by asbestos corporations to impede the spread of risk awareness among exposed workers and citizens as a crucial dynamic in the processes of AR disasters occurring worldwide. These disasters are transnational because of the economics and politics behind them, and cannot be localized to specific places because they occur and become manifest in the victims' bodies, which are the main site of the catastrophic event. In my analysis, the risk/danger experiences represent a phase of the disaster processes, which may begin in faraway countries and decades before the onset of the destructive impact of asbestos exposure on a person's life. The discrepancy between the space and time of exposure and the onset of deleterious health effects, influences the experiences of these disasters, as well as their narration. In this chapter, I will present narratives that are illustrative of the processes by which, on the one hand, the disaster victims make sense of their AR suffering and, on the other, asbestos lobbies worldwide arrange standardized communication policies aimed at minimizing or even denying the health hazards related to asbestos exposure.

Dust

'Dust', *'polvere'* in Italian and *'pò'* in Portuguese, was the most frequent term I heard throughout my multi-sited ethnography across Italy and Brazil when my interlocutors referred to asbestos. According to the study participants' narratives, the dust covered everything, lying on the workers' clothes and in their hair; it settled on machinery, and fingers could write messages on the dusty surfaces. In the parking areas, the dust blanketed the managers' cars, the workers' bicycles and the surrounding roads, and filled the furrows at the end of the workday. It covered the tables in the canteen. It created a film on the leaves of trees and plants nearby, and on any flowers in the windows. It built up on the balconies, and settled on clothes hung to dry outside the houses in front of the factory, and on the tablecloths and bedsheets inside. You could see the dust; it looked like snow, and seemed to sparkle in the sunlight. Most did not fear the dust, but there were women living near the factory who obsessively swept it from their balconies every day and never left their windows open. There were workers who wore a sort of handmade diving suit before 'diving into the dust', since 'there was so much dust that you could swim' in certain parts of the asbestos-cement (AC) factories or mines where my interlocutors had worked. To protect themselves, these workers had worn gloves, boots and overalls, which filled with dust and then needed to be washed. Before workers were allowed to leave their dusty clothes at the workplace, they would go home to their mothers, sisters and wives to wash. They too then breathed and 'ate the dust'. The Portuguese *'comer o pò'* and the Italian *'mangiare la polvere'* (i.e. 'eating the dust') are other expressions that I often heard from study participants when talking about asbestos fibre inhalation. You 'ate the dust' and it then would come into you and never leave you. Through nostrils and the mouth, the dust would reach the lungs and remain, close to the heart. It would remain stuck to your membranes and settle, insinuating itself into each fissure, slowly taking up space meant for oxygen – stifling, caging, trapping life in a vice-like grip. With these terms the disaster survivors expressed to me their knowledge of asbestos, a knowledge rooted in their experiences of exposure and its impact on their health.

Asbestos is the generic term that indicates a group of fibrous silicate minerals including amphibole, chrysotile, amosite and crocidolite.[1] Known since ancient times, asbestos minerals were celebrated up until the last century as having magical properties. In fact, asbestos minerals are made up of countless microscopic fibres, which can easily be manipulated and used in numerous ways. At the same time, the fibres are incredibly resistant, especially to fire; the Greek etymology ἄσβεστος (asbestos) means incorruptible, inextinguishable and eternal. For this reason, asbestos was believed to be, in the words of Marco Polo (1496), 'salamander's wool', since, like the small amphibian, the fibres cannot be damaged by fire (Rossi 2008). The first mention of asbestos appeared in the writings of the Greek geographer Strabo (64 BCE – 24 CE), who praised asbestos-woven textiles which were washable with fire, instead of water (Roselli 2010: 33), while in 'Historia Naturalis' [Natural History], Pliny the Elder (23–79 CE) described shrouds made with asbestos to safeguard the kings' and queens' corpses (ibid.).

Marco Polo's 'The Book of the Marvels of the World' (1496) offers one of the first descriptions of asbestos extraction activities:

> The stones, with the agglutinated fibres, were hammered in order to have smaller pieces from which the precious fibres were obtained. Once the fibres had been washed, they could be woven like wool. The resulting textiles were not completely white, but they could be whitened in contact with fire. Moreover, every time they became dirty, to clean them it was sufficient to leave them in the fire. (Polo 1496; and cited in Roselli 2010: 34)

The massive exploitation and industrial use of asbestos minerals began at the end of the nineteenth century with the opening of an asbestos mine in Quebec in 1877 (Roselli 2010: 34), and boomed in the early twentieth century. In 1902, the Austrian chemist Ludwig Hatschek patented a mixture of asbestos and cement (asbestos-cement) in a 1:6 ratio, and named it 'Eternit' from the Latin etymology *eternus* (eternal) to emphasize the extraordinary quality of the resulting items. The patent was then sold, and asbestos-containing products [ACPs] were (and still are) manufactured worldwide, with huge profits for asbestos companies, due to the low cost of the raw materials (Altopiedi 2011).

The principal asbestos mines massively exploited throughout the twentieth century were situated in the former Soviet Union, Canada, South Africa, Zimbabwe, China, Brazil, Italy and the United States (Iocca 2011: 144). In Europe, the largest asbestos mine was in Balangero (Italy, Piedmont Region), less than 150 kilometres from the largest Eternit plant in Europe, situated in Casale Monferrato, the second context of my multi-sited ethnography. The Balangero mine was active from the 1920s to the 1990s. In an investigative report for the newspaper *L'Unità*, the Italian intellectual, writer and journalist Italo Calvino used the following words to describe the environment at the quarry:

> When a new work shift starts, the workers arrive from the forest paths, those from Balangero, those from Coassolo, those from Corio, with their appearance of mountaineers, with their corduroy jackets, big boots, and caps with balaclavas.
>
> They look like hunters out for hares or just for mushrooms, as they have no guns. But there are no hares in the woods, and mushrooms do not grow in the red soil of chestnut husks, wheat does not grow in the hard

> fields of the surrounding villages, there is only the grey asbestos dust cloud from the quarry, which, wherever it spreads, burns leaves and lungs. There is the quarry, the only one of its kind in Europe, and their [the miners'] lives and deaths. (Calvino 1954)

Balangero's quarry supplied asbestos chrysotile to the majority of factories using asbestos in Italy, and with 3.86 million tons of asbestos produced over the course of the twentieth century, it played a leading role in the European as well as the global market of asbestos until the early 1990s[2] (Iocca 2011).

In Brazil, at the beginning of industrial use of asbestos, the raw material was imported. Brazil began to use and export its own asbestos from the 1930s, when, according to my interlocutors' narratives, the asbestos deposit in the *fazenda* (farm) São Felix was discovered in Bom Jesus da Serra (Poções, Bahia) by a French geologist. At that time, the local population, who used the term *pedras cabeludas* (hairy stones) for asbestos stones, used to consider these stones as sacred, even though they were common in the region. When asbestos extraction began, the wealth brought by the local mining industry reinforced the idea that the 'hair' (i.e. fibres) of the asbestos stones represented a blessed treasure for the villages around the São Felix mine (De Oliveira D'Arede 2009; Mazzeo 2018a).

The mining industry in Brazil began with the involvement of two multinational corporations: Pont-à-Mousson, succeeded by the French Brasilit S.A. (currently divided into Saint-Gobain do Brasil for industrial products, and Ltda Divisão Brasilit for construction), and a subsidiary of the Swiss–Belgian joint venture Eternit do Brasil Cimento Amianto S.A. (currently, Eternit S.A.) (Giannasi 2012: 65–71).

The French firm began asbestos mining in Brazil before the Eternit group, soon after the São Felix mine was discovered. The French participated in the foundation of the company S.A. Mineração de Amianto (SAMA) in 1939, and soon afterwards they obtained authorization for asbestos extraction. On the very same day of the authorization, SAMA was bought by Brasilit S.A., belonging to the French group Compagnie Pont-à-Mousson, and later changed its name to Saint-Gobain (Giannasi 2012: 65–71). The Saint-Gobain firm exploited the São Felix mine until 1967 when, with the Eternit group (including the Brasilit S.A. with 55 per cent of the shares and the Eternit S.A. with 45 per cent), mining activities were transferred to Minaçu (Goiás, Central Brazil), where the larger Cana Brava mine had recently been opened. The partnership lasted until 1997, when Eternit S.A. took control of all the activities and, in so doing, inherited the social and environmental responsibilities of the management and abandonment of the area occupied by the São Felix mine in Bahia (Giannasi 2012). To date, the abandoned mine of São Felix holds the major environmental liability of the asbestos market in Brazil for the extent of asbestos contamination (Novello 2012).

Until 2017, the major asbestos producing countries were China (26 per cent), India (25 per cent), Brazil (9 per cent) and Russia (8 per cent) (US Geological Survey 2017). In Brazil, all the extracted asbestos came from the Cana Brava quarry in Minaçu, the only active mine left. In February 2019, following the decision of the Supremo Tribunal Federal – STF [Supreme Federal Court] in 2017 that prohibited asbestos use and extraction in the whole country, activities ceased in Minaçu. However, a controversial and heated debate on the possibility of reactivating the mining industry, for export purposes only, then began. In July 2019, Law number 20,514 was passed by the State of Goiás, where the Cana Brava quarry is situated, and so extraction activities were allowed to start again.

The Global Entanglements of the Asbestos Market

After the invention of the 'Eternit' label in 1902, asbestos minerals were used extensively in multiple industrial sectors such as construction (e.g. for roofing, water reservoirs and pipes), shipyards, railways and textile industries (Iocca 2011). By the mid-twentieth century, the asbestos market had spread worldwide, influenced by a handful of lobbies with particular interests in asbestos extraction and AC production. Among these asbestos lobbies was the Swiss family Schmidheiny, which had built its economic empire on the asbestos and cement industry from the beginning of the twentieth century.

The dynasty's forefather was Jacob (1838–1905), father of Ernst (1871–1935), who founded the Rheintalische Cementfabrik Rüthi AG in 1906 in the Sangallese valley of Reno (Roselli 2010). Four years later, facing a crisis threatening the cement market, Ernst Schmidheiny founded the first cement cartel, called Eingetragene Genossenschaft Portland. Then, in 1920, Ernst, who had entered the Eternit Belgique group, acquired the AC plant Eternit AG in Niederurnen, managed by Jean Baer since the plant's opening in 1903. Soon afterwards, Baer and Schmidheiny together founded Amiantus S.A., a network of AC firms, to control the industrial group's geographic distribution and, in this way, they became part of the administrative boards of several AC industries, such as the Belgian Cimenteries & Briqueteries Réunies

S.A. (ibid.). Dozens of firms and plants rapidly began to be intertwined in an increasing web of companies. For instance, the Schmidheiny family managed Eternit plants in sixteen countries, with twenty-three thousand employees in total. Moreover, in sixteen other countries, the Schmidheiny family joined the Emsens family in the management of the plants belonging to the Belgian Eternit Group (ibid.). It is almost impossible to know exactly how the shares were distributed among the shareholders, although it is reasonable to assume that the Schmidheinys controlled the German-speaking countries, Middle East and Latin America, while the Belgian group controlled plants situated in Benelux, Africa and Asia. In 1929, the asbestos cartel Societé Associé d'Industries Amianteciment – SAIAC [Associated Society of Asbestos-Cement Industries] was founded in Europe, and asbestos firms from Austria, the United Kingdom, Spain, Italy, France, Belgium and Switzerland joined it to control the global asbestos market (ibid.).

The Schmidheiny family divided shares with Belgian industrial companies in the management of plants in more than thirty countries. For instance, the family was involved in the management of Eternit AG Niederurnen (Switzerland), Eternit AG Berlin (Germany), Everite Ltd. Johannesburg (South Africa), Ricalit, APC and PPC (Costa Rica), Tubovinil (Guatemala), Tecno Plásticos (El Salvador), Bobicasa (Honduras), Saudi Arabian Amiantit Co. Ltd. Dammam (Saudi Arabia), Eternit Colombia, Eternit Venezuela, Eureka Mexico, Eternit Ecuatoriana (Ecuador), Hondulit (Honduras), Duralit Bolivie, Nicalit Nicaragua, Eternit SpA Genoa (Italy) and Eternit S.A. Brasil (Roselli 2010). The production and plant management, as well as the politics of risk communication on the dangers of asbestos, followed standardized procedures and policies designed in a transnational agreement by the asbestos lobbies.

The Eternit Plant in Osasco

The historical and ethnographic data from my fieldwork in Osasco reveal the entanglements between the local and global dimensions of the asbestos market. In 1941, Eternit S.A. Brasil opened the first and largest AC factory in Latin America. The chosen location for the plant was Osasco (São Paulo), and production there run until 1993. The factory was completely demolished in 1995.

Once back in Italy, several months after the conclusion of my fieldwork, I was sitting on the sofa in my living room, and I found myself touched and almost crying. I had in my hands a map that a former

Eternit worker from Osasco – I call him Teodoro – drew and gave me as a present during the celebration that anti-asbestos activists organized for my birthday and my imminent end of fieldwork, in September 2015. Teodoro, 79 years old at that time, was one of the oldest participants in my study. He had been one of the founders of the Associação Brasileira dos Expostos ao Amianto – ABREA [Brazilian Association of Persons Exposed to Asbestos], and he was recognized by other association members as 'the person who knew everything about the factory'. When I visited Teodoro at his home for our scheduled interview, he proposed drawing a map of the entire area occupied by the Eternit plant in Osasco, where he had worked for eighteen years, from 1952 to 1953 and then from 1969 to 1986. He said that for him reproducing the map of the plant would not be a problem, because he 'had everything in his mind'. He told me that he remembered everything, even the smallest details. Months later, I was sitting in my living room, looking at the map, and I began to follow with my finger the black contours on the white sheet of paper where Teodoro had indicated the various sectors, the offices, the restaurant, the warehouse and the doctor's surgery. Teodoro's accuracy for the details and the erasure of pencil lines revealed the care that he had dedicated to the drawing. That map was a precious gift to me, as it bore the time devoted to its creation, and it shared the traces of a past time, inaccessible to me.

During my fieldwork, I often reflected on the fact that I could never have the direct experience of the 'worlds' in which my interlocutors had lived, and which had been so decisive for their lives. In this regard, the risk of over-contextualization and giving authority to the researcher's interpretations based on the simple statement 'I was there, therefore it is true' could be avoided (Wikan 1992), although it was quite challenging to deal with those 'worlds', which I could only access through the study participants' narratives and memories. Moreover, my knowledge of a factory and its workings was only theoretical, based on what I had read in books or watched in movies. My interlocutors used to ask me: 'Have you ever been in a factory?' or 'Do you know how this machine works?'. To my repeated 'no', they replied by trying in various ways to get me into the 'world' they were talking about; they made their explanations as simple as possible, mimed working processes or made drawings, as Teodoro did.

Now, I would ask you the reader to look into the world of the Eternit factory in Osasco – the world of the *trabalho pesado* (hard work), of machines and work shifts that from dawn until late at night had uninterruptedly marked the lives of the former workers I met. Here is Teodoro's narrative:

You know, here we are in the Third World. You needed to learn a profession to survive and have a life a little better than others had, otherwise you could only dig holes in the street. I had to study to learn a profession and find a job. As soon as I got my qualification as a mechanic, I got a promotion. I liked mechanics. I worked happily all my life ... I was responsible for the plant's workshop; for this reason, I knew every corner of the plant and I knew all the people working there, from the cleaners to the managers. I knew everything and everybody ... I still have everything in my mind. Every night, I still work at Eternit! [His wife, participating in the interview, although silent most of the time, smiled. Teodoro referred to the dreams he had almost every night]. Every day I work, until now I haven't had a day of rest! [He laughed]. It was like a 24-hour working day, because when a machine had a problem or did not work correctly, they called me back to the plant to fix it, even if I was already at home. At any time, during the night or very early in the morning. It was normal. It happened at least twice per week ... Today... I dream of my tools or of having a debate with my boss. I see the whole plant. In my mind, I see all the machines. I know everything. If you want to know something, I can tell you. If you want, I can draw a map of the plant with everything: the various entrances, the offices, the restaurant, the recruitment centre... there was even a lake. I used to fish there... [He began drawing; in the background, dogs barking and the sounds of cars passing close to the house; the silence in the room was only broken by Teodoro's whispers to explain to me what he was drawing]. I am drawing a map of the plant as it was when I began working there. Then, it changed a lot. It enlarged. Now I am drawing the *sessão de acabamento e moldagem* [finalization and moulding sector]. Leandro [another of ABREA's founders, and like Teodoro one of the oldest anti-asbestos activists I met] was responsible for this sector, which was one of the dustiest ones because workers cut the products there. Eliezer [ABREA's current president] worked there. [He continued drawing] Here, there was the punch clock. Everybody passed by it, the managers, the workers, the cleaners... In this other sector, there were two rotating bridges above ...

The plant was very large. In the end, there were five machines. For instance, 'Machine One' was for *telhas e canaletas* [roof tiles and pipes], while 'Machine Two' was for *telhas e chapas lisas* [roof tiles and smooth sheets] [He wrote down the products' dimensions].

Have you ever seen one of the Eternit machines? [I answered: 'No, I haven't']. That's a pity! Water, asbestos and cement were put into the machine. For every 1,500 kilos of cement there was 12 or 14 per cent of asbestos. In the machine, there was a filter. The material passed through it and became a very thin film.

It worked more or less in this way [he explained the machine's mechanism]. The mixture of asbestos and cement came down onto the filter, which was made of felt. The dimensions of this filter were around 1m x 1m. There was a hole in it, through which the water passed and pushed

> the mixture below. The mixture then passed under a rotating press… I can draw a machine for you as well. I could have taken a picture! Never thought about that before!
>
> Here, there was the *carregamento* [loading] sector, with a rotating bridge. From there, the trucks went outside through entrance number two. While here [he kept drawing], there was the workshop. Beside it were placed large amounts of asbestos. Here, the *britador* [crushing machine], the *injetora* [spraying machine], the *marcenaria* [carpentery]… every sector was full of dust, even the offices… everybody *comia pó* [ate dust] because everything was so close together … There were barracks close to the plant; the textile factory Santista – I worked there for ten years – was situated where today there is Carrefour, while the Eternit was where today there is Walmart. The whole neighbourhood was called Morumbi. Asbestos from Canada, Goiás and South Africa arrived by truck, but there was also a railway arriving directly from Osasco's train station to the factory.

Eating Dust

According to Teodoro, 'a veil of dust covered the parked cars and the trees around the plant. It was visible, especially on those trees situated close to the machinery. The sector dedicated to tube production was the worst, it was awfully dusty' (from an interview conducted in Osasco, May 2015).

At the Eternit plant in Osasco in the late 1970s, measures to limit workers' exposure to asbestos began to be systematically taken. My interlocutors' narratives that referred to a previous period, especially during the first decades of activity, described a dusty working environment, as well as practices that favoured the dispersion of the dust (i.e. the asbestos fibres), inside and outside the factory. The workers 'ate the dust', as did their wives and their children – in fact, probably all Osasco's inhabitants, who lived near the factory and those who reused the dust given away by the firm.

The waste material containing asbestos was ground in order to be reused. There were men who spent their whole lives working at the *britador* (crushing machine), in an incredibly dusty sector of the factory where workers had to crush everything: pieces of tubing, roofing and water tanks. The excess *pó* (dust, meaning asbestos) and that which could not be used anymore in production was given for free to any workers who asked for it to make flooring in their homes or gardens. 'Did you also take it?' I asked Teodoro.

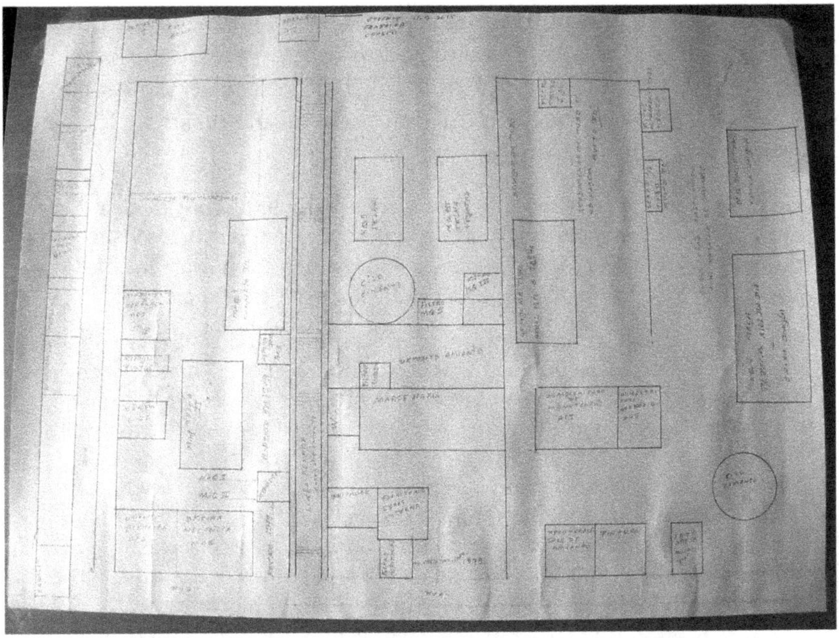

Figure 1.1 Map of the Eternit plant in Osasco (demolished in 1993), drawn by a study participant. Osasco, São Paulo, Brazil, 2015. Photograph by the author.

> No, never. I used to bring home just the residual felt filters so that my wife could make small carpets from them. She beat and washed them; those filters were full of dust … The dust was used also in public spaces, for instance in the neighbourhoods where the streets had not been paved yet. You could see trucks in Osasco transporting the residual dust containing asbestos. People came to the plant asking for the dust in order to pave the streets in their neighbourhoods – and the firm gave it to them for free.

The same practice also occurred in Casale Monferrato (Italy), and in both places it contributed to creating risk and dangerous situations beyond the factory. In the long term, it worsened the impact of asbestos exposure on public health by enlarging the size of the exposed community, and contaminating people who were often unaware of either their own exposure or even of the dangers of asbestos. In particular, the habit of workers coming home still dressed in their dusty overalls directly exposed their wives and children to the asbestos.

Paula was one of the few women to have joined ABREA. She was Ricardo's widow. Ricardo, who had worked at Eternit in Osasco between the late 1970s and the early 1980s, died in 1995 from a pulmonary oedema that was not recognized as asbestos-related, despite his occupational exposure to asbestos. Paula had a story of domestic exposure to asbestos – she 'ate the dust' at home while washing Ricardo's overalls. Here is her narrative:

> He came home, had a shower, drank some milk and went to sleep. We did not have time even for a conversation. I was very busy with four children to look after and I did not give him much attention. Our life was just eating, sleeping and working hard. He never missed a day of work.
>
> He used to drink a lot of hot milk because they said that it was good *para tirar aquele pó* [to pull out that dust, i.e. asbestos]. Then he went to bed and slept. The next day, the same. While he was sleeping, I washed his clothes. I left them to soak. There was no soap powder at that time, I used bar soap. Well, there was already soap powder on the market, but we could not afford it. It was expensive, and only people who could afford the costs bought it. When he came back with dirty boots and clothes, I washed them by hand, since we did not have a washing machine at the time. I put the clothes in a tub and got rid of the dust, which in the meantime had become stiff, with a broom. The clothes were very dirty. Now [after three decades], my hands itch, and I do not know why.

At the Eternit plant in Osasco there was no obligation (at least before the end of the 1970s) for workers to take showers or remove work clothes before leaving the plant to prevent their dusty bodies and clothes becoming potential sources of contamination outside the factory – in the city generally, but especially in their homes. The majority of the former workers I conducted interviews with said that they used to come home still wearing their dusty yellow or brown coveralls – the colour depended on their assigned task within the plant. The wives then washed their clothes, without taking measures to protect themselves.

Recent research in the biomedical field has shown the increasing incidence of asbestos-related diseases (ARDs) among asbestos workers' wives (Raile 2008; Raile and Markowitz 2011). During my fieldwork in Osasco, the majority of the women I met (all wives or daughters of former workers, now engaged in activism) did not consider themselves to have been exposed, and so rarely undertook the medical examinations proposed by ABREA to check their respiratory systems. I relate women's role in patriarchal societies such as Brazil or Italy, marked by invisibility and abnegation, to the processes leading to a woman's own exposure being unrecognized, and consequently to ARDs from domestic exposure being underdiagnosed. Similar phenomena relate to specific contexts and historical processes moulding the cultural dimension of risk perception, as I further discuss in the next sections.

The Global Health Disasters of the Asbestos Market

According to global estimates of deaths related to occupational lung cancers reported by Cullinan et al., the number of global AR deaths was 33,610 in 2010, and ARDs represent 'the commonest cause of mortality and morbidity of workers exposed to occupational hazards worldwide' (Cullinan et al. 2017: 2). Although the carcinogenicity of all asbestos minerals has been largely demonstrated, only sixty-seven countries have prohibited asbestos (Kazan-Allen 2019a), and to date it is estimated that approximately 125 million people are still exposed to asbestos in their workplace (WHO 2018; Cullinan et al. 2017: 2). Considering the long latency period of ARDs and the level of asbestos-containing materials still present environmentally, even where asbestos manufacturing and extraction have ceased (Cullinan et al. 2017: 2), the burden of AR diseases and deaths represents a global health disaster – a silent catastrophe, started in the past, affecting the present and threatening the future.

In Brazil, according to the data reported by the *Boletim Epidemiológico* [Epidemiological Bulletin] published by the Secretaria de Vigilância em Saúde [Secretary of Health Vigilance] of the Ministry of Health, 1,192 ARDs were diagnosed from 2007 to 2013, and 90.4 per cent of the identified cases were registered by public health research centres in the municipality of Campinas, São Paulo (Ministério da Saúde 2016). This information is relevant for two aspects. First, the concentration of diagnoses is in the most industrialized and populated region of Brazil, where anti-asbestos mobilization began. Second, there are documented difficulties in obtaining an ARD diagnosis in settings where the awareness of asbestos effects on health does not inform the illness experiences. This last aspect is related to the phenomenon of particularly frequent underdiagnosis in countries where asbestos use is still legal (see Terracini, Pedra and Otero 2015; Marsili et al. 2016; Cullinan et al. 2017). Moreover, the data reported by the *Boletim Epidemiológico* published in 2016 refer exclusively to ARDs diagnosed in workers exposed to asbestos. The survey did not consider the cases of diseases developed as a consequence of environmental and/or domestic exposure, workers with irregular job contracts or those whose traces have been lost in the frantic worker turnover that has characterized Brazilian industrial economics in past decades.

Unrecognized cases relate to a silent suffering, and substantiate the moral and scientific commitment to the effects of the toxic market of asbestos on health in terms of 'invisible disasters' (Mazzeo 2017a). In this regard, the role of anthropology is crucial in creating and proposing new paths to 'reimagine global health' (Farmer et al. 2013) and to take into account 'elusive data' and 'unmask the culture of silence' (Scheper-Hughes 1997: 203) when tackling global health issues.

I have adopted a critical interpretative approach (Lock and Scheper-Hughes 1990) to epidemiological data related to AR diseases and deaths.

> In a critical interpretative approach, what matters most are the means through which research data are acquired, the various and complex meanings these findings might have, and the relations between the kinds of knowledge generated and the maintenance of powerful ideologies and forms of dominance, both social/political and biomedical/scientific … Reductionist science is reappraised as a product of its historical and cultural contexts … There is often a striking lack of awareness of the ways in which the culture of their science [epidemiology and/or demography] structures the questions asked and overdetermines the findings. (Scheper-Hughes 1997: 202–3)

By analysing statistics about the incidence of AR deaths and diseases, I was able to confirm Fassin's argument about the necessity of ethnography in order 'to obtain a realistic view of the epidemiological landscape … [It] allows one to apprehend the diversity and complexity of the mechanisms through which social factors insinuate themselves into the body … This means renouncing simplistic determinisms and statistical reasoning' (Fassin 2007: 192).

How the Disasters Happen

The so-called 'Eternit trial' – which took place in Italy between 2009 and 2014 and in which the victims of asbestos contamination in Casale Monferrato accused the Eternit firm, represented by Stephan Schmidheiny and Luis de Cartier de Marchienne – made crucial documents publicly and internationally accessible, proving that the debate on AR health hazards had already been underway among asbestos lobbies since the 1970s. In this regard, the acts of the congress held in Neuss (Germany) in 1976 were emblematic; they became important proof, which the transnational anti-asbestos movement can now refer to as support for its allegations.

The congress of Neuss was organized by the agency Amiantus-Protection of Work and Environment, an institution established in 1976 to face the 'practical and political problems' that were destabilizing the asbestos market, as written in the congress report. I had the opportunity to analyse the document thanks to a legal expert supporting the anti-asbestos movement who gave me a copy. Among the listed political problems were the relationships with trade unions, journalists, mass media and competitors. The issues with the last of these had to be solved by the 'elimination of competitors producing asbestos-free products'. However, the Neuss congress was not focused on political problems, but rather on practical ones and their solutions (e.g. promoting the use of masks, moistening asbestos material before proceeding with disposal, and washing work clothes inside the factories). Projects designed to deepen knowledge on 'asbestos and health' were discussed, together with the necessity to adequately divulge such knowledge and to adopt technical measures in the plants, while taking local differences into account.

In the introduction of the congress's report, the history of biomedical studies investigating and demonstrating the carcinogenicity of asbestos fibres was documented, and referred to crucial steps in the advancement of biomedical knowledge and the prohibition of asbestos. Among the others, seminal studies on the relationship between asbestos exposure and MM were mentioned (Selikoff, Churg and Hammond 1964, 1965). In 1968, the SAIAC cartel debated the health hazards related to asbestos exposure. A WHO congress organized in Lyon (France) in 1972, with the participation of renowned experts on the health dangers of asbestos, debated the worldwide prohibition of asbestos crocidolite (so-called blue asbestos), and the process leading to the prohibition of all kinds of asbestos in Sweden, which later happened in 1977, was mentioned. It was clearly stated that the congress participants (managers of the major AC factories in the world, including Herman Straub representing Eternit S.A. Brasil) agreed to adopt strategies to manage the 'problem of asbestos', meaning the health hazards linked to asbestos exposure. The lobbies' position towards the 'problem' might be inferred from the report, but particularly from the conclusions made by Stephan Schmidheiny. Schmidheiny summarized discourses explicitly and primarily oriented to safeguard companies' economic profits, since 'competitors would do everything, legally and illegally, to disturb the AC industry' as was written in the first pages of the report. I quote from Schmidheiny's conclusion:

> Hundreds of people are engaged full-time with the problem 'asbestos and health'. They operate in government offices, companies, unions, competitor firms, mass media, medicine and groups interested in the protection of the environment. Considerable means are in motion against asbestos, and such means take advantage of the fact that the public are eager for sensation.
>
> The industry is not prepared for an attack at this level, and it is not organized collectively. A defensive action does not produce anything sen-

> sational. The problem 'asbestos and health' will become more difficult, heavy and urgent in the coming months.
>
> The critical point focuses on the fact that asbestos is accused of being a dangerous substance, and competitors take advantage of this.

In the report, there was also an explicit reference to the contributions of biomedical professionals, and biomedical studies were cited to support the possibility of establishing a safe threshold of asbestos exposure: 'The responsibility [to cause pathologies] only resides in fibres longer than 5μ and with a diameter shorter than 3μ. Asbestos considered as a simple material is by no means dangerous'. Asbestosis, lung cancer and MM were listed as ARDs; 'pleural plaques are not considered as pathology in the majority of countries worldwide', it was reported. When the policy adopted by the group of the congress participants was announced, it was introduced as follows: 'Since the 1960s, we have followed scientific studies about asbestos with the utmost attention. The rarity of diseases among workers makes us think that the security measures taken to date have been valid. However, the latest knowledge requires measures that are more cautious'.

The congressional acts, together with the broader documentation of archive material, clinical reports and testimonies made public by the Italian lawsuit, revealed the intentions behind the strategies to deny and minimize the health dangers related to asbestos exposure. This criminal management of the asbestos market (Altopiedi 2011) was designed to prevent exposed workers and citizens from framing their own experiences of danger into risk categories. I quote again from Schmidheiny's conclusions:

> We have to live with this problem. Today, we acknowledge that asbestos is a potentially dangerous material, if it is not handled correctly…
>
> It is very important that we do not fall into any type of panic. The technical directors were shocked by what they have learned during these three days. The same must not happen with the workers. The struggle against the dust must take place in each plant in a natural way and without fuss.

Schmidheiny concluded by affirming the impossibility of adopting a standard procedure in all plants, because the management conditions varied in each country. In particular, Central America had standards that differed from Europe and South Africa, and union organizations used asbestos and health issues to advance other claims. For this reason, AC companies were warned and invited to be cautious. The workers' low level of education, smoking habits and unwillingness to use masks were all mentioned as eventual obstacles to effectively implementing new safety measures as designed by the congress.

I read these last considerations as indicative of strategies intended to transfer blameable behaviours (e.g. smoking or incorrect use of the masks) and the responsibility for having contracted ARDs to the workers. The measures, transnationally elaborated and negotiated, were then put into practice locally by considering the characteristics of each context. Through similar dynamics, the transnational dimension of the 'politics of asbestos' (Waldman 2011) came to define both the AR market and disasters.

The lack of knowledge about the carcinogenicity of asbestos made workers take risks that seemed acceptable and less dangerous than other risks. Moreover, brainwashing the workers with the idea that smoking was more dangerous than inhaling asbestos fibres transferred the firm's responsibility to the workers' habits.

In Osasco (Brazil), among the strategies adopted to deny and minimize the health hazards represented by asbestos exposure, managers of AC factories elaborated discourses and practices to brainwash workers, particularly about issues concerning health and environment. I refer to ABREA's archival documents, including the periodicals *Telhadinho: Orgão Informativo e de Congraçamento dos Colaboradores Eternit* [Small Tile: Informative and Reconciliation Institute of Eternit Collaborators], edited and distributed to the workers by the firm in the 1980s. During one of the numerous afternoons spent together with my research partners at the ABREA office, we read these periodicals and even made jokes about their covers and contents. The cover of Number 70 (Christmas 1982) in particular made us laugh bitterly; it showed the Virgin Mary holding an Eternit water reservoir as if it were a cradle. A text in one of these periodicals, Number 68 (Christmas 1981), was written in collaboration with a company doctor and titled 'A sua participação no ciclo da vida' [Your participation in life's cycle], with a section dedicated to explaining pollution. I quote this section, because it represents the kinds of discourses on environmental issues elaborated by the firm and addressed to the workers – or 'collaborators', as workers used to be called by the company.

> **What is pollution?**
>
> It is a case of alterations introduced by humankind into the environment, provoking imbalances or, better, leading to new equilibria different from those previously existing, and we call the agents that cause these changes pollutants. These changes may occur in the air, water or

> soil, and can be produced by solid, liquid or gaseous substances. Pollution is relative. For example, an antibiotic is beneficial for man but it is a pollutant for the bacterium causing the infection.
>
> Nowadays, much has been said and heard about pollution. News accusing industries of polluting the environment by throwing their debris in the rivers and causing contamination are common…
>
> The problem exists and the reality is that government authorities are already worried about pollution control. Regulations and laws have already been elaborated for this purpose, and many others will appear in the near future.
>
> Aware of the problem, Eternit has invested millions of *cruzeiros* [the old Brazilian currency] in de-polluting equipment (e.g. aspirators and filters) for the well-being and comfort not only of its community of collaborators, but also of the surrounding inhabitants. Today we can say that the water that Eternit releases into the streams is free of pollutants, the dust remains trapped in the filters and is not being released into the air, and that the aspiration system in the workplaces allows clean and healthy work [*a trabalho limpo e saudável*].
>
> However, unfortunately, environmental pollution control does not depend exclusively on Eternit. We all have our part in the responsibility. The aspiration equipment provided by Eternit is useless if it is not used properly.
>
> Collaborator! Try to work respecting the rules by using the equipment and machinery correctly. Play your part in combating pollution by keeping your workplace in a good condition of cleanliness, by throwing garbage into the appropriate containers and by cleaning the machines you use. Keep your work tools in order and in the right places, because order and cleanliness are signs of culture and civilization, and we all have our share of responsibility.
>
> If we all work on this venture, we will be able to win the battle against pollution. Otherwise, we will be fatally marching towards a clamorous defeat. Together we can save the lives of the fish, the gentle singing of the birds, and the fertility of the land. Will is power and you can…

The absence of perception of risk (and consequently, disaster) was exacerbated by the trust that workers had in their employers, who they believed would never have acted against the community of workers and their families. A similar feeling characterized the narratives of my interlocutors, regardless of whether or not they were actively involved in the anti-asbestos mobilization. 'I speak the truth, that company never mistreated the workers', one of the oldest ABREA members who had been engaged in the mobilization since the beginning once told me. Another activist, during an informal conversation, told me that he had had two families: Eternit and ABREA. A similar emotional attachment to the company is related to the industrial paternalism (cf. Burawoy 1979) informing the policies adopted by the firm. Local governments in Osasco and in the two Italian contexts investigated during my previous research (Bari and Casale Monferrato) had welcomed the establishment of AC industries in their region. By emphasizing the social and economic benefits the asbestos market would bring, the decisions made within local policies contributed to a consensus and trust among the general population towards the firms. This attitude led to the removal of risk, both at public (e.g. in institutional discourses) and private levels. Working for AC firms was considered to be a great opportunity in life, a privilege, and it was a common habit to invite one's relatives to apply for positions in the same plant. These habits and feelings of trust increased the vulnerability of the community of exposed workers and citizens. AR disasters also became invisible because of similar logic and dynamics.

The last aspect I wish to draw attention to in this section concerns the experiences of disasters and dangers that have been made invisible because of particular practices and dynamics related to the routine medical examinations that workers had in the workplace. In my analysis, these tests and encounters with biomedical doctors can be included in the processes through which disasters caused by asbestos economics have occurred and continue to occur. Based on study participants' narratives (from both Casale Monferrato and Osasco), those medical encounters could have been an occasion to break the silence surrounding the dangers related to asbestos exposure. Instead, the company doctors contributed to making the veil of invisibility of risk more impenetrable, since even in cases of visible respiratory problems, asbestos contamination was always denied.

My research partners in Osasco did not remember being given a diagnosis, or their colleagues being given one, even with the presence of lung pathologies that were later read as symptoms of ARDs. Test results were never delivered to the workers, who were only verbally informed about their health conditions. In fact, only the employers received and saved the certificates from medical doctors. In this regard, I quote an interview conducted with an ABREA activist suffering from asbestosis and pleural plaques.

> We underwent periodic examinations provided by the company's doctors, but no worker ever received the diagnosis of any ARDs, even in the presence of coughing and shortness of breath [*falta de ar*]. They told us that smoking was very dangerous, especially for those of us who worked with asbestos, but they did not say why. Anyway, I followed that advice and one day decided to stop smoking. I remember I was having a break

> in the plant's yard and a guy came up to me asking for a cigarette. I gave him the whole packet and, in that very moment, I decided that I would never smoke again. I haven't smoke since that day …
>
> Nobody ever talked to me about asbestosis or told me that I had asbestos in my lungs. I only found out later, when I underwent medical checks at public health centres where there were doctors with whom ABREA was in touch.

The gap in communication increased the employers' power to control and delay the spread of risk perception among workers. Numerous times, I heard ABREA activists advising new members and reminding older ones that it was their right to ask for the certificates from their medical tests, regardless of whether they had taken place at public health centres or at private clinics in agreement with the firm.

Workers' 'experiential knowledge' (cf. Blume 2017) of the unhealthy asbestos-laden environment to which they had been exposed daily turned out to be a political tool only decades later, when engagement in activism provided them with the words that had been denied to them until that moment. The exposed workers' new awareness of being at risk of becoming sick and dying from ARDs represents a further cause of suffering. At the same time, not being recognized as contaminated victims leads to another, albeit distinct, experience of violence related to the invisibility determined by 'the processes of neutralization of truth and denial of the cause–effect relationship' in ARDs (Ferraro 2015: 123–59).

Risk communication and awareness campaigns to increase the perception of health hazards are strategies put into practice by grassroots movements addressing environmental and health issues at a local and global level (Zoller 2005; Barca 2012; Rossi and D'Angelo 2012). Practices and policies of risk communication are part of the negotiation processes to develop a risk category, recognize a risk situation, legitimize the suffering caused by exposure to a given risk, and take action to manage a given risk situation.

Anti-asbestos activists I met across Italy and Brazil had entered similar processes to fight against the socio-cultural, political and economic dynamics causing the global health disasters provoked by the toxic market of asbestos.

Conclusion

Contrary to what the Supreme Court of Rome stated, in my analysis, the 'disaster event' coincides with the death/disease event, and the epidemic disaster is the disaster, not just an aspect of it. In this chapter, I have discussed aspects characterizing the dynamics through which

AR disasters occur, are lived, and can be denied and silenced. I have discussed how specific strategies adopted by AC companies prevented workers from developing a theoretical knowledge to canalize their experiential knowledge of asbestos dangers into risk categories, which worsened and prolonged the disaster's impact on the exposed communities of workers and citizens.

Around the world, asbestos lobbies have adopted and continue to adopt denial strategies that have made the dangers related to asbestos exposure invisible, thus worsening and prolonging the contamination of entire communities (Brodeur 1985; Braun and Kisting 2006; Braun 2008; Waldman 2007, 2009, 2011; Jobin 2013).

The processes of AR disasters are characterized by dynamics making risk and the disaster itself invisible and silent (Waldman 2011; Petrillo 2015). Asbestos fibres are microscopic cancer-causing factors that can be inhaled imperceptibly. Thus, I refer to them as 'invisible'. Furthermore, asbestos lobbies have promoted strategies to prevent the spread of risk awareness among exposed workers. Consequently, a risk situation became an invisible danger, since the exposed workers and residents could not perceive it (Slovic 2010; Di Giulio et al. 2015). MM's long latency period is a further aspect influencing the experience of a risk that is perceived only when the danger becomes manifest, decades after exposure, by which time the polluting source can be distant in time and space, or may not even exist anymore. In addition, the workers' trust in the employing AC firms deserved the removal of risk while the employees were living and working in environments whose visible dustiness, although perceived and experienced, was not recognized or not admitted as a source of fatal danger.

Risk as an objective reality does not exist; it is always a culturally and historically produced cognitive category through which the correlation between real events can be represented and consequently managed (Boholm 2003). By referring to the contribution of Douglas and Wildavski (1982), Boholm reflects on the relationship between risk and culture, and the role played by various forces (political, economic and cultural) in defining a risk category (Boholm 2003). Moreover, the subjective experience and perception of risk are influenced by other factors that concern the emotional and bodily 'worlds' of an exposed social actor, as the phenomenological approach to risk theory emphasizes (Renn 2008; Di Giulio et al. 2015). According to Boholm (2003), reflecting on the cultural dimension of categories and discourses related to a risk does not mean denying the objectivity of a particular situation of danger. I agree with Parkhill et al., who argue that 'while many environmental threats (e.g. air pollution, ionising radiation and climate change) hold very real consequences for both people and ecosystems, our knowledge and understanding of them can only ever be viewed as socially constructed' (Parkhill et al. 2010: 40). However, in AR disasters, I found that the severity of the hazards may have increased because of the lack of risk perception, or due to discourses that tended to deny or minimize risk (cf. Cappelletto and Merler 2003; McCulloch 2006; Michaels 2008; Oreskes and Conway 2010; Waldman 2011; Terracini and Mirabelli 2016). Based on the cultural theory of risk, the conceptual category of risk is necessary to manage what is indefinable, unusual, uncertain, unclassifiable, and threatens an established order (Douglas and Wildavsky 1982; Boholm 2003).

The dynamics at stake in one's elaboration of risk perception have been investigated by a number of scholars from various disciplines (e.g. sociology, anthropology and psychology). Cappelletto and Merler, whose study with the Italian miners at the Australian asbestos mine of Wittenoom offers a significant contribution to the understanding of these dynamics, combine anthropological and epidemiological approaches. The authors show the extent to which the lack of knowledge about asbestos dangers prevented miners from transforming their own perception of the unhealthy working conditions into a perception of risk of asbestos dangers (Cappelletto and Merler 2003).

In AR disasters, which can remain invisible for decades, there is procrastination when managing the 'critical event' (Das 1995). The seriousness of disasters is exacerbated by the fact that the dangers reside in familiar environments, where there are no elements of 'extraordinariness' to make the exposed persons notice or think about an eventual risk situation (Parkhill et al. 2010). In similar circumstances, the risks remained unperceived and, for this reason, became more dangerous (Douglas and Wildavsky 1982; Douglas 1991; Ligi 2009).

Notes

1. To date, chrysotile is the only kind of asbestos allowed in those countries that have not passed a general prohibition of asbestos minerals yet, while the other types of asbestos are prohibited worldwide for their ascertained carcinogenicity.
2. In Italy, the prohibition of all kinds of asbestos minerals dates back to 1992, when Law Number 257 was passed, and from that point any activity involving any kind of asbestos minerals was prohibited.

2

Osasco

City, Work and Struggles

Two hammers and two cogs accompanied by the words *cidade* (city) and *trabalho* (work), evoking the importance of urbanization and industrialization, feature on the Osasco city seal, easily visible on buses, flags and public office buildings around the city centre. The narratives proposed in this chapter will confer dynamicity to the concept of *cidade*, and will substantiate the word *trabalho*. My aim is to recognize the role that men and women, children and the elderly, each with their own story, have played in the processes moulding the cultural, sociopolitical and economic fabric of Osasco. To the words *cidade* and *trabalho*, I add *lutas* (struggles) to recall Osasco's history, marked as it is by a significant legacy of civil and workers' mobilizations, strikes, protests, and cultural movements, through which imaginaries, values and practices of citizenship and civil engagement have circulated.

This chapter will offer an insight into the fertile soil from which the anti-asbestos activism emerged in Osasco, and how it then expanded throughout the whole country. The historiographical trajectories that I followed combine with the narratives of the Osasco inhabitants I met – male and female workers I came across when they had already left the world of work, without it, however, ceasing to be part of their lives. They will lead us into the Osasco of their youth and aspirations, while moving across regions and continents, as well as into the distinct seasons of both Brazil and their lives.

A substantial part of the historical reconstruction proposed in this chapter is provided by the ethnographic data collected during the face-to-face encounters I had with study participants. During our meetings, my interlocutors made their 'embodied past' (Fassin 2008) communicable, and kept it alive through the narratives we interweaved together, enriching Osasco's history with private life stories and memories.

Movements and the City

Starting from the 1870s, with the prohibition of the slave trade and abolitionist campaigns supported by laws that were gradually being promulgated, the necessity to promote 'free' paid work in substitution for slavery was functional to redress the reduction in the workforce (da Cruz Paiva and Moura 2008).[1] Thus, the Brazilian government began to adopt a number of measures to encourage immigration from Europe. Between 1870 and 1949, almost 5 million foreigners arrived in Brazil, more than 50 per cent of whom were Italian and settled in São Paulo state. Between 1890 and the First World War, Italians comprised a quarter of the São Paulo inhabitants. At the beginning of the immigration process, the majority of Italians, with their tickets paid for by the Brazilian government, moved to the coffee plantations. Those who arrived autonomously stayed in the capital and looked for jobs there as artisans, industrial workers, or mechanics.

The Italian immigrant Antonio Agù, who left for Osasco from Piedmont (around 150 kilometres from Casale Monferrato, Italy) and arrived in Brazil in 1872 (Marquetti Rocha Negrelli and Collino de Oliveira 2003), is considered to be the founder of Osasco, São Paulo, according to the official historiography. Agù, who had an initial amount of capital available, invested his money in lands adjacent to Kilometre 16[2] of the *Estrada de Ferro* (railway) Sorocabana, intuiting the future relevance of the railway for the transportation of goods, raw materials and people. These movements favoured the transformation of 'Kilometre 16' from a rural area into an industrial city, Osasco. Agù promoted the arrival of Italian immigrants and the investment of capital from the São Paulo agrarian oligarchy, which was making profits and increasing its economic and political power through the cultivation of coffee (ibid.).

In 1890, together with Barão Sensaud de Lavaud, another entrepreneur, Agù, founded the first factory in the area that would later be called Osasco. The factory was the 'Companhia Cerâmica Industrial de Osasco', a ceramics plant. Afterwards, Agù collaborated in the foundation of other two factories, a paper mill (in 1892), and a textile factory (in 1895). In 1895, Agù financed the construction of the train station. During the opening celebration, when asked what the name for the

Figure 2.1 City seal drawn in a graffiti. Osasco, São Paulo, Brazil, 2015. Photograph by the author.

station (and consequently of the village) would be, refusing to name it after himself,[3] he answered Osasco, in homage to his hometown in Piedmont.

Until his death in 1909, Agù favoured the arrival of his compatriots, who could work both in the industry sector (including his factories) and in business activities (Marquetti Rocha Negrelli and Collino de Oliveira 2003: 25). According to his will, the lands he owned in Osasco were donated for the construction of the Igreja Matriz (Osasco's main – Catholic – church, devoted to Saint Anthony, Patron Saint, in homage to Antonio Agù), the Grupo Escolar (school complex), the Mercado Municipal (municipal market), and the Cemitério (cemetery) (Marquetti Rocha Negrelli and Collino de Oliveira 2003).

In the meantime, the village, recognized as a *distrito* (district) in 1919, was gradually taking on the shape of the industrial neighbourhood of São Paulo (Sanazar 2000). Osasco's inhabitants first voted for emancipation from the capital in 1958, but the São Paulo government did not recognize either the results or the validity of Law number 5,121, promulgated on the 27 December 1958 by Osasco's administration to regulate its autonomy. New elections were organized four years later, in 1962, and this time Osasco became an independent municipality (Zampolin Coelho and Moreti 2005).

Starting from the end of the 1930s, numerous international firms chose to set up their factories in Osasco, because it was well connected to São Paulo, the economic hub of Brazil, and had a good railway (Collino de Oliveira and Marquetti Rocha Negrelli 1992: 81). The acceleration in the industrialization process coincided with a reduction in immigration from Europe. In fact, in the Vargas Era (1930–45), characterized by a nationalistic and populist policy (Ribeiro 2006; Schwarcz and Starling 2015), internal migratory fluxes – especially from north-eastern states, Minas Gerais, and inner and rural regions of São Paulo state – were favoured. On the contrary, the arrival of European immigrants, among whom there might have been communists, anarchists and unionists who could represent a threat for the political establishment, was restricted (Zampolin Coelho and Moreti 2005).

Waves of *Nordestinos* (people from the north-eastern Brazilian states), *Mineiros* (Minas Gerais inhabitants) and *Paulistas* (São Paulo state inhabitants), escaping from the misery and hard working conditions in the *roça* (rural area), moved to Osasco and joined the communities of previously arrived immigrants, especially from Europe's Mediterranean countries and Japan (Sanazar 2000). While Osasco's population in the 1940s was less than 16,000, in the 1950s it rose to roughly 41,000, and by the 1960s the number had reached approximately 115,000 (Zampolin Coelho and Moreti 2005: 105). In the broader context, the Brazilian urban population tripled from 1920 to 1940; in the same period, the population of São Paulo state increased by 40 per cent (Santos 1993).

The Brazilian geographer Milton Santos relates the processes of 'macro-urbanization' and industrialization to the processes by which an increasing part of the urban population lives in conditions of poverty (Santos 1993). In fact, in addition to the proximity to São Paulo and the railway, the availability of a large workforce was a crucial factor in determining the readiness of international firms to invest in Osasco. There, these global players could have easy access to a large, cheap workforce of women and men desperately looking for the opportunity to improve their life conditions. Often, during the interviews conducted with former asbestos workers, I heard about the preference of firms to employ young men who were from the *roça*, because they had strong, healthy bodies, were used to hard working conditions, were obedient, and did not question anything. In the narratives that emerged from our encounters, study participants usually recalled memories of their arrival in Osasco, and life stories were narrated as the achievement of (or as the attempt to achieve) a project to improve their life conditions and to guarantee an easier, better future for their children. The majority of them began working when they were underage (between 12 and 14 years old) to help their parents to support their large families. The childhood memories of a large number of my research partners evoked starvation, poverty and a lack of means to attend school.

Zampolin Coelho and Moreti (2005) describe Osasco's particular context as being different from other industrial Brazilian districts. They argue that in Osasco the alienation typical of capitalist societies did not affect the relationships among its inhabitants. A sort of solidarity persisted in a context where the modern urban profile failed to eliminate the old rural values and practices of a large number of Osasco's new inhabitants. In fact, the authors refer to the 'double identity' of Osasco's citizens.[4] Zampolin Coelho and Moreti consider a second aspect that characterized the urbanization process in Osasco. Generally, the workers in Osasco lived in houses that were their own property. This was unusual in other cities, where workers used to live in houses owned by the firms employing them, to which they paid rent. The authors relate this phenomenon in Osasco to an urbanization that was less chaotic than in the larger cities of São Paulo and Rio de Janeiro. However, such differences did not mean that in Osasco there were no social conflicts or exploitation. Child labour, long working days and unhealthy working conditions equated Osasco to other industrial contexts, as my interlocutors' narratives recalled.

Work and Life Trajectories

Lucas

Osasco, 6 May 2015, a grey morning. I just arrived at the central train station and I was going to the corner where Lucas, a member of the Associação Brasileira dos Expostos ao Amianto – ABREA [Brazilian Association of Persons Exposed to Asbestos], would pick me up to drive me to his home for an interview, the first I scheduled for my research in Osasco. I was not particularly anxious, but I was worried about being late. I walked fast. During the first months of my fieldwork, I noticed that ABREA activists always showed up on time, if not early, for their appointments, and so I did not want Lucas to have to wait for me. I was not late but, as I imagined, I found Lucas was already there.

Lucas, 68 years old in 2015, had worked at Eternit in Osasco from 1978 to 1992, when he was fired, one year before the closure of the plant. His job at Eternit was the first and only one with a regular contract that Lucas had had in his whole life. He was 5 years old when he emigrated from Portugal to go with his family to Brazil, which in the 1950s was under the Salazar regime, and they arrived at the seaport of Santos on board the *Castel Verde*.

As soon as I got into his car, Lucas began talking to me about his homeland. He described the place where he was born in Portugal, Ilha da Madeira. 'It is a very tiny island, where there are no streets. Now, it has turned into a touristic place – I watched a documentary on TV – but in the past, there was nothing there but stones. I've never been back, but someday – who knows? – I will', he told me. Later on, during the interview, he would frequently recall his Portuguese origins, and he explicitly mentioned his dream to visit Ilha da Madeira once again in his life. 'A relative of ours wrote the *carta da chamada*[5] (invitation letter) for us to come and work in the lands he had bought in Paraná [Southern Brazil]. So, on our arrival in Brazil, we moved there. Then my family also bought some land, but we did not become rich. I do not miss working in the *roça*. There was so much suffering there', he explained.

Like the majority of the former Eternit workers who joined ABREA, Lucas grew up in the *roça* where he began working in plantations when still a child. Entering the garage on the ground floor of his house, smiling and visibly proud, he pointed up to the terrace where he had built a little vegetable garden. After the interview, we went upstairs and an explosion of life and colours appeared in front of us. There were even four green parrots on the power lines. The contrast with the grey sky and dreary neighbourhood was strong – salad plants, white grapes, little strawberries and chilli peppers. Lucas had covered the more delicate, tiny plants with plastic sheets. He showed me the plants while explaining the amount of water and light needed, and the blooming season of each of them. There was a bird feeder hanging near the balcony railing. 'That is for the parrots that come to visit me', Lucas told me with a smile. When we went back downstairs, I noticed two tools, but could not understand what they were for. Curious, I asked Lucas what they were. He took one and, miming, told me that they were for sowing. He'd brought them from the *roça*.

During our encounter, Lucas showed me old letters, photographs and documents, among them his Brazilian identity document for foreigners, issued in 1969. He also showed me his medical examinations records. In 2015, he had not yet developed any asbestos-related disease

(ARD). I asked him if he had any old photographs from the time he worked at Eternit. He opened a drawer in the same room (the living room), and took out several photo albums. He sat on the floor and started browsing through them. I joined him on the floor. His daughter did the same and they began to show me some pictures. I recognized Lucas as a young man in a couple of photographs taken at Eternit. He narrated how he had come to work there in Osasco:

> One of my father's cousins worked there. I told him that I was looking for a job. I was 32 years old and had just arrived in Osasco from Paranà, where I had been working in the *roça* … It was very hard to live and work there. As soon as my relative presented my application, Eternit employed me. They preferred employing men from the *roça* because we were used to hard work. Except for in the offices, 90 per cent of the workers at Eternit were from the *roça*, because, especially in the beginning, it was hard work, you needed strong arms, because it was all manual work, the machines arrived later … I was in charge of the cleaning activities. I also worked early mornings on Saturday and Sunday. I did night shifts as well. I didn't like to work at night. However, working at Eternit was good. The salary was good and never late. Everybody liked working there. They fired me in 1992 [the plant closed in 1993], otherwise, I would have continued.

In the photo albums, among black-and-white portraits, photographs of birthday parties and photographs taken at Eternit showing Lucas with his co-workers dressed in khaki overalls or dressed smartly for official ceremonies in the presence of the managers. There were also various photographs of flowers and fruit; Lucas told me that his daughter had taken them on the terrace where the little vegetable garden was. Again, a smile and a proud expression appeared on his face.

Leandro and Elisabete

> *A vida é uma história, filha, uma história muito comprida* [Life is a story, my daughter, a very long story]. (From an interview conducted in Osasco, July 2015)

Osasco, 17 July 2015, early morning, sunny. I was going to Leandro's house on foot from the central train station. It was a half-hour walk. I identified the house when I saw Leandro waiting for me on a couch on the veranda. I approached and greeted him. He guided me into his living room. Elisabete, his wife of 61 years, come to greet me. She invited me for lunch, which she was already preparing.

The interview began in the morning and concluded after lunch, in the early afternoon. By that time, warm sunlight was flooding into the living room where Leandro and I sat on the sofa, highlighting the yellow, red and brown colours of the wooden handcrafts he had made during his life. He was 87 years old in 2015, and sadly died in 2018. The most vivid image of him I have is him sitting cross-legged on the couch on his veranda, with the sunlight brushing his elegant features.

Leandro was born to parents of Italian origin in the inner region of São Paulo state, where he began working in the *roça* as a child. Together with his family, Leandro moved to Osasco in 1941. In that same year in Osasco, Eternit do Cimento-Amianto do Brazil S.A. opened the plant that would become the first asbestos-cement (AC) factory of that firm in Brazil, and the largest in Latin America. Leandro worked at Eternit in Osasco for thirty-two years, from 1945 to 1977, when he retired.

Here is Leandro's narrative of his work and life story:

> I was born on a farm in the inner area of São Paulo state. Then my father bought a small plot of land and we lived and worked there until 1941, when we moved to Osasco. My father did not know how to do anything, and my grandfather never had a house to live in. I was 12 years old and my father arranged a false ID for me to start working, since the legal minimum age for working was 14. I began working in a matchstick factory in Osasco. The salary of a 12-year-old kid was good enough to pay three months' rent. I worked there for three years, until a doctor told my mother that working there was unhealthy for a kid … My father was illiterate, but my mother went to school. She was from a richer family, but then, after the marriage, with six children… it was a miserable life … When I began working at Eternit, the plant was as small as a matchbox. When I stopped working… it was as large as a 1,000-litre *caixa d'agua* [i.e. water reservoir, among the most common asbestos-containing products in the world] … I saw the factory grow and employ up to 1,700 workers. Eternit was one of the best factories in Osasco. The salaries were good and always paid on time. Everybody wanted to work there because of the good, slightly higher salary compared to those that you could earn at other factories. For instance, if a carpenter's salary was on average 14 cruzeiros per hour, at Eternit it was 17 or 18 cruzeiros …
>
> I began working as a trainee carpenter. It was quite hard for a teenager. One day, a boss told me that he wanted me to be his secretary. I began working in his office, but I did not like that kind of job. I could not stand sitting at a desk all day, I wanted to move. A couple of months later, I told my boss that I wanted to learn the profession of carpenter. I told him, 'I do not like such sluggishness here, in the office'. You know, I spent just three years at school, a rural school. Then soon after, I began working in the *roça*. I never went to a vocational school, [although] after my marriage I studied a bit of technical design by myself … When I got promotion and began earning the salary of a carpenter, I was happy with life! [*eu fiquei feliz da vida!*].

> I was able to buy my own house, where I made my own family [*eu criei a minha familia*]. When my wife and I got married, we lived for ten months without electricity, but for the first time in our life, we could take a shower instead of a bath in a tub. I put an Eternit *caixa d'agua* on the roof: we even had hot water during the day!

Paula and Ricardo

Osasco, 22 July 2015, a grey, rainy morning. I was on a city bus going to a peripheral neighbourhood, where I had an appointment with Paula, one of the few women in ABREA. Paula, 58 years old in 2015, lost her husband, Ricardo, in 1995 owing to pulmonary oedema when he was only 59 years old. Ricardo had worked at the Eternit plant in Osasco from 1976 to 1983, but his death had not been recognized as AR. Paula had only recently joined ABREA, where she had come to know about the dangers of asbestos. She was a taciturn woman, and I had hardly spoken to her during the ABREA monthly meetings.

Entering the neighbourhood, I felt dismayed. It was my first time there and I had never been so distant from the Osasco city centre. Everything looked unfamiliar. I was relieved when I saw Paula waiting for me at the bus stop where I had to get off. Paula drived me to her home, a house made of bare bricks at the top of a steep, unfinished staircase. The ground was s muddy due to the rain. She took my hand and hold on to me. At the top, I could see that besides Paula's house, there were others, where her children and grandchildren lived. I saw a fair-haired child playing on a terrace. 'She is one of my granddaughters', she said. Paula was black. Later on, during the interview, she would tell me that Ricardo had been white and fair-haired, of Italian descent, and twenty-two years older than her. They had four children, two black and two white. Throughout their twenty-one-year marriage, they faced a lot of rumours and prejudices due to their age and colour differences. In particular, Ricardo's family did not accept Paula into their family at the beginning of their relationship; 'I am black and I was dirtying his family'.[6]

When Paula and Ricardo got married in 1975, Paula was seventeen. She was born in Minas Gerais and moved to São Paulo, together with her mother, in 1969, when she was twelve. During the interview, she described the sense of astonishment at the Estação da Luz [Luz train station] on her arrival in São Paulo. 'Isn't it beautiful?', she asked me. I agreed, the Luz station was still an elegant building, a beautiful crossroads of trains and people when I visited it in 2015. Paula told me: 'The Luz station was the first place I saw in São Paulo. My mother and I had to take a train to Osasco from there. I had never travelled by train. We had moved from Minas Gerais to São Paulo by bus. At the Luz station, I took the train for the first time in my life'.

As soon as they had settled in Osasco, Paula's mother arranged a job for her as a housekeeper and babysitter. During the interview, Paula explained to me that her mother was jealous of the attention that her stepfather gave her and so she preferred to send her daughter away from home. Paula said that both her mother and her stepfather mistreated her, and that working as a housekeeper and babysitter was hard work for her. She quickly had to learn to cook, do the housework and take care of the children, even though she herself was still a child.

Aged seventeen, Paula met Ricardo. When he proposed to her, she did not hesitate for a moment. She accepted immediately and has never in her life regretted that decision. Below, I quote parts of her narrative:

> I met Ricardo one night after a party at my aunt's house. I was coming back to the house where I was working at the time. It was dark, and I felt a bit scared of the cars and could not decide whether to cross the road. He offered me his arm, and we crossed the road together. Then he asked me if I wanted to 'escape with him' [*fugir com ele*, which means spending at least one night together in order to make a marriage necessary to save the girl's honour]. I really did escape, but you know what? It was worth it. He was a good partner. He was mother and father to me, beyond being my husband. I loved him. I took care of him and he took care of me. When you are alone in the world, when you meet somebody who'll take care for you, you love him.
>
> We 'escaped' in January and we got married in March 1975. In 1976, he began working at Eternit. He was happy ... Before working at the Eternit plant, Ricardo had worked in another factory situated in Osasco.
>
> He did not speak much about his work. The only thing he used to say was that the company was good, the work was hard but well paid, and that the salary was always paid on time. We were the first family in the street to buy a colour TV. Our neighbours used to come here to watch it.

Paula described how she washed her husband's overalls in the evening, so encrusted with dust that it seemed to be hardened like cement. Paula and Ricardo did not have a washing machine and could not afford to buy powdered detergent. Paula used to put the dirty overalls to soak for a while and then rub the dust off with a brush and wash with a piece of soap. She remembered how the climate in Osasco was much more humid at that time than today. 'It was never sunny here, just misty and rainy all the time; we never saw the sun', she told me. For this reason, the clothes would not dry; she had to use a red-hot iron to dry them so that Ricardo could go to work with clean overalls. She continued:

> Ricardo never lost a day at work. When not working, he used to take care of the plants and the vegetable garden at home. At the time, there were plenty of bamboo trees here, which we used for the stove. Ricardo loved gardening. We had a variety of vegetables and fruit, including mango, pineapple, lemon, gourd, pumpkin and lettuce. We also had roses. It looked like a *sitio* [croft] here. He took care of everything. One day he told me: 'When I die, if you cannot afford to buy flowers for me, at least bring me one leaf of that mango tree' [I had noticed it in front of the door at my arrival]. So, every November, on All Souls' Day, I go to the cemetery and take a leaf from that mango tree to him. I have removed all the other plants and trees, apart from that one.

Paula began attending ABREA at the invitation of an acquaintance, a former Eternit worker engaged in the anti-asbestos activism. During our meeting, she told me that she was enjoying attending ABREA. Taking part in the association's activities forced her to leave home and talk to people. She said that she had always been extremely shy, but she was now learning to overcome her shyness and not be afraid to talk to strangers. Together with her youngest son, she had recently begun to discover neighbourhoods of the cities of Osasco and São Paulo where she had never been before. She was taking the subway for the first time, starting to 'know the world' as she said, and she looked happy and proud of herself.

Because of her domestic exposure to asbestos, Paula had begun to undergo periodical check-ups at local public health centres whose doctors were in contact with ABREA. By engaging in their activism, she understood that asbestos was dangerous and she believed in the importance of the mobilization, 'not to get money, but justice', she said. She hesitated in using words like 'asbestos' and 'justice'; she asked me to confirm their correctness. She also asked me to explain which diseases asbestos exposure provokes. She had never even heard of asbestos before attending ABREA. She told me that she barely knew how to read and write, but now she was learning new words and learning not to be afraid of 'knowing the world' and new people.

After Ricardo's early retirement for health reasons, Paula had worked at a couple of factories owned by multinational companies based in Osasco. In 2015, she was living on her husband's pension of approximately 800 reais [Brazilian currency, corresponding to approximately 200 US dollars] per month, with financial help from her children.

Struggles

The city of Osasco has been crossed by active socio-political and cultural movements since the early years of its urban and industrial growth. Beginning in the early decades of the twentieth century, union and workers' organizations inspired by anarchism and socialist ideals operated there and handled the claims raised by workers, most of whom were immigrants, illiterate and minors.

In Brazil, working-class struggles began in the first twenty years of the twentieth century. Until the 1930s, laws guaranteeing basic rights to workers did not exist, and governments reacted to workers' claims as matters to be solved by police intervention (Giannotti 2007). Anarcho-syndicalism brought by Spanish and Italian immigrants played a crucial role in accelerating the process through which Brazilian working-class awareness developed and mobilizations spread. Anarchism was based on anti-clerical, anti-military and anti-capitalistic ideals in favour of an international proletariat. It developed especially in southern European countries, which were less industrialized than the northern ones; workers who emigrated to Brazil came from precisely these countries, especially Spain and Italy (ibid.: 76), and a relevant number of them settled down in São Paulo state.

> From the anarchic perspective, syndicates were the most important form of workers' organizations. The main form of struggle was 'direct action': spontaneous struggles with the maximum of autonomy for workers' organizations. The anarchists refused the idea of any central union organization. They only accepted the idea of confederations, which did not impose their decisions and respected the autonomous decisions of the bases instead. Striking was a lobbying instrument, in addition to other kinds of manifestations and protests. The main instrument of struggle and opposition to the bourgeois class was the general strike. (Giannotti 2007: 77)

The history of Brazil's industrialization cannot be dissociated from the history of slavery and coffee plantation economics. With the official abolition of slavery in 1871, it became necessary to import a foreign workforce; thus men and women lived and worked in de facto slave-like conditions, especially those who worked on plantations or as non-specialized workers (Pignatari Werner 1981). In the early 1900s, with the increasing needs of the flourishing industrial sector, governments and entrepreneurs incentivized the immigration of specialized workers from Europe. This immigration did not just produce economic changes, but also had a relevant impact on the sociopolitical scenario in regions devoted to plantation economics and the recent industrializing regions such as São Paulo. Unlike the new Brazilian proletariat, the European one was already politicized. Consequently, 'Brazil did not just import a workforce, but also ideas. The social movements of the beginning of the twentieth century were linked to the anarchist, socialist and union ideas imported together with the specialized workforce' (ibid.: 5).

In 1901, a group of workers employed at the Vidraria Santa Marina glassworks in São Paulo began to mobilize for better working conditions. Most of them were Italian immigrants with a strong working-class awareness (Pignatari Werner 1981). At the time, São Paulo was becoming one of the most industrialized regions of Brazil. High demand for specialized labour attracted specialized workers from European countries, particularly Italy, France and Spain (ibid.). Soon, the first signs of conflict emerged between (a) local entrepreneurs with a mentality anchored in slavery, large landed estates and coffee plantations, wishing to enter the international market and capitalist bourgeoisie, and (b) the foreign workers with a class awareness rooted in European workers' struggles and political thought, especially anarchism and socialism (Giannotti 2007).

The Vidraria Santa Marina was one of the most prosperous industries in the São Paulo region, as the glass industry was an almost non-existent sector in Brazil at the time, and there was a dependence on imports. Hundreds of workers were employed, most of them Italian, and a large number of minors also worked there (Pignatari Werner 1981).

A first strike was organized at the plant in 1901, when workers mobilized for better job contracts. A second strike, in 1909, was organized by 130 workers (all of them minors) requesting higher salaries (Pignatari Werner 1981). This strike led to a mass firing. However, the workers, who were now unemployed, continued to stay in touch with unionists who had supported them during the strike. Particularly incisive was the role played by Edmondo Rossoni, an Italian anarchist and unionist who, on his compatriots' invitation, worked as a teacher to the workers' children (ibid.). The workers' relationship with the unionists led to the formulation of a project for a glass industry cooperatively managed by the workers themselves, who would become *operários-proprietários* (worker-owners). The industry was to be called Cooperativa dos Vidreiros and the chosen site was Osasco, not by accident. In fact, Osasco's inhabitants, the majority of whom were Italian, welcomed and supported their unemployed fellow compatriots by providing them with food, hospitality and help in finding new jobs. Antonio Agù, celebrated by official local historiography as Osasco's founder, even donated land to the workers where they could build a new glass industry; it is interesting to note that not only Italian immigrants gave their support, but also other groups that 'adhered to union values and working-class identity' (ibid.: 50–51). The building for the new factory was erected with the highest quality materials and with the support of unionists, workers and citizens. Companies holding the monopoly of the glass industry in São Paulo soon began to perceive the workers' project as a serious threat, and so mobilized efforts to prevent the start of production. In the end, they reached their objective by illegally corrupting the cooperative's treasurer, who escaped with all the documents and the money that had been collected to buy a furnace, thus depriving the workers of the material conditions to realize their project (ibid.: 54). Nevertheless, this cooperative, despite production never starting, is evoked by local and national historiography as an emblematic example of the start of working-class struggles in Osasco – and in Brazil to a broader extent (ibid.: xiv–xv) – as the following quote suggests:

> The experience and the memory of all this has been transmitted to the descendants of the glassmakers of the Vidraria Santa Marina. They [these events and memories] moulded Osasco into how it appears today, and more than their ancestors, they [the descendants] have been aware of their structural position, as the events of 1968, when they formed a heroic group of student-workers, have demonstrated. (Pignatari Werner 1981: xv)

The strikes organized at the Vidraria Santa Marina are emblematic of crucial aspects characterizing Osasco's history, and they help to situate anti-asbestos activism within a broader process of local dynamics and struggles whose traces were still alive in my interlocutors' narratives and practices of activism. These traces emerged from the stories of emigration, accelerated industrialization, urbanization, child labour, exploitation and displacement. At the same time, the life stories I listened to recalled the trajectories undertaken by men and women who were moved by needs, aspirations and passions in their search for a better life and improved working conditions. By engaging in an everyday struggle for survival, they established new social and affective relationships that became their roots in a rapidly changing world.

Worker-Priests and Liberation Theology in Osasco

The impact of Liberation Theology (LT), whose principles and methods have been put into practice by worker-priests living in the poorest neighbourhoods of Latin American cities and rural regions, has been relevant in the sociopolitical processes in Latin America since the end of the 1960s (Rowland 2007). LT's spread across Latin America is intertwined with the consequences of the accelerated industrialization and urbanization processes that have deeply marked the social and economic contexts of entire regions (Dawson 2007: 140), such as Greater São Paulo, within which Osasco is situated.

> In a situation where, because of international demand for economic growth to service foreign debt, hundreds of thousands of peasants have been driven off land that their families farmed for generations, and where many have drifted to the shanty towns that have sprung up on the periphery of large cities, Liberation Theology has flourished. (Rowland 2007: 2)

In Osasco, the activities promoted by worker-priests operating at the Base Ecclesial Communities (BECs) situated in *favelas* (shanty towns) and *bairros operários* (working-class neighbourhoods) have been crucial in moulding the local social fabric, having also played a fundamental role in the organization of resistance to the military dictatorship in 1964–84 (de Jesus 2006). Starting from the 1960s, worker-priests following LT principles have promoted educational activities at the BECs situated in the most vulnerable neighbourhoods of the city, and contributed to the development of a sense of community based on bonds of friendship and social justice ideals (de Jesus 2006).

The economic growth of the São Paulo region was intertwined with the emergence of urban populations living in conditions of extreme poverty due to the high unemployment rates caused by the imbalance between the number of job opportunities and the much higher number of men and women who moved to the industrializing centres with the aim of improving their lives. Similar phenomena are not just preventable by capitalist economics, but they are critical for its being perpetuated, as the constant availability of such a workforce allows for continued low salaries and the consequent increase of private profits (Martins Rodrigues 1974). Rowland quotes the words of one of the most representative exponents and inspirers of LT, Gustavo Gutiérrez, who said: 'The question in Latin America will not be how to speak of God in a world come of age, but rather how to proclaim God as Father in a world that is inhumane. What can it mean to tell a non-person that he or she is God's child?' (Rowland 2007: 3).

In places such as Osasco, uncontrolled industrialization and the effects of unplanned urbanization combined with the cultural legacy of colonization and an economic system based on slavery and coffee plantations. Governmental institutions operated to safeguard investors' interests (Brazilian and foreign), and did not hesitate to deploy military and police forces to prevent any protests by workers and disadvantaged groups (Martins Rodrigues 1974). In similar settings across Brazil, displaced men and women, living in conditions of extreme vulnerability due to illiteracy, poverty and the lack of a support network, had no guaranteed rights. As reported by local historiographical monographies, 'every social and economic right needed to be conquered' by workers (Pignatari Werner 1981), and the weapon they used most, starting from the early twentieth century, was the strike (Giannotti 2007).

Throughout the decades, Osasco's sociopolitical and cultural life has been particularly vivid due also to the student-workers' groups, including workers studying evening courses at the Ginasio Estadual Antonio Raposo Tavares (which opened in the 1950s) (Pignatari Werner 1981). Moreover, students from the University of São Paulo working in the local factories joined workers' mobilizations (de Oliveira Rovai 2014). The critical thought and resistance practised by all these social groups (worker-priests, student-workers and others) culminated in July 1968 in one of the largest and most uniquely overt strikes to be organized against the military dictatorship.

Starting in the 1960s, these social groups animating Osasco's political life referred to Freire's pedagogy, believing in the importance of education and the key concept of *conscientização*, which literally translated means the process of developing critical thinking (Freire 1980). Under the military dictatorship in Brazil (1964–84), social movements found a substantial coincidence between education and revolution. The combination deeply influenced not only their strategies and ethics of struggle, but also inspired their projects for democratic governmental institutions to be organized after the military regime (Tassan 2012: 139).

The Brazilian historian Semeraro offers an interpretation of Brazilian social movements in the light of two key concepts: liberation and hegemony. In particular, he underlines how Freire's idea of liberation and Gramsci's (1975) concept of hegemony are fundamental references for an understanding of Brazilian mobilizations in the 1960s and 1980s (Semeraro 2007). These theoretical and political tools became deeply intertwined, and they influenced 'social movements, political organizations, and Brazilian working-class educators whose political-educational practices achieved a sort of unity by conferring a peculiar accord of language, theoretical formulations, and sociopolitical projects' (ibid.: 95). They are still useful tools to understand the struggles currently undertaken by oppressed and subaltern groups, in Brazil and globally (Semeraro 2007).

At the end of the 1970s and the beginning of the 1980s, the lexicon of Gramsci's political thought was popularized by social movements and academia. According to Gohn, 'Gramsci is the author most incisive in the analysis and in the dynamics of struggles and urban grassroot movements in Latin America in the decades of the 1970s and 1980s' (Gohn 1997: 188, quoted by Semeraro 2007: 100). Moreover, Gramsci's concepts have been fundamental in the elaboration and implementation of the new institutions of a democratic State to be erected after two decades of military dictatorship. Gramsci's acknowledgement of the ethical and political dimensions of the State legitimized the flow of the numerous sociopolitical forces that fought against the dictatorship into the new State institutions, avoiding the risk that they might disaggregate or disappear (Semeraro 2007).

The legacy of Osasco's sociocultural and political history was still affecting the strategies and practices of anti-asbestos activism I researched in 2014–15. The anti-asbestos activists I met gathered each month in meetings favouring discussions, reflections and proposals for action that might be feasible in the local context, but with constant recall of social justice aims to be pursued worldwide. A connection can be found between those practices and the tradition of civil engagement characterizing Osasco's history. The *conscientização* process starts from the involvement of the oppressed, the marginalized and the sufferers, who develop knowledge and therefore acquire the power to act. The following step of *conscientização* consists of making others acquire knowledge, and in so doing, making one's own oppression – and suffering – visible and recognized, while at the same time making others aware of specific dynamics producing disparity and vulnerability. I relate the category of the 'anti-asbestos activist' who is generally a person suffering from the impact of asbestos exposure on his/her life to that of the 'oppressed', because both categories pivot around the centrality of the social actor living concrete experiences of suffering. The awareness developed through *conscientização* provides the 'activist/oppressed' with new tools and words to understand, name and live his/her own suffering, and such critical thinking creates the conditions for the passage from subjection to subjectification of the victim (Semeraro 2007). In a similar way, Gramsci's idea of catharsis evokes 'the transformation of a passive individual, dominated by economic structures, into an active subject, able to make decisions and carry on a personal project of society' (Semeraro 2007: 99). To achieve this project, both liberation and hegemony's conquests are necessary, and coexist in a complementary relationship.

Anti-Asbestos Activism in Osasco

In the mid-1990s, in Osasco, where the sociopolitical scenario was rooted in the above-illustrated processes and dynamics, a group of asbestos workers, experiencing symptoms of illnesses that they could not understand, began to gather and seek together explanations and truths concerning their health conditions. Many of them had worked at the Eternit plant in Osasco (closed in 1993), but there were also workers from other factories, such as Lonaflex (Osasco) and Brasilit (São Caetano do Sul, São Paulo). These workers, the majority of whom were already retired or unemployed due to the closure of the factories, found interlocutors willing to listen to their voices, to start a dialogue and to form a collaboration that has lasted until today. These interlocutors worked in public institutions such as the Ministério Público do Trabalho – MPT [Public Ministry of Labour], and the research institute Fundação Jorge Duprat Figueiredo de Segurança e Medicina do Trabalho – FUNDACENTRO [Jorge Duprat Figueiredo Foundation of Safety and Occupational Health].

In the first phase of the anti-asbestos mobilization, social bonds of friendship, work and political militancy, rooted in Osasco's specific social fabric, were decisive for the foundation of the Associação Brasileira dos Expostos ao Amianto – ABREA [Brazilian Association of Persons Exposed to Asbestos] in 1995. Moreover, biosocial connections which emerged from sharing the same asbestos-related diseases (ARDs) that were gradually becoming manifest and diagnosed in the workers, strengthened those bonds.

Based on my interlocutors' narratives, the first reactions of the Eternit firm aimed to damage the activism precisely through its strong relational (political, social and affective) dimensions. In response to the accusations and mobilization of former workers, the firm tried to weaken and crumble those bonds by proposing alternatives imbued by the industrial paternalism that had moulded the firm's management policy in the previous decades. Moreover, the firm reacted to the workers' mobilization on a practical and economic level as well by offering compensation and health insurance to the former workers.

Below, I conclude this section with a quotation from an interview conducted with a former Eternit worker who was among the founders of ABREA, the non-governmental organization whose members became my main interlocutors while researching in Osasco:

> When the workers founded ABREA, the activities at the plant had already ceased, but the firm came back and opened an office to attend

> to former workers. They even reopened the club for former workers, whom they used to refer to as collaborators of Eternit. There, they organized barbecues and parties to which they invited all of us except those most visibly engaged in the activism. Along with this, they began to offer health insurance. When their doctors diagnosed an ARD, they offered compensation. The amount depended on the seriousness of the disease. They offered 15,000 reais [just under 4,000 US dollars] for a very serious disease. The majority of former workers who signed the agreement got 10,000 reais [approximately 2,500 US dollars] on average. They recognized just one or two of the ARDs that can develop because of exposure. For example, they did not recognize heart fatigue [*o cansaço do coração*]. They recognized only asbestosis, a disease that gets worse as time passes. They proposed that we sign an agreement not to file lawsuits against the firm and not to complain, even if the worker should later develop a more serious disease. There were many pressures on us, and many accepted and signed the agreement because they needed money.

Eliezer

My understanding of anti-asbestos activism in Brazil, and more specifically in Osasco, has been deeply influenced by the encounters and conversations I have had with the current ABREA president, Mr Eliezer João de Souza. Mr de Souza has authorized me to use his real name, so I share his suggestions and narratives with true authorship.

Mr de Souza, seventy-four years old in 2015, was born in Minas Gerais, where he lived and worked from when he was a child in the *roça*. He was aged approximately twenty-five when he first arrived in São Paulo and then, in 1968, he began working at the Eternit plant in Osasco, where he joined friends from his hometown who had previously migrated. 'They told me to come to Osasco and work with them at Eternit. The salary was good, many young men were there, and it would be nicer and more enjoyable [for me] than continuing to work in the construction industry as I was doing, in a very isolated area of São Paulo state', he told me.

In Osasco, Mr de Souza started living in the working-class neighbourhood called Vila Yolanda, where a group of worker-priests from France and Italy were active. Referring to the principles of LT, these ecclesiastics decided to share their daily lives with the poorest and most vulnerable Osasco citizens, most of whom had recently arrived from Brazil's north-eastern states and countryside. During the day, the priests worked in the plants, while in the evening they promoted local inhabitants' participation in meetings and educational activities organized in the working-class neighbourhoods, based on the method called 'Ver–Julgar–Agir' [See–Judge–Act] (Gutiérrez 1972).

Based on 'ordinary people's everyday experience of poverty', LT 'involves a use of Scripture, the interpretation of which is closely related to that experience' (Rowland 2007: 1). Through the 'Ver–Julgar–Agir' method, people were prompted to reflect on their daily troubles and events around them by referring to the Bible and main Christian doctrines. Conversely, the Scripture was interpreted in light of daily life experiences considered important sources of knowledge. The activities promoted at the BECs focused on this praxis, and were intended to develop a sense of belonging based on the active role of marginal and vulnerable communities, which in this way engaged in bottom-up processes to achieve better life conditions and social rights (Dawson 2007).

During our conversations, Mr de Souza often referred to his encounter with the worker-priests living in Osasco as a crucial experience that had influenced all his life as an individual, worker and militant. I could see how this influence on his ethics had affected the way he conceived of, designed, and carried out ABREA's activities. In particular, the encounter with the French worker-priest Domingos Barbé had a significant impact on Mr de Souza's life. In the 1960s, Domingos Barbé settled in Osasco, in the same neighbourhood where Mr de Souza lived, Vila Yolanda. There, Barbé proposed the importance of 'active non-violence' in Brazilian resistance against the military dictatorship (Barbé 1983), and participated as a metallurgic industry worker in the strike organized in Osasco on 17 July 1968 (de Oliveira Rovai 2009, 2014). For this reason, Barbé was expelled from Brazil. The military government expelled immigrants they considered subversive, and this practice was especially used against unionists and anarchists from European countries who divulgated their ideals and supported grassroots mobilization in Brazil (Giannotti 2007).

One morning, as I was nearing the conclusion of my fieldwork, Mr de Souza gave me a book as a present, saying that it had been a fundamental reference point for civil struggles in Brazil, and that many militants had studied it. The book's title was *Jesus: Sua Terra, Seu Povo, Sua Proposta* [Jesus: His Land, His People, His Proposal] (MTC 2001). 'Agata, our struggle against asbestos, here in Osasco, in São Paulo, Brazil, is deeply related to these movements', he told me. I quote the conversation that followed, during which Mr de Souza explained the positive effects of the strong relationship between anti-asbestos activism and other social movements in Osasco. These relationships, originating from shared stories of militancy and civil engagement beyond the specific mobilization against asbestos, were rooted in the historical processes that had taken place in Osasco – a context distinguished by a vivid movement of people, capital and ideas.

de Souza: Agata, look at the cover! There is Jesus' profile drawn among workers in protest. This is a historical book; do you know why? This book helped a lot in the democratization of Brazil, at the time of withdrawal, during the military dictatorship here, from 1964 to 1984. Many courses have been organized based on this book, not only for Christian militants, but also for all the leftist militants in Brazil. The Catholic Church in Brazil had an organization through the worker-priests, who were mostly from France and Italy. Father Domingos Barbé was my teacher many years ago and he used this book to deepen the reflection on the Christian faith's examples within workers' lives. Many of the militants who studied with workers-priests were tortured, imprisoned and killed during the dictatorship ... Our movement here in the São Paulo region and Osasco is connected to trade unions and social movements together, [and] to religious groups too. Many support us today because they know and respect our struggle.

AM: Doesn't similar support occur in other cities?

de Souza: No, it doesn't – not with the same assiduity at least. Here, there is joint work that is plural work with different entities. In Osasco, each trade union is represented in the inter-union board, from the largest to the smallest. ABREA is also represented, and there we defend workers' health and support the unions' unity in the workers' joint struggle for health and rights.

Worker-priests adhering to LT, through their activities at the BECs situated in the poorest neighbourhoods, operated at the margins and occupied those interstices of social life in a violent, individualistic and competitive context. In those interstices, ideals of social justice and equity were thought of, elaborated, discussed, and eventually partly achieved jointly with other social groups – student-worker organizations and trade unions in particular, which were then declared illegal during the military dictatorship.

I found several parallels between the Liberation Theology practices that started in the 1960s and anti-asbestos activism in Osasco as it was in 2015. First, LT took on a fundamental role in legitimizing and providing a language – 'God's Word' – for the social struggles that emerged from suffering that was being socially experienced and had been structurally produced. Similarly, anti-asbestos activism has provided ARD sufferers with language, including political, judicial and biomedical words, to think about and name their private experiences of exposure, illness and grief in terms of injustice. In both cases, such language made the sufferers 'no longer willing to be the passive objects of abuse and exploitation, but now determined to be active subjects, increasingly responsible for the construction of their own history' (Dawson 2007: 148).

A second parallel is in reference to the global dimension of the socioeconomic injustices produced by capitalist economics, to which both the Brazilian civil struggles over the past decades supported by Christian groups guided by LT and current anti-asbestos activism have enacted by reiterating the necessity of transnational mobilization. Although commonly associated with the social and historical processes occurring in Latin America beginning in 1968 (the year of the Medellín conference in Colombia, considered to be the official start of LT) (Rowland 2007), 'LT can be considered as a worldwide movement for human emancipation' (Berryman 1987). In a similar way, anti-asbestos activism is performed in various contexts, aiming to achieve a global asbestos prohibition and operating through transnational activities. The universalism preached by theologians in the name of the suffering Christ struggling together with the poor in shanty towns across the world is recalled by anti-asbestos activists in the name of the suffering that affects each person involved in AR disasters throughout the world, wherever asbestos pollution has existed or still exists.

A third parallel concerns the emergence of so-called *comunidades de destino*, or 'communities of fate' (de Oliveira Rovai 2009), which built on the social relationships triggered by activities promoted by worker-priests through the BECs, on the one hand, and by anti-asbestos activists through the association ABREA, on the other. This parallel is particularly significant in relation to a context characterized by the mass movement of people who followed the market's demands and found themselves displaced in a new life and working environment. The engagement in sociopolitical activities can be seen as a process through which the social actors developed a sense of belonging to the specific context of Osasco, based on new social and affective relationships instead of familial bonds.

> Upon being opened to the everyday concerns and events of the poor, it is within the formal ecclesial arena that the people find acceptance, resolve and encouragement from the knowledge and experience that God is not only on their side, but also calling for an end to the massively unjust and unacceptable conditions in which so many at the base spend their entire lives. (Dawson 2007: 148)

Deep connections and mutual influences among the various social forces active in Osasco have existed for many years, and are documented by a large local historiography (see Pignatari Werner 1981; de

Castro Andrade 1998; de Jesus 2006; de Oliveira Rovai 2009, 2014). By considering their impact on anti-asbestos activism, I have taken into account the role of these social forces, religious groups inspired by LT and promoted by worker-priests, jointly with trade unions and workers' organizations. They share common struggles for the achievement of social and political rights, and in the theological doctrine they find a common language to elaborate and legitimize their claims.

Conclusion

My approach to Osasco's history of urbanization and industrialization stems from the consideration of the meanings my interlocutors attributed to their settlement in Osasco and work at the Eternit plant. I have quoted narratives that best illustrate the incisive impact on the lives of workers arriving in Osasco from the *roça*, and consequently starting work in the factory, which proved to be a turning point, or at least a temporary improvement, in the quality of life for the majority of the participants in my study.

I have situated the startling population growth that occurred in Osasco, especially between the 1940s and the 1970s (Sanazar 2000; Marquetti Rocha Negrelli and Collino de Oliveira 2003; Zampolin Coelho and Moreti 2005), within the broader immigration process that contributed to defining São Paulo state as Brazil's industrial and financial hub (Bernardo 1998; Ribeiro 2006; da Cruz and Moura 2008). I retraced these historical processes based on my research partners' narratives and documentation through bibliographic research and visits to museums and archives. Ethnography has been fundamental in grasping the implications of the transnational movements for an individual's life. On the one hand, face-to-face encounters have facilitated an empathetic relationship between myself and the study participants, thanks to whom I collected substantial, nuanced qualitative data. On the other hand, the multi-sited dimension of my research (begun in Italy in 2009) has allowed me to identify and reflect on the transnational connections characterizing the political, economic and social processes at play in the toxic market of asbestos and in AR disasters worldwide.

During the interviews with my interlocutors in the field, I entered worlds that I could only access through their memories. The narratives that emerged during our conversations, supported by old photographs, documents and objects, helped us to make communicable and meaningful the past, as embodied in the men and women I met. However, the question Fassin (2007: 123) poses is worthy of reflection:

> How can we infer the existence of a lived link between the past and the present? How can we read the mark left by the events that took place years, decades, even centuries ago in the experience of people today, some of whom confronted them directly, others through what they heard from parents or friends, or yet again imperceptibly or surreptitiously when memories are triggered by images or worlds? Of course, there is what people say, but everyone knows that reference to history or memory does not necessarily tell all the truth about what really happened. Conversely, there is what is left unsaid, and we also know that repression allows one to cover up the most painful traces of the past.

During our ethnographic encounters, I tried not to 'restrict myself to what I was told or ignore what was being kept back' (Fassin 2007: 123). Gestures, tone of voice, teary eyes and changes in breathing helped me to grasp the meaning or the importance of a past event, a memory, or a lost affect as it was lived and perceived in the present. This is because

> the ordeals lived through in one's flesh and blood say more about the social world than the developments reshaped by the mind, because they connect the present to the experience of the past in order to build the future, rather than connect the present to the project of the future in order to erase the past. There are things one does not forget. (Fassin 2007: 169)

The reconstruction of the worlds of my interlocutors' youth and work at the plant – worlds physically inaccessible to me – was achieved through narratives and bibliographic research. Beyond the importance of a historical contextualization, my concern was being able to read the traces and the resonances left by that past in the present. Accordingly, the 'thickness' (Geertz 1973) of ethnography has been fundamental in both data collection and analysis to grasp and reflect on the affects and meanings shared, lived and elaborated in the present, and triggered by the evocation and experience of the past.

Once again, I found in Fassin's reflections on the fruitful combination of a historiographical approach with an ethnographic one (Fassin 2007: 201–2) the theoretical tools to which I referred.

> Historiography and ethnography put the flesh back on the society being investigated. … My aim is to allow the social configurations to come alive in individual histories. Or yet again, using a classical distinction, to reveal the constraints of structure and the freedom of agency. But perhaps we must go further – not beyond, but within the narratives. As we all know, interviews render more or less linear and coherent stories that sketch a life or fragments thereof, thus representing a privileged medium to attain people's experiences. Nevertheless, they are not the whole story. Not only do observations and archives come to complete and elucidate them, but their very materiality must be explored from the point of the speech forms and the interactive situation. (Fassin 2007: 201–2)

A 'historiography-informed ethnography' (Fassin 2007: XIV–XV) was essential to understanding the sociopolitical and economic processes inscribed on and lived through the bodies of the social actors involved in the processes I wanted to investigate. At the same time, a phenomenological approach has been crucial in relating the past to the present of the participants in my study.

Notes

1. In 1871, the so-called 'Lei do Ventre Livre' [Free Belly Law] was promulgated; it established that slaves' children had to be considered free. The official abolition of slavery in Brazil came through the 'Lei Imperial' [Imperial Law] n. 3,353, known as 'Lei Áurea' [Golden Law] in 1888 (see Schwarcz and Starling 2015). Compare with Freyre's seminal investigations into slavery for a deeper understanding of the processes that led to the abolition of slavery in Brazil (Freyre 1933).
2. So-called because it was 16 kilometres by rail from Praça [square] da Sé, in downtown São Paulo.
3. The names of numerous Brazilian cities reveal that was a common habit for the first settlers to play a relevant role in a city's industrial development and growth to give it their name.
4. For a deeper understanding of the processes of identity construction among migrating social groups, with particular focus on cultural flows from countryside to urban contexts (and vice versa), compare with the seminal studies conducted by anthropologists from the School of Manchester in Africa (Epstein 1958; Mitchell 1960; Gluckman 1960; Mayer 1961).
5. Immigrants often arrived in Brazil because of the *carta de chamada* written and sent to them by relatives who had emigrated earlier and were already settled in Brazil. In the Museo da Imigração [Museum of Immigration] of São Paulo, these letters are permanently exhibited.
6. Compare with Ribeiro Corossacz (2004, 2005) for a deeper understanding of Brazilian 'racial democracy'. In contemporary Brazil, racism against black people, the majority of whom are from the north-eastern regions of Brazil, still represents a human rights issue. The non-governmental organization Anistia Internacional no Brasil [Amnesty International in Brazil] reported that 77 per cent of the thirty thousand young people murdered in Brazil in 2012 were black (Pellegrini 2014). In this regard, Anistia Internacional no Brasil launched the campaign 'Jovem Negro Vivo' [Alive Black Youth]. For further information, see the website https://anistia.org.br/campanhas/jovemnegrovivo/ (last accessed 1 February 2020).

3

Suffering and Embodied Disasters

> The incarnate body (in contrast to the merely biological) is the living site of a contested hegemony of power.
>
> —Ronald Jonas Frankenberg, 'Preface', in Scott et al., *Private Risks and Public Dangers*

'A time bomb': Often, during my multi-sited ethnography across Italy and Brazil, I have heard this expression to describe the existential – bodily – condition of those who have been exposed to asbestos, and had fibres nestled in their bodies for decades.

The trajectory connecting Casale Monferrato in Italy and Osasco in Brazil follows the dynamics of the global market of asbestos, the transnational grassroots mobilization in the name of social justice, and the suffering experienced by the exposed communities.

After a civil mobilization began in the 1980s and with the elaboration of epidemiological evidence (Magnani et al. 1987), asbestos-cement (AC) production at the Eternit plant in Casale Monferrato has been recognized as the main cause of the almost two thousand AR deaths in the city since the start of the activities in the early 1900s, due to both occupational and environmental exposure (Rossi 2012). During an interview conducted in Casale Monferrato in 2012, an anti-asbestos activist who had lost her husband to malignant mesothelioma (MM) related to environmental exposure to asbestos, described her suffering experience as a caregiver in terms of a nightmare comparable to an Alfred Hitchcock horror movie (Mazzeo 2018c).

Asbestos fibres silently wound and stiffen membranes covering vital organs. Bodily laceration starts when the besieged body is young and strong, and can run fast over long distances and work over long stretches of time. Then comes slow unceasing erosion that continues as the body ages, hair whitens, and wrinkles on the face and hands seem to retrace the map of paths and encounters drawn over a lifetime.

I was often told that day by day your breath shortens; you notice you can no longer easily climb stairs, and that you are now always coughing and have a pain beneath your shoulder blades. 'Shortness of breath' (*falta de ar* in Portuguese and *mancanza di respiro* in Italian) was the most frequently used expression I heard: 'I feel this shortness of breath', and 'my breath is trapped, it is not free'. Suddenly, you feel like something is crushing your chest, close to your heart. Time is about to run out. After hiding for decades, a bomb is going to explode soon and devastate everything, including your life. During our encounters, relatives and friends of people who died from ARDs recalled the most acute episodes of pain of their beloved ones: 'It was as if she had a plastic bag over her head'; or 'He spent all night sitting in bed, coughing and wheezing. It was cruel being a powerless witness to that atrocious pain'.

Asbestos-related (AR) disasters become visible in crumbling bodies and disruption. The 'embodied past' (Fassin 2008) then comes to the surface and becomes manifest through the decaying body, threatening an irreversible absence. A secret guarded for years is announced and then revealed, understood and narrated when the body's symptoms are translated into signs making the individual experience of suffering part of a collective disaster. The past is lived and relived in the crises of the present, and the traces of the processes through which the toxic market of asbestos has disseminated its 'time bombs' then become visible in the flesh and the intersubjective experiences of suffering.

This chapter includes stories of AR suffering of previously exposed former workers, their widows and children, whom I met in Brazil. Illness, contamination and grief are interlaced experiences of the impact of asbestos exposure on a person's body and life. Suffering, considered in a cultural context, is an experience that is as intimate and individual as it is intersubjective and social. What are the fleshy dimensions of the fading processes of global health disasters? How do exposed people live with their contamination and the risk of developing an ARD? How do survivors experience the disaster's impact on their physical and social worlds?

The voices of the 'sufferer-activists' (Mazzeo 2017b) I met, and which I report in the next sections, constitute a polyphonic narrative that reveals the pervasiveness and nuances of disaster processes of global dimensions. These processes occur in local and intimate contexts consisting of dangerous workplaces, contaminated neighbourhoods and unsafe homes, lacerating bodies and affective relationships threatened with irreversible losses. The narratives that this book is based on emerged from conversations with my Brazilian interlocutors. Anguish and sorrow pervaded these stories. The same feelings were expressed by the Italian anti-asbestos activists I met during previous research, while describing similar experiences of AR disaster.

Leticia and João

Leticia had a resounding voice on the phone. I called her from the bus to confirm the stop to get off. She reassured me that I would find her there waiting for me. As soon as we met, she congratulated me on my ability and courage to move alone across São Paulo and Osasco, and to live alone away from my family. She also confessed that the day before she had been going to call me to cancel our appointment, as she doubted that she could have anything interesting to tell me. Several times she repeated that she was not as organized as João, her husband. She said she did not remember much and she knew nothing of the work at the factory because João never talked about his work. Leticia described João as a lonely man who rarely spoke and was always on his own. Later in the interview, I would read a medical certificate stating that João, 83 years old when he died of lung cancer in 2013, had suffered from severe depression during his retirement.

Leticia, 73 years old in 2015, and João had migrated together to Osasco (São Paulo) from Bahia (north-eastern Brazil) in the late 1950s to escape poverty. In the old document photographs that Leticia showed me, João was a young, white, clear-eyed man. His appearance preserved the traces of centuries of white presence, colonization and exploitation in a region that is still among the country's poorest.

After picking me up at the bus stop, Leticia took me to her house and invited me into her living room. On the couch was a collection of documents and papers. The darkness in the room contrasted with the sunshine outside. Before starting the interview, Leticia told me that she had a gift for me. It was a religious book that 'João would definitely have given [you], if he were still alive'. Leticia and her family were members of the Seventh-Day Adventist Church. João had been an ABREA activist, but he had left the association when he began to join his family in religious activities. The ABREA monthly meetings on Saturday mornings were not reconcilable with the religious principle of not working on Saturdays.

Leticia had never actively engaged in ABREA. A biomedical doctor from the local occupational health centre promoting epidemiological surveillance of women exposed to asbestos in Osasco had given me Leticia's contact details. Most of the women involved in the surveillance project were wives and widows of former workers at the local Eternit plant.

João had worked at Eternit for twenty-two years (from 1958 to 1980). Initially, he worked as an unskilled worker and was paid 17 cruzeiros per hour. Then, in June 1966, he was promoted to office assistant, and was paid 198,000 cruzeiros per month. By the time he retired, he was responsible for the warehouse. Leticia highlighted that thanks to her husband's promotions, their family's life conditions had improved. 'Thanks to the work at Eternit, we could build our house, raise our children [*criar nossos filhos*], let all six of them attend college and guarantee them a good life', she said. Several times during the interview, Leticia thanked Eternit – and once she said that she would never sue the company. As she stated, taking the firm to court would have meant not being thankful for the good that she and her family had received.

> In his last months, João had a horrible pain in his chest. He was hospitalized and spent his last two months in the hospital. The doctors told us that he could not return home and could not undergo chemotherapy because everything was already taken [by the disease that had affected his vital organs. I asked Leticia: 'Did he have cancer?']. He had cancer. On the death certificate, I think, it is written that it was cancer, isn't it? Here, it should be written that it was cancer [she gave me the certificate], but yes, it was cancer, because I know it was… [She read] Malignant neoplasia of the lung. This neoplasia, what would that be? [I answered 'cancer'.] Cancer, malignant neoplasia of the lung. I remember what the doctor told me: 'He cannot come back home anymore, and he cannot stand chemotherapy… there is nothing to do'… He died in a nursing home. There, he was very well looked after, but he died alone.
>
> On his last day, he called me and told me he wanted a lemonade soda. I could not find one. A girl from the hospital gave me another drink. I told him I would go and buy whatever he wanted. I came back to Osasco [he was hospitalized in São Paulo], I bought everything he liked, I went home and washed the fruit I had brought for him. I thought of going back to São Paulo, but it was already late and my daughters told me that it would be better to go the next day in the morning, very early in the morning. They told me to rest, so I lay down, but I had a pain in the heart [*uma dor no coração*]. When it was almost midnight, the phone rang. At such an hour, there is no good news. They said that he had just passed away. For a long time afterwards, I felt guilty for not having been with him when he passed away, but many people have told me that maybe

it was good not to be together because they say that it is very painful: those with such problems in their lungs suffer so much from shortness of breath [*falta de ar*]. He had already had two crises for shortness of breath, and the doctors had connected him to an oxygen tank, but they had already warned me that at any time the oxygen might not solve the crisis anymore. People told me, 'you don't know, maybe God had a plan for you not to see all that suffering'. People say that is horrible when a person dies from shortness of breath.

It is ok, I know that he went to rest in peace. Even in my prayers, I asked God not to allow him to suffer… because suffering… we are very selfish and want a person we love to stay in a bed suffering, even though we know he will never get well again. I am not in favour of taking life nor am I in favour of death, nor is God. We die for the original sin, but we have hope in a new heaven, in a new land, where God will let all the injustices cease… Are you Catholic? [she asked me the question in a rhetorical way. I felt I couldn't answer anything but yes. I nodded]. So you already know that Jesus suffered too; he died suffering on a cross for us and is now preparing a place for us where there will be no more injustices. This is our hope and solace. ['Did your husband suffer a lot?' I asked.] The first three months he suffered a lot. A year before he passed away, I already saw that he was not doing well. I noticed that he was always tired and he was no longer the same person. When he began to feel bad and could not sleep at night, I begged him to go to a doctor, but he did not want to go, he thought that if a doctor treated him, his suffering would last longer. He did not want to go to a doctor, even though he didn't know that there was nothing to do. He didn't know and neither did we. … My husband was hospitalized and then his condition got worse. The pain he felt was horrible. The nurse gave him sedatives and he slept for half an hour, but soon the pain began again. In the end, it was necessary to use the oxygen to make him breathe, but he violently refused that. I had to hold the tube and prevent him from removing it. Sometimes, he squeezed my arm because he was very angry. A doctor entered the room and I told him that he was mad at me. The doctor explained to me that he was not angry, but that his mind was confused because of the oxygen. ['Did he know that he had cancer?' I asked Leticia.] We never talked about that, but I think he knew.

In a corner of the living room was a chair. When I stopped recording and noticed it, Leticia told me that João had spent his last year sitting there in 'his' corner. Two years later, everything was still in the same place: the chair, the fan and João's favourite painting by his daughter, representing 'The Last Supper'. In those objects and in the way Leticia and her daughters avoided that corner as if it was a forbidden place surrounded by a kind of sacredness, I felt the strong presence of an absent loved one. That feeling returned and accompanied me through the encounters and while listening to the narratives that I describe and

Figure 3.1 Absence–presence of an anti-asbestos activist who died of lung cancer in 2013. Osasco, São Paulo, Brazil, 2015. Photograph by the author.

report in this chapter, in order to let you, the reader, enter the intimate worlds of AR disasters.

In Italy as well, these intimate worlds were marked by the absence–presence of a beloved one in the lives of the men and women who participated in my study. In Casale Monferrato, where, as previously mentioned, the toxic production of asbestos-containing products (ACPs) has to date provoked the death of almost two thousand inhabitants, an entire community has had to learn how to cope with the absence of many fellow citizens who had an irreplaceable role in their lives. At both an individual and collective level, coping strategies are deeply intertwined with the strategies of local activism, which are triggered by the search for a meaning to make the disaster itself understandable and manageable – such a capacity to imagine a different, better and more equal future is inextricably rooted in the past, moulding the story of a community and its members (Appadurai 2013). Remembering and narrating the past then become practices of activism and, at the same time, of care for individual and collective suffering.

Irene and Roberto

Osasco, 18 May 2015, morning, with a grey, rainy sky. By bus I reached a peripheral neighbourhood in Osasco, where I had an appointment with Roberto's family. Roberto, who had been one of the most committed ABREA members, died of malignant mesothelioma (MM) in 2009 when he was 72. Roberto and his family received the diagnosis of MM while he was undergoing medical examinations to treat a persistent pain provoked by a fall. Roberto had worked at the Osasco Eternit plant for just three and a half years, from 1964 to 1967, when he was 30. That had been his first job with a regular contract. Before that, he had lived with his Italian-descendant family and worked in the *roça* on coffee and corn plantations in the inner region of the state of São Paulo. Several of the study participants had only worked at Eternit in Osasco for a short period. This is related to the high and rapid turnover characterizing Brazilian occupational life, especially in the past, and it differentiates the narratives heard in Brazil from those in Casale Monferrato, Italy, where this phenomenon was less frequent.

With the first salary earned at Eternit, Roberto and Marcia, his wife, bought a piece of land and then built a house. Marcia still lived there in 2015, together with two of her children, Irene and Renato, both in their forties, and present during my visit. Irene showed me a picture of the first wooden house that Roberto had built on that land and Marcia told me that in the beginning, since there were no doors, she could not go outside and leave the house unguarded.

As soon as I sat at the kitchen table with Marcia, Renato and Irene, I realized that Irene would be my main interlocutor during the interview. Soon after the interview began, Marcia stood up and continued preparing the lunch to which she had invited me as soon as I arrived, while Renato went outside to photocopy some documents for me. Before I could ask any questions, Irene began talking to me about the MM experience they had lived through with her father. I could feel the importance that she attributed to the fact that I was there as a witness to her family's tragedy. At the beginning of the interview, I did not ask any questions, but let Irene narrate her story.

Irene brought a book from the living room and sat with me. 'Look at this! My father used to read this book every single day. There are the traces of his fingers on its pages'. She was showing me her father's book of prayers. More precisely, she was indicating the pages of morning and evening prayers, which had the yellow traces left by her father's fingers. 'He used to sit on the sofa and pray. He desperately tried to take strength from God. He did not want to die. Look at the page with the morning prayer – the trace he left is so visible!', she said. Irene delicately turned the book's pages, lingering on those that still held the most visible traces of her father's presence. As in Leticia's living room, I felt the strong presence of an absent loved one. Roberto came alive through Irene's gestures and memories. During my fieldwork in Osasco, I had already heard about Roberto many times from ABREA members who had loved and survived him, and had seen pictures of him. A large portrait of Roberto was always exhibited during asbestos awareness campaigns and at the events organized by ABREA.

Irene started her narration:

> Probably, the fall squashed his lung and heart. To understand why the pain persisted, we went to the doctor and afterwards we discovered that the lung was 'full of water' [*cheio de agua*, meaning that there were pleural effusions. I had already heard a similar expression during my previous research in Italy]. As soon as the doctors aspirated the liquid, it [*agua*] reappeared again. When he saw that yellow liquid mixed with blood he said: 'Look! They are really removing the dust [i.e. asbestos] from me. He was really sick. His belly became swollen. Before the fall, he just suffered from shortness of breath [*falta de ar*] and tiredness. After the fall, his condition got worse. Deeper examinations revealed the presence of cancer, close to the heart. When the doctor communicated his diagnosis, he [Roberto] became furious – he did not accept it, he refused it, he got angry and did not want to know anything more about it. He had many comrades who had already died, and he did not want to undergo the same experience. He was a close friend of Carlos, who was very sick and then died in that period [2008/2009]. He said that the doctors had made a mistake and that the diagnosis must be wrong. Because of his poor health condition, the doctors told us that surgical treatment was not an option; he could undergo just chemo and radiotherapy. The cancer was growing fast and expanding to the heart, to the stomach, which began to swell, and to the prostate. He could not eat anymore. His belly, full of water, hardened. The cancer took all his organs; the doctor said there was nothing that could be done. He [Roberto] did not accept it. He

> was not the same person anymore. After a while, he began to consult spiritualists and to pray a lot. He was really afraid of death. He searched for help everywhere, and began to ask anybody who came to visit him for prayers, regardless of their religion – Catholic, spiritualist or evangelical… it didn't matter.
>
> Before the diagnosis, he used to talk all the time about ABREA and asbestos dangers. He was very active in the association, and he participated in every activity that they organized. He was talkative and very talented at explaining things, so other ABREA members always wanted him to give talks during awareness campaigns. But… when he got sick… everything stopped. He was too weak. The disease consumed him and it finished him [*acabou com tudo dele*]. On communicating the diagnosis, the doctor said that he had six to twelve months of life expectancy. His faith helped, because Daddy lived for one more year after the diagnosis, but… the last months… he suffered a lot. It was painful standing by him. He did not drink or eat. In the end, he weighed just 55 kilos. When my father received the diagnosis, the doctor asked him if he had ever worked at Eternit and if he had ever heard about MM. My dad answered that yes, he had worked at Eternit, although only for a few years, and that a dear friend of his had recently died from MM [he was referring to Carlos]. The doctor told him that he had MM too. My father became sad and hung his head [*baixou a cabeça*] … I spent his last night [the night of Easter 2008] awake looking after him. In the early hours of the morning, he told me '*Papai não aguenta mais. Estou dipartindo*' [Daddy can no longer stand (the pain). I am leaving].

Irene was crying as she said those last words. I was also crying while listening to her. I was not just witnessing and being empathetic with her suffering (Throop 2012), I was suffering with her because her story recalled some of my most painful memories too and made them present in the encounter between the two of us. We were daughters still mourning the loss of a parent. My understanding of Irene's suffering was painfully emotional, more than theoretical.

Pedro

Pedro, 73 years old in 2015, worked at the Eternit plant in Rio de Janeiro, from 1962 to 1969. I met him during anti-asbestos campaigns organized in Rio de Janeiro in which ABREA activists from Osasco participated. The interview with Pedro took place at his home, in the same neighbourhood, Barros Filho, where the Eternit plant was situated and still functioning, and where the majority of the members of the local anti-asbestos organization (ABREA-Rio de Janeiro) lived. Below, I report a quote from our interview, conducted in June 2015:

Figure 3.2 Absence–presence of an anti-asbestos activist who died of malignant mesothelioma in 2009. Osasco, São Paulo, Brazil, 2015. Photograph by the author.

Pedro: I visited six workers a few days before they died. They told me that the pain they felt above the heart was unbearable. Usually the pain attacks the heart, but also the liver and kidneys… it's horrible. I have asbestosis and pleural plaques. The latest examinations showed the presence of small nodules in my lungs. Now, I have to undergo computerized tomography.

AM: How did you discover that you had plaques and asbestosis?

Pedro: I was living while dying little by little [*Eu vivia morrendo ao pouco*]. I found out that the firm was contacting former workers to undergo medical examinations and eventually proposed signing the transaction [*acordo*]. I went to the company doctor and I explained how I felt tired all the time, with shortness of breath [*falta de ar*], and problems walking. To walk a short distance, I had to stop a dozen times. As soon as the doctor heard me, she called the manager and said: 'We have another bomb here, another bomb has appeared' [he smiled, and emphasized the doctor's inopportune sarcasm]. I underwent radiography and the results showed that I had asbestosis and pleural plaques. It's too much! [*É muita coisa*] … A friend of mine suffered many crises.

AM: What crises?

Pedro: The crises due to asbestos, don't you know them?

AM: No, I don't.

Pedro: These crises are awful. Horrible coughing. Pain in the legs. Tiredness. You cannot breathe, you have headaches, pain in your heart, in your shoulders, a horrible tiredness, and a sick body, but really, really sick. It looks like the person is going to die, to fall and die. In this way, many friends of mine have died. One friend was losing weight; this was a bad sign. Another friend survived just twenty days with the disease [*doença*]. When these asbestos crises become more frequent, people die. I have already had them [the crises] three times, but my time to depart has not arrived yet, otherwise, you would not be chatting with me now [he smiled] ... If you see somebody dying from asbestos... it is horrible... he becomes a 'dressed bamboo tree', it seems that an animal is going to eat him. He becomes skinny. The eyes sink. Everything collapses. The person becomes like a cave. It is horrible. We arrive at that point just to meet God. It is very sad.

The suffering related to the impact of an exposure that occurred decades earlier does not exclusively manifest itself in the onset of diseases such as asbestosis or MM, but also in the anguish experienced because of having powerlessly witnessed your friends' deaths and in the awareness of being at risk of becoming sick and dying in the same dreadful conditions. The past exposure then represents an 'immediate threat' that comes 'at an intimate level: within our own bodies' (Kleinman 2006: 5), and, from there, reactivates the memory at each crisis, each asbestos crisis, such as those Pedro experienced and described.

During our walk from the association's site to his home, Pedro showed me the factory where he had worked four decades earlier. The industrial plant was vast, and it dominated the tiny bare brick houses situated nearby. In front of me lay an area with a multiplicity of contrasting images: on the one side, the factory, the trucks and thousands of piled Eternit awnings; on the other side, garbage bags stacked in a corner, the houses, and children coming back home in their public-school uniforms. In between, a sea of vivid green trees and plants, among which I glimpsed a horse, which increased my sense of estrangement.

The local anti-asbestos NGO in collaboration with public health professionals is promoting actions to monitor the health conditions of exposed workers and inhabitants, and to give them priority access to adequate health care services.

Figure 3.3 Eternit plant in Rio de Janeiro, Brazil, 2015. Photograph by the author.

Chico

I interviewed Chico on a cloudy morning in June 2015, when he was aged 79. He had worked at Eternit in Osasco from 1952 to 1985. After an occupational exposure of over thirty-three years, he was given a diagnosis of asbestosis and pleural plaques in the early 1990s. Chico lived in the Kilometre 18 neighbourhood (Osasco), so called because it was 18 kilometres by rail from Praça [square] da Sé, in downtown São Paulo. I met him in front of the Teodoro Sampaio train station and together we walked to his home, where the interview would take place. On our way, he showed me a public garden known as Praça do Samba [Samba Square], because there the first singers and bands performing the Musica Popular Brasileira – MPB [Brazilian Folk Music] used to play. He was visibly proud of the neighbourhood where he had been living since he was a teenager. Chico was one of the few ABREA activists I met who had been born in the city of São Paulo, to parents of Portuguese descent. While we were walking, he told me that when he was a young boy [*moleque*], and was already working at Eternit, he attended a vocational school in São Paulo. He used to take the train in Osasco and leave from the Bras station (now a metro station in São Paulo centre). He used to run from the station to the school. He smiled while telling me this. He emphasized his strength. I remembered this story when, a couple of hours later, he spoke to me about his frustration at not being able to walk long distances, because after a few steps he was no longer able to breathe. Below, a quote from the interview with Chico:

> Chico: Before I acquired knowledge [of asbestos], I didn't feel anything, because when it becomes manifest, it begins with plaques. The first illness that nestles in the lung is the plaques. When they get large and numerous, they become… [cancer, but he did not say the word].
>
> AM: Before that, didn't you feel anything?
>
> Chico: No, I didn't feel anything; I even used to run… Gradually, the plaques become larger and the capacity of your lungs diminishes. Now, I can't even run 50 metres, because I have shortness of breath [*falta de ar*]. The doctor advised me to walk, instead of running… If I think about who I was and who I am today… anguish and sadness don't help at all. I have to learn to live with the illness I have, but without going back to my memories and thoughts all the time, otherwise I won't be able to survive. I have to live with this illness and go forward. I know that I can't run, so I don't. I know that I am not a kid anymore, but I also know that if my lungs had not been injured by asbestos, I could play sport. I have this shortness of breath and I know that there are things that I can't do anymore. I try not to think too much about them, because it's useless to think about them. Thinking makes me feel sad and angry. Thinking doesn't help with anything. I have to live with the damage I have.

In addition to asbestosis and pleural plaques, Chico had a serious hearing impairment. During our encounter, he asked me to sit beside him and speak loudly. He related his hearing difficulties to his work at Eternit because the noise there had been deafening. However, he had not received compensation for his deafness, as that was not recognized as being a consequence of his thirty years working in the plant as a carpenter. His three brothers worked at Eternit too. One of them was very active in ABREA, and I had seen some photographs of him. He had died a few years earlier from a disease that although not diagnosed as AR, because it had been impossible to establish an unequivocal cause–effect relationship between asbestos exposure and the pathology, relatives and comrades were sure it had been provoked by the inhalation of asbestos fibres. Chico continued his narrative:

> The firm did not want to acknowledge that asbestos caused diseases, but they gave us a kit that we [the workers] used to call the *kit-morte* [death

kit]. It included an oxygen tank and a hose; they gave it to you if you had the company's health insurance. When you cannot live anymore by breathing naturally, then you have to attach the tube to your nostrils and stay with that day and night. We still use the expression *kit-morte* to refer to the oxygen tank, the hose and, unfortunately, to the wreath of flowers when it arrives at the time of the burial. For those who retired and did not sue the company, the firm paid for their hospitalization. I don't remember which hospital [in São Paulo] it was, but sometimes I went there to visit some friends. If you had become sick and had not sued the firm, you might go to talk to the firm's doctor; then, when you were hospitalized, the company paid all the costs. If the conditions got worse, the firm would come in with the *kit-morte*. The firm did not acknowledge that asbestos was killing us, but they knew that it was. This triggered in me a feeling of revulsion. The firm could have alerted us or adopted measures to protect us… I feel indignation, because no one has the right to harm others, and the firm injured so many people… the company was 'a wolf in sheep's clothing'. They injured and caused harm, while not warning anyone about the dangers of asbestos. They knew that they were killing people, and that twenty-five or thirty years later, people would start dying from ARDs. They were just interested in profit and money, not in workers' lives. Simply, when an employee had health problems and could not work anymore, they fired and substituted him. We have been deceived, no one wants to be deceived; the children themselves when they are deceived, feel indignation. If a friend of mine sues the company, I go to the court to give my testimony, moral support, and strength. Our hope is that the firm will be condemned and obliged to pay for the harm they provoked.

Many have died without knowing anything about asbestos. Many people died with lung problems and never knew that those problems were asbestos related. When we organize the week of awareness campaigns in April, you were there with us this year, there are so many curious people who come to us and, after a short conversation, exclaim: 'so that's why my father, my neighbour, my cousin died… he worked at Eternit! He had the same symptoms you're describing! No one talked to him about asbestos! What is asbestos?' I think that three thousand employees worked at Eternit; there were three working shifts, it was a lot of people. And there are even more people who never worked at Eternit but who lived nearby, had lung problems, died and didn't even know … No one suspected anything. We were very innocent. We were too innocent. No one ever tried to investigate or find out.

During our interview and other informal conversations, Chico reiterated several times that he had been betrayed by the firm, and this awareness made him feel furious. He pointed out the criminal management of a company that, although aware of the carcinogenicity of asbestos, did not opt to implement changes in the productive process (especially the substitution of the raw material) and guarantee safe working conditions for its employees. On this crucial aspect, the impacted community of Casale Monferrato in Italy, which shared similar feelings of anger and outrage as Chico, mobilized for the so-called 'Eternit trial' – the first trial against an AC firm accused of environmental disaster manslaughter.

Chico trusted the firm, he loved his work, and he was happy with life [*ficava feliz da vida*], while unaware that a disease had settled inside him [*uma doença estava lojada dentro*].

> Every year, I undergo examinations: radiography and spirometry; periodically, I have tomography as well, but radiography is every year. The spirometry is to evaluate the capacity of the lungs; it is also called pulmonary function. Radiography and tomography are good, but the pulmonary function is very bad – it forces you too much, it requires too much force, you have to blow and reach a certain level. You have to blow with your mouth open until you cannot bear it anymore. This examination hurts you a lot, but it is necessary to see how your lungs work. No one likes to undergo spirometry, but we have to. When we [he and his ABREA comrades] arrive at the hospital, we have already prepared ourselves. You have to sit down and rest. You must be very calm. Among all of us who undergo this examination, nobody likes it because it is too troublesome. You already do not have enough breath, but you have to force yourself and you get exhausted. Generally, I go alone to the hospital, and I take the train and bus, but there are friends who cannot reach the hospital alone. In those cases, we always arrange a car. There is always somebody available to help.

Chico's words gave concreteness to the meaning of 'care-activism', by which I refer to the support that anti-asbestos activists regularly provide, as I observed them in Italy and Brazil (Mazzeo 2018c). ABREA, in particular, were playing a fundamental role in providing its members with practical and emotional help, which proved to be essential in caring for those suffering due to the impact of the asbestos market on their lives.

While Chico was showing me his clinical documentation, I noticed that his next examinations had been scheduled for the next month. I shyly asked if I could accompany him. I took several minutes and many words to ask him that question, as I did not want to appear too intrusive. My tone of voice became lower. I had to repeat my question a couple of times and that made me feel even more embarrassed. In the end, when he got my question, he answered with a large smile that there were no problems and he would be very happy for me to go to the hospital with him. I felt relieved. He told me that he realized it would be important for my study and 'for the struggle' [*para a luta*] to go with him and, hopefully, to talk to his doctor. I thanked him and told him that I would be happy to meet his doctor, but that my main concern would be to just stay with him in the most discreet way possible. I would not enter the medical laboratories, but rather to wait with him before and after the examinations. He accepted with another smile, and we arranged the details for meeting up. Below, I report some quotes from my fieldnotes, written on the day of Chico's medical checks.

> São Paulo, notes written in the bus, 7 July 2015, 7.30 A.M.:
>
> I am going to join Chico. We arranged to meet at 8 A.M. in front of the hospital. I hope to arrive on time, I am anxious. At this time, the bus is slower than usual, because at every single stop there are people boarding. It is very crowded. I am also a bit afraid at the idea that I will soon be sitting in a hospital waiting room with Chico, witnessing his vulnerability. Yesterday, he called me and told me that it was probably not necessary for me to come, and that the next day of examinations scheduled in two weeks would be more interesting for me as there would be the opportunity to talk to the doctor. I repeated to him that I would be happy just to accompany him and stay with him, and that I did not need to talk to the doctor today – I could arrange a meeting with the doctor on another day. For a moment, I thought that he had changed his mind and did not want me to go anymore, but then his words and tone of voice reassured me: my presence was not a problem, he was sincerely concerned that accompanying him could be a waste of time for me. I repeated that I had already planned my day based on his examinations and that no, it would not be a waste of time at all.
>
> Notes written in the waiting room of the pulmonology unit:
>
> I arrived on time, even a few minutes before 8 A.M. Chico was waiting for me in front of one of the hospital entrances. He smiled at me. He told me that he had arrived early and had walked in the meantime. He was carrying a grey folder containing his clinical documentation. Now he is undergoing the spirometry; the thoracic radiography is scheduled soon after that. Before he entered the room, we chatted a bit. He told me that he woke up at 5.30 this morning and took two buses to reach the hospital in São Paulo from Osasco. I told him I woke up at six. I asked him if his wife sometimes comes with him to these medical check-ups. He answered no, that's not necessary. He explained that he undergoes these examinations every year. If nothing has changed, as he hopes, the doctors will tell him to come back in a year, otherwise in six months, and they will already schedule the next appointment. The waiting room is crowded. Chico does not sit until two chairs become free for both of us.

Notes written in the waiting room of the radiology unit:

Now Chico is undergoing radiography. I asked him how the first examination went. He looked tired. He told me that it had been difficult for him. He described how this examination consists of blowing into a tube from a sitting posture. He had to breathe and then release air. The nurse had asked him to repeat this act several times, because his breath was too short and she could not measure it. After the examination, his face was flushed and his eyes shiny. I had the impression that he had suddenly become shrunken and unbalanced.

Notes written in the garden of the University of São Paulo, Faculty of Public Health (where I went after the encounter with Chico).

When Chico and I left the hospital, it was raining heavily. I had an umbrella and I offered to accompany him to the bus stop. We had to be very close to be covered by my tiny umbrella and we soon started to walk arm-in-arm. It was the second time since I had known him that we had touched each other. The first time was after the interview I carried out at his home. On that day, when I was leaving, unlike when I had arrived and we just shook hands, he gave me two fatherly kisses on my cheeks. Today, when his bus arrived, he thanked me and gave me a large smile. We said goodbye by kissing each other's cheeks again. We were both smiling. We had shared an experience and built a connection based on it. I felt enriched and incredibly alive.

Beatriz and Carlos

I met Beatriz on a cold and rainy morning in June 2015. The interview took place at her home, which I reached on foot from the Osasco train station. Walking was an enriching, pleasant way to explore the city and the neighbourhoods where the participants in my study lived. Because of its large size, I could not easily have a saunter in São Paulo itself, so when it happened that my interlocutors in Osasco lived in neighbourhoods that I could reach on foot from the train station, I seized the rare opportunity, regardless of the weather.

Beatriz, aged 71 in 2015, was one of the few women actively engaged in the ABREA activities; she was the widow of Carlos who had worked for four years (1964–1968) at the Eternit plant in Osasco, employed in the administrative sector. Carlos died from MM in 2008, aged 66. Only after Carlos's death did Beatriz join ABREA.

Beatriz's home was on the upper floor of an elegant building. During the interview, she told me that Carlos had liked that building, one of the first tall residential buildings in Osasco, and he used to say that it would be nice to live there. After Carlos's death, Beatriz sold the detached house where they had lived together, and where Carlos had had his office, 'his corner', because 'that house was too big [for her alone]', and also 'the past had impregnated everything' and was overwhelming to her, she explained.

Beatriz welcomed me into the living room. The room was spacious, with elegant furniture and just a few ornaments. We both sat on the couch, but distant. Unlike other study participants, Beatriz did not show me any documents or medical certificates. She told me that she had thrown away all those documents and any papers related to Carlos's work and disease. To prompt the conversation, I asked her if she had any pictures of Carlos as a young man to show me. She said yes, and asked me if I had enough time. Of course, I had. Anthropologists always have plenty of time in the field, I thought, remembering my first readings on ethnographic research when I was a university student. I smiled. Beatriz stood up and went to the bedroom to fetch a couple of boxes containing old photographs from above the closet. I offered to help, but she said it was not necessary. I stayed in the living room, alone, looking at the few framed photographs on the shelves. Carlos, Beatriz, their daughters, and the grandchildren whom Carlos had never known. After a few minutes, she called me and I went into her bedroom.

I took the boxes while she was getting off the ladder, then she put them on the bed, opened them and began showing me the photographs randomly as they captured her attention: lunches, barbecues [*churrascos*], birthdays and trips; Carlos and her, hugging with young smiling faces. Yellowed Polaroid pictures of the honeymoon in an envelope, and the black and white photographs of their wedding laid out in a leather album. Together, we were digging into the past she had shared with Carlos, and weaving the plot of their story. I felt that the images I saw and the anecdotes Beatriz was telling me were enriching my knowledge of Carlos's story. The photographs also brought back my own memories, related to my parents who had married in the same year as Beatriz and Carlos, 1970. Although the weddings had been celebrated in two different countries – Italy and Brazil – the clothes, the ceremony in the church, and the poses of the newlyweds in the photographs were the same. I could see my mother's expression in the smile and the liveliness of a happy, beautiful young bride, who looked to the future with confidence and optimism, and bittersweet feelings and memories took over my attention for a few moments that to me seemed unbearably long.

Beatriz was one of the few women taking part in ABREA's activities. However, during the association's events and monthly meetings we had only chatted briefly, as she used to leave as soon as the assemblies finished. During the interview, I came to understand that what I had perceived as an attitude of escape was related to her shyness and profound difficulties in speaking about Carlos and the experience of MM they lived through together: Carlos, as a contaminated man, and she, as his wife and then widow. Several times, Beatriz' eyes became red and her voice broke as she was talking about Carlos. I tried to tone down the intensity of our conversation when I realized that remembering was becoming too painful for her. Even for me, controlling my distress in the face of her sorrow was becoming particularly difficult.

Here I report an extensive quote from Beatriz' narrative:

> Through the association [ABREA], Carlos got to know a lot about ARDs and MM. He used to say 'Thank goodness, I am one of the few ABREA members who has not been touched by asbestos'. He always thought that he was a lucky person, as he had worked there for four years yet he was fine. He periodically underwent check-ups and everything was fine. However, the fibre was already there, and when it appeared, it appeared as an exploding bomb. When he began to feel bad, it was not long before [his departure]… he began to feel something… I noticed that he had a mild cough in September 2007. It was just an annoying little thing, but I asked him: 'Aren't you going to the doctor?'. He answered no, and said that he was fine. Actually, he was still feeling fine for the rest of September, and into October. He had this very mild cough, but he was fine. He had undergone examinations in July and the results hadn't shown anything.
>
> In April 2008, he began to feel very tired. One day, he wanted to go on foot to the bakery near our house, but he came back soon and said: 'I don't know what I'm feeling – I wasn't even able to get there'. On that same day, he went to talk to a doctor who supports the ABREA struggle. The doctor took X-rays of his thorax; the results showed a large pleural effusion. When Carlos saw the radiography, he exclaimed: 'Gosh! I have mesothelioma!' He made the diagnosis himself. He didn't talk to me immediately after the visit. He came back home very nervous, but he didn't say anything. He arranged another visit to the hospital, and, at the scheduled appointment, I accompanied him. He didn't want me to go, but I did. The doctor asked for the radiographs he already had and then drained the liquid; the blood, the pus, everything was already infected. When the results were ready, they did not give a different diagnosis. It was mesothelioma. In the period before the hospitalization, almost one month, he underwent four drains [because of the presence of pleural effusions]. As soon as the liquid was drained, it appeared again. It was a lot of suffering, a lot of pain [*Era muito sofrimento, muita dor*]. He was hospitalized, but it was… it was so rapid. Doctors told us that surgical treatment was a worthwhile option to prolong his life expectancy. They could remove the left lung because the mesothelioma had affected only the left one. We agreed to surgical treatment, but… it didn't work. At that time, our youngest daughter was pregnant. He hoped that

surgery would allow him to see his granddaughter, but it didn't. It was very difficult [*Era muito difícil*]. On the last day of his life, he put his hand on my daughter's belly to bless the granddaughter he would never see [Beatriz was crying]. It is too much. I do not want to remember his suffering. Those were very painful days. While he was hospitalized, he was conscious and he saw people dying, he suffered a lot there [in the hospital]. He had refused the tube to an oxygen tank, but in the end, it was inevitable. He was particularly afraid of the night. During the day, it was fine, but at night, he said, it was terrible…

When he knew… because he saw so many friends fall… Gosh, he shut [himself] in the room that was his office. He locked himself in and stayed there all the time. Gosh, we suffered a lot, a lot, a lot… because we knew what his illness was. It was very painful to see it happening to such a lively person, and to know that he was doomed. He felt like that. His only hope was surgery. He knew that he had a very short time, a year, a year and a half at most, but he didn't think it was going to be that fast. His hope was surgery to survive a few months more, but… I think that his greatest suffering was knowing that he was doomed. He was so aware of his imminent departure that before being hospitalized, he wrote on a piece of paper what I would need to do after his death, and he left this piece of paper and other documents in his room for me to find. When I discovered he had prepared everything… Gosh, it was so painful for me.

As soon as he felt bad, he understood everything. His last weeks were very sad and painful. He was so aware. He had been such a healthy person, so full of life, with so many dreams in his head, but when he received the results, he said 'Everything has been decided'. He knew that he could survive for about six months, a year at most. He was so discouraged. Who could ever imagine a person so full of life, who loved life, entering the room and preparing his funeral? It was painful. He cried so much! He cried there, in his room. Sometimes he closed the door and I let him cry. It was a moment to be by himself, while I ended up crying in another room. What we went through, I believe many families went through the same illness, but they did not have the same knowledge he had. I think they suffered less. He had an in-depth knowledge of the disease because he had friends who were sick; he stayed with them, talked to doctors for them, accompanied them to the medical examinations. I think that it was more painful for him because of the awareness he had about ARDs, so I think he suffered more.

Carlos died in July 2008, aged 66, from MM that he had diagnosed himself three months earlier. Through his engagement in the activism, he had developed the tools and acquired the words to translate the symptoms and images of his lungs into signs that he had contracted MM like many of his friends. He knew that the 'time bomb' that had been hidden inside him for fifty years was going to explode soon.

As I have observed and heard during my fieldwork across Italy and Brazil, a diagnosis of MM is often conceived of by those receiving it as a death sentence. Considering that life expectancy is on average nine months from the diagnosis (INAIL 2018) and that quality of life can be seriously compromised by the development of the cancer as well as by the side effects of chemo, radio and surgical treatment, sufferers (those affected, but also their loved ones) may experience the illness as if they are trapped in a horror movie, as a study participant from Casale Monferrato (Italy) once told me. Moreover, in contexts where the awareness of the disaster is low or non-existent, getting the right diagnosis may be difficult. This is something that emerged from my first study conducted in my hometown, Bari (Italy) (Mazzeo 2014, 2017a), and such invisibility is related to the underdiagnosis of ARDs, a phenomenon that is still frequent today, especially in those countries still using asbestos (Pasetto et al. 2014; Marsili et al. 2016). The uncertainties and delays about diagnoses may provoke a sense of despair and abandonment among the sufferers, who in their search for a meaning to pain and sorrow that may be intimately lived as nonsensical, may gather, when favourable conditions occur, in communities through which knowledge and practical and emotional support are exchanged. In this regard, the NGOs with which I have so far conducted fieldwork across Italy and Brazil seem to have acted in order to guarantee the sufferers' 'right to meaning' (Quaranta 2012a), and have opened up unexpected and unpredictable pathways of care for their members.

Before arranging my appointment with Beatriz for this interview, I had already heard about Carlos from other ABREA members, who told me how committed he had been to the association, and how he had participated and helped with the organization of every event and activity. ABREA activists recalled how much they missed their *companheiro* (comrade). Throughout the years, the memories of Carlos and his story came to represent essential references in the narratives that ABREA members were collectively elaborating to fund and negotiate their identities as members of a community. Most of the time, ABREA activists remembered Carlos along with another ABREA member, Roberto, who had also contracted MM and died in 2009 (one year after Carlos). Roberto and Carlos had become friends through ABREA. One of the first photographs Beatriz showed me during our interview was of the two men sitting in the sun during an anti-asbestos campaign.

As previously mentioned, Carlos had only worked at Eternit in Osasco for four years back in the 1960s. During his professional career in another factory, he had continued his studies and obtained a Master's degree in Law. His friend Roberto, before working at Eternit and then in other plants in Osasco as an unspecialized worker, had worked in the *roça*, with no opportunity to study. Carlos and Roberto established a friendship strengthened by biosocial bonds rooted in their shared somatic condition of having been exposed to asbestos. In contrast to other disasters wherein the disruption accentuates class differences (Saitta 2013), AR disasters cross class barriers like the microscopic fibres that permeate all parts of a factory. These microscopic 'time bombs' are spread not only among the workers and their family members, but also among managers and clerks, and residents living and working near an asbestos-polluting source. Eventually, awareness of the existence of an AR disaster only emerges through the direct experience of it, through crumbling worlds and decaying bodies. For some, the ABREA members' bonds of friendship began in the factory, while for others, friendships were born in the community that emerged from the experiences of the disaster. In contexts affected by disasters, the survivors may tend to gather into a community performing grassroot practices of citizenship marked by an increased participation in the local sociopolitical life as it had happened in Casale Monferrato (Italy), site of my previous research). The majority of ABREA members had a similar working-class background, thus differences based on the type of the work done in the plant did not appear to reflect a hierarchy in the relationships observed in 2015. Specialized workers responsible for a work unit in the factory fought side by side with unspecialized workers who were formerly under their supervision. Roberto and Carlos's friendship is an example of how the ties born from sharing a hazardous exposure, namely asbestos contamination, broke down class differences in the face of their common fragility.

With a broken voice, Beatriz concluded her narrative with the words below:

> He was everything to us. He was a father who gave everything to us and saved nothing for him[self]. Outside the family, there was only ABREA for him, and I respected that. If we had to go to a wedding and on that day he happened to have a meeting at ABREA, we would not go to the church, but just to the party. In this way, he could go to the ABREA meeting. I understood how dedicated he was to ABREA and I never impeded his involvement. It seems as though it was already planned that in the future I would join ABREA too …
>
> On the day of his wake, the first person I saw was Roberto. He was upset. Like my husband, he knew a lot about ARDs. He came to me and said, 'I have mesothelioma too. Like Carlos'. I perceived his words as a desperate request for help. It was as if he was asking me, 'Please, please, help me, for God's sake!' I heard a request for help in his voice. I said, 'No, you are going to be fine, you are alive, you are going to get out of

this, try to be calm'. He could not even speak, but I saw his despair. When I arrived at the chapel, Roberto was already there and came to hug and talk to me. That encounter was so painful [she cried]. The firm is responsible for the suffering of all of us. There is no way that one can say that the firm gave so many benefits to people. There is no way to say that. They could have given protection or warnings or changed the production system. They could have warned people that asbestos was dangerous, that workers needed to be careful and take measures not to inhale the fibres. They could have at least given a warning communication so that someone could decide to take the risk or not, because there may be someone who says, 'Well, anyway, I am going to die someday!' No, they did nothing. They exposed poor innocents to risk, and the firm made profits at the expense of these innocents. Where did workers get sick? Why did they die of asbestos? The firm knew that asbestos was dangerous. My husband died very early in relation to his family – his grandmother and his parents, for instance, they all died very old, over 80 or 90 years old, while he… he died when he was 66 years old; he still had a life in front of him.

He was totally dedicated to the association, as the current president is. What he needed to do, he did. After he passed away and I realized the importance of ABREA in his life, I began to take part in the association. Previously, I just went to the parties they organized at the end of the year, but I didn't pay much attention to their struggle. My participation now is a sort of contribution; a way to thank ABREA because it was good for him. It is also a way to help and do something to prevent other families like mine in the future undergoing the same suffering we passed through, and to try to get asbestos prohibited. ABREA is part of this fight, and it helps families to avoid what we have suffered.

I went to Paris in 2012 to attend an international meeting organized by the French anti-asbestos movement. I had to carry something that might represent Carlos… it was for a manifestation. [Beatriz showed me a white T-shirt with a photograph of Carlos.] I asked my daughter to cut the photo you saw in the living room, where he was sitting with Roberto, and have it printed on the T-shirt I would take with me to Paris. On the day of the manifestation, it was very cold and rainy, so I could not wear the T-shirt; I had to wear a coat because it was too cold, but I held the T-shirt with his photograph on my chest for the whole march… many people from various countries took a picture of him. When we went to Casale Monferrato in 2014, I took the T-shirt with me again. It was photographed again and it even appeared in an Italian newspaper. Now, I want to order another T-shirt with his photograph, together with the photographs of other Brazilian victims from asbestos, because it was not just Carlos who died. My husband represents all the victims. To put a picture of my husband alone may seem like an act of selfishness… how many people died? On that day in Paris, I cried a lot. The organizers called a couple of Brazilian activists onto the stage and they talked about

> my husband. Soon, all the people in the square began to call my husband's name as a sign of tribute. It was so emotional. It felt like a vibration. I knew that in that moment Carlos was being gratified. I felt that. I do not even know how to explain that feeling. After that, I take part in ABREA, and I do what I can do [for the anti-asbestos struggle]. He was a good father and a good husband. I think he deserves it [her participation]. God willing, someday we will see our country free of asbestos.
>
> That picture in the banner… I think it was taken when somebody from ABREA went to visit him in hospital, in his last days. I think he asked someone to take that photograph, which is very sad for me. I do not have it here at home. With that picture, he wanted to show to the world how dangerous asbestos is and that it is a matter of life or death to prohibit it. He was very dedicated to ABREA and he asked for the photo to be shown on any possible occasion, so now when there is an event or a manifestation, ABREA members exhibit that photo. I cannot prevent that, although for me it is very painful and difficult. I cannot ask ABREA not to show it. It would just be my cowardice speaking, because if he had asked them to take that picture and show it to the world, I cannot say: 'No, I do not want to!' I have freed the use of it and said: 'Let the will of him who fought so hard with ABREA be done'.

I read Carlos's request to be photographed while he was confined to a bed, skinny, attached to an oxygen tank, and looking fiercely at the camera as his final contribution to remaking a world in which the younger generations, including his granddaughter, would live, while he would soon pass on from that same world. Through activism, Beatriz was trying to ease her suffering triggered by the loss that had destroyed her world. By relating her individual story to processes of disasters affecting entire communities of workers and citizens around the world, she became involved in a globally mobilized grassroots movement. Perhaps the great awareness of sufferers like Beatriz gives a moral responsibility for 'ensuring that others understand the social injustice our worlds routinely create' and for doing something to subvert those processes that deny and impede justice (Kleinman 2006: 24).

Unveiling Disasters

For many, the perception of our finitude produces a crisis, while some of us see it as a natural part of our current existence. The discovery of having been deceived for decades produces anger and indignation. No resignation seems to be possible (cf. Benson and Kirsch 2010). Pain, illness and death are then read through the words of activism as the wounds provoked by a subtle violence suffered in the past but still existing in the present. In fact, violence continues to be perpetrated every time suffering is not recognized, disasters remain silent, or a widow is unable to condemn a company because of the good her family had received in exchange for the 'lethal work' (Johnston and McIvor 2000) done by innocents, as Chico referred to asbestos workers.

The engagement in activism provides those affected by asbestos with a common language to live and situate their illness experiences within a specific frame through which the sufferers recognize each other as victims of the same injustice and deception. Even the most intimate experience of suffering, which tears the body from inside and exiles the sufferers to impenetrable terrains of anguish, fear and death, reveals its cultural and social dimensions. The paths to giving sense to nonsensical suffering made more acute and unbearable by the awareness of what is destroying one's body are emblematic of the mutual exchange between the body and the surrounding world, an exchange that runs along inextricable ties (Quaranta 2006c, 2012b).

Involvement in ABREA gave João, Roberto, Pedro, Chico and Carlos the words to translate the symptoms of their physical pain into the language of activism and name it as the result of a merciless crime of social injustice, the nefarious outcomes of invisible disasters. On a public level, they actively participated in ABREA activities, including awareness campaigns, as strategies of grassroots mobilization to promote recognition of the disaster. However, on an individual and intimate level, according to their own or their survivors' narratives, their awareness had exacerbated their suffering. Knowing exactly what they were going to face, having seen their friends fall and die one by one, and knowing that there was no escape, led João and Roberto to not accept their diagnoses, and Carlos to delay the medical examinations that would have confirmed his suspicions and fears. Survivors also suffered as powerless witnesses to the atrocious pain and decay of loved ones. Leticia, Irene and Beatriz, disoriented by the loss of reference points in their lives, had to learn how to cope with the absence of their loved ones and how to live and act in worlds that had been devastated by the disasters occurring in the intimate though social worlds of contaminated bodies and affective bonds. According to a moral and cultural Western perspective to which I inevitably refer, the experience of physical pain is the most emblematic part of the loneliness that characterizes us as human and defines our finitude (Elias 1999). However, the suffering that emerges from an experience of illness such as cancer or a debilitating disease does not necessarily belong to one person, but can instead be taken over collectively (Gordon 1991: 137–56); it can upset and destroy the worlds of those who experience the illness with the beloved one who has been diagnosed with a disease.

Below, I quote the last sentences of Chico's narrative about his experience of disaster, and the story of his own engagement in anti-asbestos activism:

> My life changed as I knew about the injury I had. I did not know anything before that. Then I began to go to the doctors, to undergo examinations… and the doctors talked to me. The change began at that moment and I began to live differently. As I told you, I know that I cannot run or move quickly. I have had to learn to live with the injury I have. When I began to take part in ABREA, I thought it was a good thing, because in the association I would be together with others who have the same problems as me. You see that it is not just you who has this problem – a friend has it too. We strengthen each other, because we see that we are not alone, and we can share what we feel. When we know that a friend of ours is dying, we visit him to give support to him and his family. We share a sad experience, but in that moment, a word pronounced by a friend can console.

Chico highlighted the role of the association as a place where contaminated workers like him might with others live the suffering provoked by the impact of asbestos exposure on their bodies. ABREA provided the activists with the tools to make sense and take care of their suffering. The reconstruction of a collective history of injustices and disaster opened up new possibilities of sense (and care) because 'there is not any single over-determined meaning to disease; rather, the experience of serious illness offers a means of understanding in a particularly deep and powerful way what personal and collective moral experience is about' (Kleinman 2006: 156).

Practices of Memory, Care and Community

During my fieldwork in Osasco, I took part in a commemorative ceremony organized by ABREA activists. Although I had never attended anything similar during my previous fieldwork in Italy, I can find similarities between the practices observed on the occasion of this ceremony in Brazil and events in Italy involving the commemoration of asbestos victims, which I had participated in during my research. In both countries, these social facts functioned as crucial moments in the search for meaning for AR suffering at both an individual and a collective level. Moreover, through them, the survivors strengthened their sense of belonging to a community and, in doing so, elaborated their identity based on a 'collective memory' (Halbwachs 1987), which these rituals contributed to keeping alive and narrating. I quote from my field diary:

> São Paulo, 26 April 2015. Sunday. Sunny and warm. I arrived in Osasco before nine in the morning. Eliezer [ABREA's president] and his son were waiting for me behind the train station. We had an appointment to go together by car to Aquilino dos Santos – Vítima do Amianto [Asbestos Victim] Square. This square was dedicated to the first asbestos victim who died after ABREA's foundation in 1995, and is in the Vila Nova neighbourhood, where the religious commemorative ceremony would take place. The square was small, hidden in a maze of tangled roads and houses. The ABREA members thought it might be difficult for me to find the place, so they suggested having someone to meet me at the train station. On our way to the square, we stopped to pick up Teodoro [the ABREA activist in Chapter 1]. Teodoro was waiting for us in the street. The square was very small indeed, at the corner between two streets. There were large trees under whose shadow ABREA members and friends were standing in a circle. A wall surrounded a circular space, in the middle of which there was a stone table with a burning candle, informative brochures about asbestos toxicity, and sheets with the words of the hymns to be sung neatly arranged. It all reminded me of the sacredness of an altar.

All around the gathered group, large portraits of activists who had died from ARDs were hanging from the trees. They had been placed there earlier on that quiet morning. They were the same posters that had been exhibited in Antonio Agù street during the event 'Proteção Contra o Amianto' [Protection against Asbestos], a week of awareness campaigns organized by ABREA every April, the month internationally dedicated to occupational health. On the last day of the event, ABREA activists commemorate their departed comrades with a religious ceremony. In the year of my fieldwork (2015), ABREA activists had invited three spiritual guides to administrate the ceremony: one Catholic, one Evangelic Pentecostal and one Spiritualist to represent the main religious faiths of the association's members. Although this event was organized on the occasion that awareness activities were being addressed to the general citizenry, the ABREA activists did not seem to be keen to make this ceremony really public. My impression was that by not advertising it too much, they preferred to live that moment as an occasion to remember loved ones and comrades, among a few intimate friends, relatives and supporters of their struggle. During the ceremony, I felt like I was witnessing (and taking part in) a sacred ceremony. I was particularly struck by the photographs of the activists who had died, their portraits exhibited and hanging right behind their survivors. The expressions of those men and women who had passed on, and about whom I had heard from their loved ones' narratives, seemed to assert their presence and participation beyond their irreversible physical absence. Part of the ceremony was dedicated to their commemoration by a spontaneous sharing of memories and feelings: anybody could speak and say something about a friend or a relative who had died. These acts of memory, collectively performed on the occasion of the ceremony or the exhibition of photographs – casts of a presence that has been here (Barthes 1980) – were practices of activism and care for the survivors who were mourning the loss of their friends and loved ones, as well as their own decay and preannounced death. Suffering was not overcome, but it was made meaningful by a 'fate's or affective community' (Halbwachs 1987), whose relational identity was rooted in a shared narrated memory. Remembering was painful, but it was conceived as necessary and felt to be a moral and political commitment. The subversive tension intrinsic to those acts of memory, dissolving the fracture between past, present and future, undoubtedly practices of a prolonged individual and collective mourning, reminded me of the words adopted by Zhang to talk about mourning in terms of protesting. In particular,

> the refusal to end mourning becomes a political action of protest against the social injustice responsible for the loss of life. In this light, death is no longer accepted as the end of a life, but is scrutinized as the beginning of the pursuit [of] justice. The gravity of mourning moves away from death toward life along the axis of moral responsibility for the loss. (Zhang 2012: 271)

In the refusal to break the bonds with a past that continues impacting the present, in the painful traces it leaves, survivors make sense of their suffering. Survivors are living beyond life (and death), and by mourning they are affirming life because 'survival is the most intense life possible' (Derrida 2004 in Fassin 2014a: 45). Mourning primarily concerns life; as Zhang states,

> it is not new to argue that mourning is not about the dead but about the living… However, it is entirely new to say that mourning is not about death but about life, because to elaborate on Butler's argument, grievability – the eligibility to mourn in public – is about the worthiness of life – for the dead as well for the living. (Zhang 2012: 277)

Practices of mourning are practices of care and activism aimed at achieving the acknowledgement of the worthiness of the lives of those who have already passed away, those who are still suffering and those who, someday, will live in a world free from asbestos, thanks to the men and women who mobilize now against injustice and violence.

The last words publicly pronounced by the philosopher Derrida (quoted in Fassin 2014a) effectively express what I perceive to be a vibrating impulse or the will of the sufferers and activists – the disaster survivors – who did not abandon the struggle despite the disaster (and death) in their lives:

> 'Surviving is to still be fully alive and living after death. It is the "unconditional affirmation" of life and of the pleasure of life; it is the hope to "survive" through the traces left to the living.' I believe that in this revelation there is much more than the last testimony of a philosopher who has certainly not let us get used to clarity and simplicity. I consider it an ethical gesture through which life is restored to its most obvious and ordinary dimension – life that has death as a horizon, but that is not separate from life as a social form, inscribed in a story, a culture, an experience. (Fassin 2014a: 45)

The practices characterizing ABREA's activism were, on the one hand, practices of care to the extent that intersubjective relationships and experiences amplify the potentialities of a process of care (Taussig 1980; Mol 2008). On the other hand, the actions promoted by ABREA were practices of activism to the extent that reading and narrating the history inscribed in the 'bodies in pain' (Scarry 1985) represent the occasion to relate the intimate aspects of an experience of suffering to the social and political dynamics of disaster processes.

Reading the traces of the injustices suffered inscribed in the bodies was possible thanks to the lens and words provided by activism, through which the embodied history became a tool of struggle, providing legitimacy to the activists' allegations. Moreover, referring to a shared history gave individuals – bodies – in pain the possibility to recognize each other and gather in a community. In these paths of both care and activism, individual and collective acts of memory have played a crucial role. Remembering was both a practice of care for those grieving for an irreversible loss, and a practice of political action.

Memory reactivates the past, and feelings of despair, anger and indignation are lived again and again, dissolving the gap between past, present and future. The traces of the suffered injuries abruptly emerge from the ruins left by disaster processes, and hurt each time a new diagnosis is pronounced and a new death occurs. However, beyond the shared experience of suffering, the occasions of collective rituals such as the commemoration I participated in during my fieldwork represent to the sufferers – at the same time victims and activists – the motivation for never giving up (*nunca desistir*) their struggle. On these occasions, absence is not a constant and anguishing affirmation of an irremediable loss anymore, but becomes a reassuring presence instead.

Figure 3.4 Aquilino dos Santos – Vítima do Amianto [Asbestos Victim] Square. Osasco, São Paulo, Brazil, 2015. Photograph by the author.

The ruins provoked by the 'bomb's explosion', for a moment, cease to be lacerating wounds, but become scars mending a multiplicity of private stories of suffering into a collective history of a community whose members fight and live with AR disasters in their daily lives.

Conclusion

In AR disasters, the suffering body holds the traces of the cultural, sociopolitical and economic processes through which 'corporate crimes' (Altopiedi 2011) have been perpetrated on vulnerable social actors considered as cheap, easily exploitable and replaceable resources in the global and toxic market of asbestos. The body is the place where the devastating impact of these processes of disaster primarily occurs, but the body is also the place where traces indicating new paths to undertake can emerge among the ruins, 'from the dust' (Petrillo 2015). Activism provides sufferers with the lens and words to read the traces of AR disasters on contaminated bodies, and inform the suffering experiences as cultural practices even before the catastrophic eruption in one's world at the moment when the awareness of being at risk of dying from an ARD becomes part of everyday life.

I refer to Kleinman (1997, 2006) when I consider the suffering condition related to the disaster experience as a condition from which 'the lived experience of "everything that really matters" transforms the ordinary … These socio-somatic processes not only connect society and the body-self, they can transform both poles of experience' (Kleinman 1997: 331). The awareness of being at risk of suffering and dying from asbestos exacerbates the suffering of those living at risk, and forces them to reflect on contingencies, encounters and activism in their lives, which makes them consider what 'really matters', and informs their actions in the world as 'sufferer-activists' (Mazzeo 2017b):

> The things most at stake are clarified, for us and others, by the dangers we encounter. Those dangers, moreover, can and often do remake what matters most, so that what matters and who we are is not what was before, but instead becomes something new and different … Experiences of life's very real dangers are not only about injury and limitation but also hold the potential [for] creative and inspiring change. Creative because they open new realities; inspiring because, in the face of pain and death, these experiences change intimate others, offering the possibility that their moral life can also be different. (Kleinman 2006: 156)

In everyday life, practices of activism, for instance, consisted of ensuring that all the members of the association underwent periodical examinations at public health centres, both in Osasco and São Paulo. On the one hand, these medical checks safeguarded the exposed through a constant monitoring of ARDs already diagnosed. The majority of ABREA members I met had been diagnosed with asbestosis and pleural plaques. This put them at an increased risk of an AR cancer. On the other hand, the data resulting from these examinations were recorded, and they represented the basis on which epidemiological evidence and scientific knowledge emerged and were elaborated. Often, while carrying out participant observation in the association's office, I was present for phone calls made by ABREA members on their voluntary shift (*plantão*) to other members to make or remind them about appointments, to tell them that clinical reports were ready or to ask for the availability of someone with a car to accompany a member with mobility problems.

In ABREA's refusal to abandon those who were doomed to a painful and unavoidable death, I discovered what defines care, because the encounter and communication with sufferers are essential elements in any process of care. I refer to the Italian anthropologist Francesca Cappelletto, who left us a touching ethnography about her own cancer experience:

> Both an individual and a social group, by expressing their own pain, can find a sense of protection and freedom from the anxiety and despair that often accompany the suffering condition. Such a necessity to 'speak' can be linked to the traumatic nature of disease: those traumatized will narrate and re-narrate the past–present event, which becomes an object of narrative memory. (Cappelletto 2009: 217)

Engagement in activism has opened paths to face the multiple crises provoked by AR disasters, and to care for the suffering of those who have been involved in those experiences: the social actors with ARDs, those exposed to the risk of ARDs, and the grievers. Arthur Kleinman's investigations into the moral dimension of care (Kleinman 1997, 2006, 2009, 2012) have offered me the theoretical tools – and inspiration – to think about the practices of activism in terms of paths of care. Illness experiences, such as the ones lived by the anti-asbestos activists I met, can 'open eyes, break down doors, and encourage active engagement with real threats and their societal causes' (Kleinman 2006: 157). In line with Kleinman (2006), and Wilkinson and Kleinman (2016), I consider (bodily) suffering as a condition from which sufferers can reinvent their role in the world as sufferers and, at the same time, promote changes with a sociopolitical relevance as activists. 'Moral experience, especially the moral experience of suffering, holds the potential for remaking our lives and those of others' (Kleinman 2006: 157).

Acts of memory become a regular part of the rhythm of life of a sufferer engaged in activism. Reading and narrating the memory inscribed in the contaminated bodies coincide with practices of care and struggle. Basing their actions on the collective and individual narratives by which the activists keep the past alive, the disaster survivors mobilize, negotiate rights and promote changes in the local context (Petryna 2002; Brown et al. 2004). They invent new roles in the world for themselves as individuals and as members of a community (Polletta and Jasper 2001), establish affective contact and experience encounters that are therapeutic for their suffering (Goodwin, Jasper and Polletta 2000, 2001; Cappelletto 2009).

An ethics of care framed the practices and discourses of anti-asbestos activism I researched, and it was connoted by a critique towards the dominant system of knowledge and power, which had ceased to appear immutable and natural. The disaster survivors conceived of their engagement in the anti-asbestos movement as something urgent and necessary to promote change and take care of their own and others' suffering. Anti-asbestos activism emerges from (and its legitimation is rooted in) the memory guarded and reactivated by the suffering body, which becomes the 'battlefield' that bears the injustices; but the body is also the primary locus and tool for action, from which practices and meanings of struggle appear.

Based on their memory and embodied history, the anti-asbestos activists I met in Osasco were disentangling the knots of the disaster processes they were suffering from, both as individuals and as members of a community of survivors. On the one hand, activism provided the sufferers with the words to name and read the traces of disaster in their bodies as proof of the injustices and exploitation suffered. On the other hand, the allegations advanced by the activists found legitimation in the experiential knowledge kept alive by the 'bodies in pain' (Scarry 1985) and the evocation of bodily suffering experienced in the past. The practices of anti-asbestos activism aimed to break the invisibility around AR disasters, and the exposed workers used their contaminated bodies as a tool for political action in their struggle to gain asbestos prohibition in Brazil. If, as I believe, the body is 'the most immediate, most proximate terrain where social truths are forged and social contradictions played out, as well as the locus of personal resistance, creativity and struggle', it is crucial to consider the role of the 'afflicted, naturally subversive' body (Scheper-Hughes 1994: 232) to understand anti-asbestos activism. In contexts wherein those involved in the disaster experiences learn the words to name and relate their own suffering to corporative crimes affecting a community, the suffering body amplifies the potentialities for action, and questions the taken-for-granted assumptions that a society elaborates in relation to victimhood, suffering and care.

4

The Politics of Anti-asbestos Activism

> Injustice experienced in the flesh, in deeply wounded flesh, is the stuff out of which change explodes.
>
> —Margaret Mead, *Blackberry Winter: My Earlier Years*

The body guards the traces of the past and, in particular, 'the body in pain is a source of memory' (Kleinman 2006). By relying on the embodied traces of the processes of AR disasters, the anti-asbestos activists I met in Osasco were engaged in a movement aiming to break the silence about these processes, using their contaminated bodies as a political tool in their struggle to gain asbestos prohibition in Brazil. In this regard, the quote from Merleau-Ponty (1945) in Fassin (2007) is particularly appropriate:

> The true mark of history is inscribed in the materiality of the physical and psychic being. The specific past which is our body can only be seized by an individual life because it has never transcended it, because it secretly nurtures it and partly uses its strengths – because it remains its present. The body is therefore a past embodied in a present. It is the tangible trace of time, the mark that brings it up to date. (Fassin 2007: 177–78)

Since its foundation in 1995, ABREA has sought and then found among unionists, politicians, environmentalist groups, public health professionals and legal interlocutors a dialogue and collaboration to legitimize its allegations and empower its struggle. Mutual support and recognition established these connections. In the initial stages of the mobilization, workers who had noticed the traces of the disasters on their bodies sought medical examinations and diagnoses from doctors outside the firms using asbestos, and they thus gained the words to name what was afflicting them. Exposed workers approached biomedical professionals from public hospitals and occupational health research institutes who were specialized in lung diseases and epidemiology. On the one hand, relating their illness experiences to occupational exposure to asbestos was crucial in legitimizing their activism. The development of such knowledge triggered feelings of deception that motivated workers to take action against their employing firms in the name of the injustices suffered, based on their unawareness of their exposure to toxic agents whose carcinogenicity had been shown by biomedical studies since the mid-1960s (Selikoff, Churg and Hammond 1964, 1965). On the other hand, by using their contaminated bodies as proof, sufferers entered the processes of elaborating knowledge and epidemiological evidence. Starting from this premise, politicians who embraced the anti-asbestos cause then supported legal efforts to prohibit asbestos in the Osasco municipality and the São Paulo state.

The unionists and politicians who most sympathized with ABREA activists were those whose political backgrounds were rooted in the specific sociocultural fabric of the city. These interlocutors had been actively involved in the resistance against the dictatorial regime (1964–84) and then the Brazilian democratization process. To describe the fundamental 'social capital'[1] on which ABREA could count, I referred to archival documents as well as to narratives emerging from my encounters with anti-asbestos activists, unionists, public health professionals (lung and occupational health specialists), politicians and lawyers. All of them maintained that the global prohibition of asbestos was the safest and most effective measure to stop the invisible disasters provoked by the toxic market of asbestos worldwide. It is important to consider this aspect to situate my interlocutors' narratives within a clearly defined opinion on the health dangers of asbestos exposure. Looking reflectively at my fieldwork experience, I would have been given different perspectives by professionals, entrepreneurs and politicians in favour of the asbestos market if I had been able to approach supporters of the so-called 'controlled use of asbestos' (Castleman 2003).

Anti-asbestos Activism through Biomedical Paths

In the early 1990s, in Osasco, an unemployed former Eternit worker spent several months unsuccessfully looking for a new job. One day, a doctor checking his health during a selection process for a position at another factory told him that the reason why nobody would employ him was the bad condition of his lungs. The worker underwent further examinations, which revealed that his lungs were seriously contaminated with asbestos. He began to search for his former co-workers to warn them about the possibility of being contaminated. In the meantime, he made his first contact with professionals at the Ministry of Labour involved in the surveillance of safety measures in workplaces, who put him in contact with biomedical doctors specializing in lung diseases and occupational health. In the 'collective memory' of the ABREA members, the anti-asbestos mobilization in Osasco began with this specific episode, emblematic of how an individual story of vulnerability can be part of processes of disaster affecting an entire community of exposed workers and residents.

In the early 1990s, studies conducted by professionals at the Fundação Jorge Duprat Figueiredo de Segurança e Medicina do Trabalho – FUNDACENTRO [Jorge Duprat Figueiredo Foundation of Safety and Occupational Health] began to elaborate the epidemiological evidence of AR carcinogenicity in Brazil. Data were emerging from medical examinations of hundreds of asbestos workers, the majority of whom had worked at the Eternit plant in Osasco and would later join ABREA. As recalled by a biomedical doctor whom I interviewed in São Paulo in September 2015, this was the situation before the mid-1990s:

> There were no diseases because there had never been an investigation. There was no place for medical checks: a sick worker with respiratory problems used to receive treatment as if he had tuberculosis. We know about several metallurgical workers contaminated with silica or asbestos who were diagnosed with tuberculosis instead. The two diseases are completely different, but there was no diagnosis for ARDs. The concept of a relationship between occupational exposure to asbestos and disease simply did not exist.

The FUNDACENTRO and the Centro de Referência em Saúde do Trabalhador – CEREST [Reference Centre for Occupational Health] of the Freguesia do Ó in São Paulo were among the first public health centres contacted by asbestos workers who were beginning to think critically about their bodies and their occupational experiences. I refer to the interviews conducted with five biomedical doctors I met in Osasco, São Paulo and Rio de Janeiro. In them, anti-asbestos activists from ABREA and other Brazilian associations found interlocutors, supporters and biomedical professionals who cared for workers' health. My interlocutor continued

> The first contact dates back to 1995; they [the asbestos workers] began to come to our centres asking for check-ups. At that time, there was still no occupational health centre in Osasco, so they had to come to São Paulo, and this might have been a mobility problem for some. Generally, a worker informed a co-worker about the opportunity of undergoing examinations to detect the presence of asbestos in their lungs.

The Grupo Interinstitucional de Estudo de Trabalhadores Expostos ao Asbesto – GIETEA [Inter-institutional Study Group of Asbestos-Exposed Workers] made the first diagnoses of ARDs in Brazil. The GIETEA included biomedical doctors from four public health centres as partner institutions: FUNDACENTRO/Divisão de Medicina do Trabalho [Occupational Health Unit]; CEREST of Freguesia do Ó (São Paulo); Instituto do Coração-InCor/Hospital das Clínicas, Faculdade de Medicina, Universidade de São Paulo – HCFMUSP [Cardiology Institute/Das Clínicas Hospital, Faculty of Medicine, University of São Paulo]; and Área de Saúde Ocupacional – ASO, Universidade de Campinas – UNICAMP [Occupational Health Department, University of Campinas]. Over the years, the composition of the group changed, and the Rede Nacional de Atenção Integral à Saúde do Trabalhador – RENAST, Regional Osasco [National Network of Comprehensive Care of Occupational Health, Osasco Region] which had been founded in the meantime, took the place of InCor. Below, I quote one of my interlocutor's last statements:

> It was important to carry out collaborative work, especially at the beginning. At that time, we [biomedical doctors] could have had doubts and could have made mistakes, as we could not rely on a profound knowledge of ARDs. So we met periodically to discuss the test results and we signed the diagnoses together. The involvement of professionals from four important public institutions conferred great reliability to the certificates we signed together, after collectively studying each case. It was a significant learning process for us. We examined hundreds of workers; the majority of them had been employed at the Eternit plant in Osasco. From 1995 to 1998, there were a large number of workers contacting us through ABREA. The basic examinations were radiography and spirometry. The results of our first investigations were shocking: seven workers out of ten were diagnosed with ARDs, in particular with pleural plaques and asbestosis.

The biomedical doctors I met were supporters of the anti-asbestos activism and had spent part of their study and training experiences abroad. The relationships linking them to Italian researchers (especially epidemiologists and public health professionals) and institutions such as the Istituto Superiore di Sanità [Superior Institute of Health] in Rome were still strong in 2015. The majority of these connections were the continuation of dialogue and collaborations begun in the 1980s, a time of crucial reforms in public health policy in Italy which deeply influenced the elaboration of the Sistema Único de Saúde – SUS [Unified Health System], the Brazilian public health system ruled by the post-dictatorship Constitution of 1988 (Berlinguer, Teixeira and Campos 1988; Paim 2008). Brazil's democratization phase and policies addressing the active participation of civil society favourably influenced ABREA's role in biomedical knowledge and epidemiological evidence-finding processes. ABREA served as a collective social actor representing a community of 'afflicted bodies' (Scheper-Hughes 1994), and focused its struggle on biomedical paths to find interlocutors and supporters at the public health centres, in a process of renovation due to greater democratization in all the Brazilian public institutions after dictatorship. At the same time, health professionals and biomedical doctors had the opportunity to investigate the ARDs contracted by a large number of asbestos workers – an opportunity that favoured local advancements in biomedical knowledge about the carcinogenicity of asbestos fibres. This aspect is emblematic of the processual dimension that characterizes biomedical knowledge as a cultural system rooted in paradigms that are absolute and true, until they are substituted by new paradigms achieving consensus from the community of experts (Kuhn 1963). In my analysis of the processual dimension of biomedical paradigms, and their role in understanding and treating 'socially produced epidemics' (Braun and Kisting 2006), I refer to Fassin (2007) who argues:

> Epidemics are moments of truth when both knowledge and power are put to the test. Doctors test their theories, and citizens expect concrete results from the authorities. This well-known and often-recorded fact, along with the transformations it brings about in the field of science and the destabilizing effect it has on the current government, has led to interpreting epidemics as factors of social change. It would be close to reality, however, to regard them as factors that reveal states of the world that are already there but could just as well never materialize. They are revealing in the sense of unveiling ... The epidemic thus invents nothing; it uncovers. It is a biological phenomenon that shakes or strengthens the existing social structures and representations, but does not create them ex nihilo. (Fassin 2007: 32)

> The evolution of knowledge at the heart of scientific activity is what will guide the normative changes. When new discoveries are made, the norm changes. Seen this way, biomedicine is always right. At the time when it makes a definitive statement – and to the extent that it has mobilized all the scientific resources immediately at its disposal – it is speaking the

> truth, even when it declares the contrary of what it had asserted previously … However, compared to biology, for instance, the specific nature of biomedicine comes from the fact that it is also medicine. It has effects on people and on society, through diagnoses and treatments, through individual counselling and collective pronouncements, through the production of norms that in the end turn doctors into 'moral entrepreneurs'. Thus, contrary to science, when biomedicine speaks the truth it also speaks morals and, in so doing, becomes socially vulnerable. Though it can always claim it has done its best at any given moment, it is accountable to the public in the long term. And though it may forget, the public will remember. (Fassin 2007: 84)

A lung specialist whom I interviewed recalled several times that reformed Italian health policies had influenced his career and decision to work in a public hospital. He had studied in Italy in the 1980s, and that specific sociopolitical context had marked his attitude and ethics as a biomedical doctor. I quote:

> It is a sensitive matter. We care for workers who do not trust medical doctors anymore, since they have been deceived for many years. We know about workers who neither accepted nor believed in the diagnoses we gave them. Some workers are suspicious. They still have a lot of doubts and ask numerous questions. Many of them undergo tests at both public hospitals and private medical ambulatories contracted by the firm. In this way, they can compare the results. I do not judge this behaviour. It is their choice and their right, since by law the firm is obliged to guarantee periodic medical checks to exposed workers. We should always keep in mind that contaminated workers are vulnerable people. They are poor, elderly and sick. They have to face a number of practical and emotional difficulties. Those who have pleural plaques and asbestosis live with a higher risk of contracting lung cancer and MM. They suffer from this awareness; many of them have trouble sleeping … We give lectures and train new generations of medical doctors, but they [ABREA activists] play an irreplaceable role. They build a network, mobilize and, through awareness campaigns, involve exposed workers and citizens who until that moment did not know anything about the dangers of asbestos. In those cases, ABREA puts them in contact with us. In general, periodic examinations are scheduled once a year, but in cases of necessity, they know that they are free to come and talk to us when the ambulatory is open [one day a week] without an appointment. Since they suffer from chronic diseases that upset their lives and their families, the follow-up [*acompanhamento*] is fundamental, and it is important that they feel they are accompanied [*eles se sentam acompanhados*, meaning cared for and not abandoned].

The practices of activism undertaken by ABREA members consisted largely of collaboration with biomedical professionals in public health research institutes, whose knowledge and expertise they had contributed to improving and widening in a significant way. As stated in an academic article published in 2001, epidemiological data about the health hazards of occupational exposure to asbestos were almost inexistent throughout the 1990s (Algranti et al. 2001), and only a few investigations had been conducted prior to the early 2000s (Nogueira et al. 1975; Costa 1983; Amancio, Bonciani and Urquiza 1988). The same article, reporting the first results of an epidemiological survey, acknowledged the essential role of ABREA in the study, which had involved 868 asbestos workers between June 1995 and August 1999. The survey's results showed that 8.9 per cent of the workers had asbestosis, while 29.7 per cent had pleural thickening.

During this process of investigation, the ABREA was set up by former workers with the creation of a central registry. This organization took over the task of identifying and listing former workers. The principal objective of the project was to investigate respiratory morbidity due to asbestos exposure. Former workers were approached by ABREA and invited to participate in a cross-sectional evaluation and longitudinal follow-up (Algranti et al. 2001: 241).

ABREA activists collaborated with biomedical doctors in the elaboration of the epidemiological evidence of the suffering that they and their families were experiencing every day. They were living archives of the traces of processes of a health disaster begun in the past, persisting in the present and threatening the future. Keeping the memory of the past alive and making it readable and communicable through the words of biomedicine has been fundamental in legitimizing anti-asbestos activists' claims.

Leandro, one of the oldest ABREA members I interviewed, had written a long list of the names of deceased ABREA members, including his comrades who had died up until 2003. He then updated the list, and it contained 109 names by 2015. Leandro had produced tangible proof of the 'invisible disasters' provoked by the toxic market of asbestos by writing down in his jealously preserved notebook the names of his co-workers who had died from ARDs. Once again, during my fieldwork, I could feel the extent to which practices of memory were indeed practices of activism (Mazzeo 2017b, 2018c). I recall Appadurai's reflections on the practices of bottom-up citizenship and democracy, which are essential for the vulnerable social groups in the world to become aware of their own rights and role in history. As Appadurai (2013) states, vulnerable social groups can only develop the capacity to 'aspire to' and 'design' a future that is different from their present state of oppression if they develop the instruments to investigate the causes of their oppression, and make their suffering visible and communicable. By using in an unexpected way those instruments thought to favour control over the population, such as those designed by demography and statistics (Foucault 2005), vulnerable social groups can enter history, from which their role has often been silenced or left unrecognized (de Martino 1948). I agree with Appadurai when he states that research is a human right, and calls for anthropologists to commit to making their tools and knowledge public and at the service of the poor. This is because the capacity of doing research coincides with the capacity to aspire, meaning the capacity to practise bottom-up democratic citizenship (Appadurai 2013).

In ABREA's office, another informal register was represented by a package of yellow membership records called *falecidos* (deceased members). The register was on a desk with the records of the current members and of those who had abandoned the association. Each record included the member's photograph, date of birth and workplace. The membership cards belonging to current members had been placed beside those who had died. Ordered in that way, the documents evoked a proximity between the absent and the alive, the departed friends and the survivors. It was like there was a tangible continuity between past and present created by the sufferer-activists' militant memory (Mazzeo 2017b).

Conceiving of biomedical paths as paths of activism is intertwined with the consideration of the cultural dimension of scientific knowledge, whose categories and explanations are not absolute or neutral 'truths' of a monolithic institution (see Kuhn 1963), but rather the product of a permeable and fluid system of power crossed by conflicts. The practices of activism undertaken by ABREA members consisted of a daily struggle for the recognition of the carcinogenicity of asbestos fibres, which had been denied them for decades. While corporations involved in the global market of asbestos referred to the 'controlled use of asbestos' theory to continue making profit with asbestos (Castleman 2003), contaminated workers denounced the lack of biomedical recognition of their suffering as a form of further injustice. In this regard, I recall João's story narrated to me by Leticia, his wife (referred to in Chapter 3).

João had died of lung cancer in 2013, having worked for twenty-two years at the Eternit plant in Osasco. He was also a smoker. On his death certificate, there was no mention of his occupational exposure to asbestos, despite the fact that, in April 1997, GIETEA had diagnosed him with both asbestosis and pleural plaques (Prüss-Ustün et al. 2011; IARC 2012). João's family had not asked for an autopsy, which might have proved the presence of asbestos fibres in João's lungs, and the medical doctor who signed the death certificate could not state the presence of an ARD as there had been no examination of tissues or organs.

In 1997, João had filed a lawsuit against the company because of the discrepancy he found between the results of his GIETEA medical tests and those from the company's doctors who had examined him during his post-dismissal check-up, a few months before his GIETEA exam. Moreover, he found there was a discrepancy between the certificate stating his ability to work and his health condition. At that time, João was suffering from constant tiredness, shortness of breath and depression. By comparing the documents that his widow Leticia had shown me during our interview, I noticed that although João had undergone the same tests (radiography, spirometry and computerized tomography) by both the company doctors and GIETEA, the diagnoses were divergent. GIETEA had found evidence of asbestosis and pleural plaques, while the company medical doctors had not found evidence of any ARD, and had declared that João, aged 66, was still able to work.

The judges in charge of João's case requested a medical survey, which eventually did not attest to the presence of ARDs either. The lawsuit documents stated that 'the presence of asbestos in the lungs [as was evident from the images] might not be read as a disease in itself; moreover, the symptoms of tiredness and shortness of breath might be related to pulmonary emphysema, most likely due to the worker's habit of smoking'. The medical report ordered by the judges repeatedly stated that the dangers of asbestos exposure depended on a person's reaction to exposure and on a high dose–time relationship: meaning that the larger the number of inhaled fibres and the longer the duration of exposure, the higher the risk of contracting an ARD. It also stated that former workers would not run the risk of contracting asbestosis in later years. However, João's 'mild depression, sadness, gloom, bitterness and tendency to isolate himself from family and friends' were mentioned to describe his health condition.

The results of epidemiological surveys have proven the carcinogenicity of asbestos fibres since the 1960s (Selikoff, Churg and Hammond 1964, 1965). Nevertheless, the international community of health professional experts in AR issues is still involved in a debate about the so-called 'controlled use of asbestos', based on which national and multinational corporations continue using asbestos legitimately. In the literature, the debate continues, with some authors maintaining that the cause–effect relationship between exposure to asbestos chrysotile and MM onset cannot be established with certainty (Assis and Isoldi 2014), and others stating that to determine a safety threshold in asbestos fibre exposure is impossible, regardless of the kind of asbestos minerals involved (Marsili et al. 2016). The discussion takes place in comments and letters published in academic journals, such as Algranti's comments (2014) on Assis and Isoldi's review (2014) and statements of international research institutes (Collegium Ramazzini 1999, 2010, 2015), as well as in the everyday life of health professionals and researchers operating in contexts involving divergent categories, as happened at the time of my fieldwork in Brazil. In 2015, I could perceive the conflicts at play in the explanation and treatment of ARDs. I heard about circumstances in which health professionals and researchers engaged with anti-asbestos activism and campaigns aiming to prohibit asbestos worked in the same units or university departments as professionals who adhered to the 'controlled use of asbestos' theory, maintained the possibility of working safely while exposed to asbestos, and argued that establishing a 'zero risk' condition was impossible for any activity.

Asbestos Prohibition in Osasco and São Paulo

The results of the first biomedical studies and epidemiological surveys substantiated anti-asbestos activists' allegations: the diagnoses that former asbestos workers were receiving for the first time in their lives made the deaths of an increasing number of friends and comrades, the inner wounds on their lungs, their shortness of breath and their coughs indisputable proof of asbestos toxicity. By the mid-1990s, the struggle that ABREA members had undertaken and carried out along biomedical paths was strengthened as they mobilized in the name of asbestos prohibition by also undertaking political and administrative paths. Along these paths, ABREA found supporters and interlocutors among those social actors whose civil conduct and ethics were rooted in the lively socio-political and cultural context characterizing the city of Osasco, in particular between the 1960s and 1980s.

During my fieldwork, I had the opportunity to conduct an interview with Marcos Martins, in 2015 the state deputy of the Partido dos Trabalhadores – PT [Workers' Party], who had been engaged in anti-asbestos activism since the beginning of his political career. With the current ABREA president, Eliezer João de Souza, the two men shared the experience of militancy among the worker-priests operating in the peripheral neighbourhoods of Osasco, who divulgated the principles of Liberation Theology (Gutiérrez 1972), and believed in the emancipating potential of education as theorized by Freire (1967, 1970, 1980). I had first met Deputy Martins in April 2011 in Casale Monferrato

Figure 4.1 Membership cards of anti-asbestos activists. Osasco, São Paulo, Brazil, 2015. Photograph by the author.

(Italy), where he had been invited to an international conference organized by the local anti-asbestos NGO. He was renowned in the international context of anti-asbestos activism for having supported the law prohibiting asbestos use in Osasco (Complementary Law 90/2000, ruled by the Decree Law 8,983/2001) and for writing the São Paulo state law banning asbestos (Law 2,684/2007). Both had been fundamental achievements for the grassroots movement aimed at asbestos prohibition in Brazil. The municipal law prohibited the use of any kind of asbestos-containing material in public and private construction, and established that every year the city government would fund the awareness campaigns organized by ABREA in April, the month internationally dedicated to occupational health issues. The state law then prohibited the use of asbestos-containing material and products in the entire territory of the state of São Paulo. The laws included all kinds of asbestos, including chrysotile, which was then still extracted in Brazil.

On 23 November 2016, the Brazilian Federal Supreme Court discussed the Ações Diretas de Incostitucionalidade – ADI [Direct Actions of Unconstitutionality] undertaken by the Confederação Nacional dos Trabalhadores na Indústria – CNTI [National Confederation of Industrial Workers] against the laws approved by the São Paulo state and municipality concerning asbestos prohibition. The discussion was about the alleged unconstitutionality of the laws and non-conformity with the federal law allowing asbestos use. These actions were symptomatic of the conflict – and violence – intrinsic to a debate in which the right to live and work in a safe environment appeared to be negotiable and secondary to the rules governing the global market of asbestos. Since Brazil was the third largest asbestos producer in the world until 2017 (US Geological Survey 2017), its anti-asbestos activists faced numerous difficulties over more than twenty years of mobilization.

During the earliest stages of the Brazilian anti-asbestos activism, local firms responded by trying to silence the denunciations and weaken the grassroots movement by undermining the social and emotional bonds among the workers, a crucial binding force of ABREA's activism. In Osasco, several years after the demolition of the Eternit plant in the mid-1990s, the firm reactivated the Associação Recreativa dos Colaboradores Eternit – ARCE [Recreational Association of Eternit Collaborators]. In the association's magazines, periodically sent to former workers, short articles commemorated the 'good old days' by recalling the friendships born in the plant, and praised the enthusiasm and commitment of the workers, who used to be called 'collaborators'. Moreover, during our encounters, my interlocutors often showed me the invitation letters they used to receive from the firm to participate in barbecues (*churrascos*), Christmas parties with donations of baskets of food, and activities of fraternization (*confraternização*). In 1997, a series of meetings were inaugurated entitled 'Conversas com a Eternit' [Conversations with Eternit] consisting of 'delightful and relaxed reunions' intended to build a 'friendly relationship of mutual and permanent trust (*confiança mútua e permanente*)'. At the same time, former workers received invitations to reflect on the transactions proposed by the company instead of undertaking legal actions, and reminders of the opportunity to undergo periodic medical checks at the health centres contracted by the firm, as guaranteed by law. The texts of these letters contained numerous recalls of the importance of participation, fraternization, and the opportunity of meeting old friends at the ARCE.

The public debate on asbestos prohibition was still characterized by conflict at the time of my fieldwork, and it represented the background of Deputy Marcos Martins' narrative about the story of asbestos prohibition in Osasco. I quote:

> The collaboration with FUNDACENTRO and then with CEREST here in Osasco was important to empower the workers' struggle and to care

> for them, so in these centres workers might undergo medical examinations and be followed up [in their chronic illness care]. As a city councillor (*vereador*), I brought workers' cases into the municipality government's debates. Together with workers and professionals [biomedical doctors and technicians from the public institutions supporting workers' mobilization], we wrote a project for the prohibition of asbestos use in Osasco, a project that I signed and proposed to the local government. We made a very concise project asking just for prohibition. Previously, we had presented another broader project that was rejected at state level because it was considered unconstitutional. However, despite our precautions, our second project was rejected too. It was a very hard moment for the struggle, with a lot of pressure put on us. Even medical doctors [members of the municipality government] voted against asbestos prohibition. We designed another project, although we could not be confident that this would not be rejected as well. A relevant number of councillors continued to vote against it. In the meantime [in 2000], ABREA organized an international seminar, and delegations from more than thirty countries came to Osasco. On that occasion, a councillor from a party different from mine publicly assumed the commitment to propose a new project for asbestos prohibition. His project would have more chance of being approved as the councillor's party was part of the government, while I was in the opposition at that time. Therefore, I decided to withdraw my project [with less chance of it being voted through] and to support the new project, although it had been proposed by a rival political party. I made that decision because asbestos does not distinguish based on political opinion, colour or gender… asbestos is carcinogenic for everybody. We needed public health to prevail over political divisions. Eventually, the project was approved, but our struggle did not cease. I took every occasion of public assembly to denounce the dangers of asbestos and the deaths occurring among contaminated workers. At that time, there was a sort of invisibility surrounding asbestos matters even in the media, which never mentioned anything about asbestos carcinogenicity or ABREA's struggles.

I wish to draw attention to two aspects introduced by Deputy Marcos Martins in his narrative. On the one hand, the importance of situating activism and locally experienced injustice in the transnational context of the anti-asbestos movement and AR disasters; in this regard, the international seminar organized in Osasco in 2000 (see next section) accelerated the approval of asbestos prohibition laws and represented a successful strategy of struggle. As discussed by Appadurai (2013), activist groups are increasingly interconnected in the global world, where local practices of struggle acquire recognition and support from other activist groups who share similar objectives of social justice with them. On the other hand, Deputy Martins highlighted how the lack of communication and visibility had exacerbated the dangers of asbestos and the suffering of the men and women injured by the market of this carcinogenic mineral.

Anti-asbestos Activism through Judicial Paths

During my fieldwork, my gatekeepers asked me if I would be available to conduct interviews with a dozen of the older ABREA activists about their occupational experiences. A camera operator (militant in the PT party) had made himself available to record these interviews free of charge. ABREA's board believed that it was extremely important to record the testimonies of the oldest members while they were still alive and able to remember and narrate. In this way, their memories would become important resources for the anti-asbestos struggle, in the present and in years to come. For instance, the recordings might be used as proof in legal proceedings aimed at obtaining compensation and protection of access to care and medical assistance. I accepted. My task was to ask a list of questions I had written based on the instructions received from ABREA's board. The questions had to be more concise and direct than those I was used to asking during the interviews conducted for my own research purposes, which opened with 'grand tour questions' (Spradley 1979) and followed the rhythm of an ordinary conversation. My earlier questions had been designed to elicit a narrative and create empathetic communication with my interlocutors in order to grasp the nuances of their illness and activism experiences by listening to their bodies speaking through teary eyes, silences and shortness of breath. Now, instead, the purpose of the interviews was to obtain objective testimonies about the working conditions in the factory, the safety measures adopted by the company, the risk awareness among workers, and the workers' own ARD(s). Before starting the recordings, the association's director stressed that the meeting was not to be considered as an assembly of ABREA members, but rather as a reunion of former co-workers from the same plant. Personal opinions and feelings towards the firm should be left out. It was recommended that they always tell the truth and only the truth.

That admonition reminded me of when a couple of ABREA activists had shown me handwritten papers that they kept in their wallets. On those papers, they had carefully copied out the biomedical terms naming the ARDs they were suffering from, and the key dates of their occupational illness experiences. When I asked them the reason for those papers, they answered that they wanted to be prepared at all times to say without hesitation or looking doubtful the truth about what damage the exposure to asbestos had caused them. I interpreted that practice as one of everyday struggle intended to prove the biosocial condition of victimhood in which they lived, and whose recognition might guarantee them access to social and health rights.

On the day scheduled for recording the interviews, we were all feeling nervous – me for asking questions that would be recorded and heard by others, and the ABREA members (former workers) for having to answer under the pressure of holding the microphone, being recorded, and having a professional camera and lights directed on their faces. Below, I quote from my fieldnotes.

> Interviewing Chico (referred to in Chapter 3) particularly touched me. He was the last one to give testimony. He had asked to sit next to me in order to hear the questions better – he had a hearing impairment caused by the noisy working environment in the plant – but for the shoot we could not be seated next to each other. I put my chair as close to him as possible, and I spoke loudly, slowly pronouncing the words. Nevertheless, he could not hear the questions clearly. His eyes became frightened and his hands and legs started to shake. His breathlessness became more accentuated. He seemed to be visibly shrinking. I had had the same feeling when I accompanied Chico to his periodic medical checks, and saw how visibly tired he was coming out of the laboratory where he had undergone spirometry.

For anti-asbestos activists, commitment to the movement consisted of making their own (embodied) memory objective proof of their suffering, and thus making it an instrument with which to pursue justice. They also sought to be recognized as victims, and to practise new forms of citizenship based on their biosocial condition (Petryna 2002; Fassin 2007; Fassin and Rechtman 2009). In everyday experiences of activism, the 'militant (acts of) memory' (Mazzeo 2017b) were frequent and multiple. ABREA activists, for instance, used to give testimony at the collective and individual legal actions taken against companies responsible for the occupational exposure to asbestos that had been so damaging to their employees' health.

Below, I quote an informal conversation with one of my gatekeepers engaged with ABREA activism as an external supporter, as she gave a lucid, clear analysis of the reasons why the legal actions undertaken by anti-asbestos activists were indeed actions of struggle:

> How do you lobby and fight for your rights when you are a worker? By striking. Asbestos victims cannot adopt this strategy anymore; the factory where they had been exposed does not exist anymore. Therefore, what can they do in political terms? They can organize demonstrations and lobby politicians, but it is like… do these actions really bring a result for them? Not always. Lawsuits do. Political action gives visibility to your suffering that thus becomes acknowledged and respected, but at an individual level, the victims may say 'Okay, we attend the assemblies and take part in the events, we dedicate time and energy to the associa-

tion, but how do these efforts improve our life in practical terms?' How does their engagement support them in facing their everyday needs, such as buying medicine? Suing the firm represents a possibility to find a certain kind of relief. They [the victims] have concrete difficulties to face. This is the main issue. They are sick and cannot work anymore; the majority of them are retired, but many aren't yet. How can they survive with all these limitations? Compensation may represent relief and offer protection to them. They live in a condition of social exclusion. It is necessary to understand the universe of those who suffer from ARDs. Losing a job and not being able to find another one because of the disease represents a suffering condition. In low-income families, unemployment and diseases mean a catastrophe.

What struck me about the words chosen by my gatekeeper to refer to ABREA's actions was the constant reference to the world of the factory and work in general, which, although in the past, continued to represent the framework within which the actions and meanings of the activism, as well as of the suffering, were lived in the present. The link with the factory was no longer dependent on employment contracts, but on the diagnosis received and the suffering lived. The asbestos workers continued to be 'workers', although they were by then excluded from the labour market, due to age and disabilities. At the same time, the demolished factory continued to exist in the contaminated bodies, discourses and relationships kept alive by activism. The legal actions were understood as the possibility to make the bonds to the factory (and the dynamics of the AR disasters that occurred there) visible, as they continued to exist through the contaminated bodies of workers and their intersubjective experiences of suffering. In that very place of death and disruption – the plant – the sufferers from asbestos exposure might eventually see their claims accepted, achieve previously denied rights and practise new forms of citizenship. My gatekeeper's analysis highlighted the condition of vulnerability that characterized the life of the majority of ABREA members. With their young, strong bodies, their dreams and ambitions, they had been the main actors in the Brazilian economic miracle of the 1940s through to the 1970s. However, the owners and managers perhaps saw them as cheap and exploitable resources that could be abandoned once they had been totally spoilt. My gatekeeper's discourse concluded with the following lines:

I noticed that the labour tribunal [*justiça trabalhista*] is giving some interesting answers to those who have been exposed to asbestos; it is attentive to workers' needs, it is a tribunal that may be defined as civil [*cidadã*], caring for issues of social relevance. Right now, I can hardly

> see any other similarly effective ways to ensure that workers' rights are respected or that they at least receive compensation higher than the offensive one established by the agreement with the firm ... Giving the victims this possibility to have competent and zealous lawyers means giving them the chance to achieve objectives of justice and to be able to speak to the companies as equal to equal.

In the early 1990s, when former workers were beginning to mobilize and organize to sue the companies, the firms involved in the global market of asbestos began to contact them and propose an out-of-court settlement (*acordo extrajudicial*), with money and/or health insurance as compensation. The value depended on the seriousness of the ARD diagnosed. The majority of my interlocutors mentioned that the value varied between 5,000 and 15,000 reais – equivalent to approximately 1,500 and 4,500 US dollars. According to my gatekeepers, more than four thousand workers signed the transaction, and in doing so, agreed not to sue the firm in the future. However, in current legal actions, this possibility has been considered even for those workers who did sign the transaction, because the transaction concerned issues of life and death, which cannot be negotiated.

At the time of my fieldwork, ABREA and the Public Ministry of Labour were involved in two public civil actions in the name of the former workers at the Eternit plant of Osasco. In February 2016, the first judgment was pronounced and the firm was ordered to pay 100 million reais [approximately 28 million US dollars] for collective damages. The money would then constitute a fund to support research and awareness campaigns on the dangers of asbestos. Moreover, the judgment included 300,000 reais [approximately 80,000 US dollars] for those diagnosed with an ARD (or their heirs) for moral damages, and 90,000 reais [approximately 24,000 US dollars] for moral existential damage provoked by the impact of a diagnosed ARD on an exposed person's life. Other innovative aspects of the judgment obliged the company to provide lifetime medical care for all exposed workers, and to use mass media channels to inform former workers and their relatives about their right to compensation, so that they might claim the benefits established by the court's decision, pronounced in the first grade of the lawsuit (Almeida 2016). This judgment, although not definitive, represented an important achievement after many years of struggle, which had seen ABREA collaborating and establishing a dialogue with various interlocutors, including lawyers. As can be seen from my interlocutors' narratives, in the initial phase of mobilization, asbestos workers sued the firm individually through various local law firms and individual lawyers, the majority of whom did not have any deep knowledge of occupational health issues in general, or of ARDs specifically, and this compromised the outcome of many of the lawsuits. In 2001, thanks to the visibility achieved on national media, ABREA widened its contacts and initiated a dialogue with the law firm currently representing ABREA members in legal proceedings, a firm well known for its engagement in safeguarding workers' rights.

According to the association's statute, ABREA, founded in Osasco (São Paulo), is a non-governmental organization with a national identity, unlike other Brazilian NGOs dealing with asbestos-exposed people, which have a regional identity. Therefore, ABREA based in Osasco can represent any victim of asbestos exposure in lawsuits undertaken anywhere in the whole national territory. However, as ABREA is not a union, in collective actions it can only represent its own members and does not automatically represent the whole group of asbestos workers. During my fieldwork, I had the opportunity to interview a lawyer who represented ABREA members. He explained to me how the former workers came to be in touch with the law firm he represented. Here I quote from his narrative:

> Workers contact us [the lawyers] because they have first had contact with ABREA. Never does a worker look for our office first. Generally, they contact ABREA because they have been diagnosed with an ARD and want to know which procedures they should follow to claim for compensation. ABREA puts them in contact with us. In the first meeting, we explain to the worker what documentation is needed and we ask for medical certificates attesting to the presence of an ARD. It is also important to know when the diagnosis was made, since here in Brazil, people can only file an action in the judiciary within two years of a diagnosis. Often, the workers who contact us do not have reliable documentation [medical reports] proving that they have been contaminated with asbestos. In these cases, we advise them to undergo medical checks; so they then contact ABREA again, which arranges a visit to one of the public health centres with which ABREA has been collaborating for decades.

Good documentation proving contamination is an essential element, because only reliable diagnoses can give the sufferer the possibility to take action and claim his/her rights for compensation, meaning access to health care and relief while facing basic needs and everyday difficulties. The importance of the words allowing the translation of the symptoms of social and individual suffering into readable and communicable signs is related to the dynamics characterizing the politics of anti-asbestos activism discussed in this chapter.

'The Passionate' and the ABREA Networks

'To me, it is like she is genderless. She is above everything. She is a fighter, a comrade, a friend, a sister, a technician, a great expert on asbestos matters. I totally trust her.' The current ABREA president, Mr Eliezer João de Souza, used these words to refer to engineer Fernanda Giannasi, whom the popular Brazilian magazine *Época* defined as a fighter woman (*uma mulher de combate*) and the 'Erin Brockovich of Brazil', when a special issue dedicated to anti-asbestos mobilization was published in 2001. Internationally renowned as 'The Passionate' (*Pasionaria*), Giannasi has been engaged in anti-asbestos activism over the last four decades, and she contributed to placing the locally performed ABREA struggles in the national and international context of the grassroots activism aimed at the national and global prohibition of asbestos. I met her for the first time in Casale Monferrato (Italy) in 2011 (on the same occasion that I met Deputy Marcos Martins), at a time when I did not imagine that I would later carry out research on the practices of activism related to the AR suffering afflicting her compatriots.

Upon my arrival in Osasco, Fernanda Giannasi acted as one of my gatekeepers and introduced me to ABREA members whose struggle she had joined as a militant, professional and supporter. Being introduced by her undeniably facilitated my access to the field, where I then acted autonomously. At the beginning of my stay in Osasco, she voiced her concerns about the difficulties I might face being a woman among a community of elderly men imbued with a strongly masculine culture. She attributed the activists' acceptance of her leading role in activism to the fact that acknowledgement of her professionalism and commitment made the activists 'forget that she was a woman' or think of her as a 'genderless fighter', as the ABREA president used to say. The cover of the *Época* magazine, with a half-length photograph of her in front of numerous close-up portraits of asbestos workers, strongly expressed her role in the activism. As I observed during my fieldwork in 2015, she continued to represent a fundamental point of reference for the anti-asbestos activists, who still conferred upon her the moral and technical authority to represent their voices.

During the numerous informal conversations and formal interviews we had, Fernanda Giannasi mentioned several times that her participation in the Global Forum that had been held in Rio de Janeiro on occasion of the 'Earth Summit' in 1992 had been a turning point in her professional and private life. I quote one conversation I recorded with her consent.

> For the first time, I came into contact with environmentalist groups. I had been working with the Central Única dos Trabalhadores – CUT [General Confederation of Workers], and I had studied the history of working-class struggles and the Italian movement, but in the debates held in 'Rio 1992' there was pressing attention to environmental issues related to industrial policies that I had never seen before. 'Rio 1992' introduced me to the world of environment-based social movements, and I began to reflect on occupational issues and safety in workplaces from a different perspective.

Giannasi played a crucial role in making anti-asbestos activism and the multifaceted disasters caused by the asbestos market worldwide visible. She contributed to constituting ABREA as a collective social actor operating in the national and international context to prohibit asbestos and to gain social justice against human exploitation and 'environmental racism'.[2] Her network and skills supported ABREA in establishing contact with external interlocutors and improving their communication strategies through various channels (from awareness campaigns in public gardens to the use of social networks). Maintaining contact with national and international organizations was part of the activists' everyday lives, and Giannasi's role was fundamental in mediating communication with English- or Italian-speaking social actors. She had had a long-lasting correspondence since the 1990s with some of these social actors, including the Associazione Familiari Vittime Amianto – AFeVA [Asbestos Victims and Relatives Association] of Casale Monferrato, with which I had conducted previous research in 2012.

On 17 November 1995, Giannasi sent a fax to the Italian activists she had met two years earlier at the seminar 'Bastamianto' ['Stop Asbestos'] organized by the Associazione Italiana Esposti Amianto – AIEA [Italian Association of Persons Exposed to Asbestos] in Milan. The association would later circulate the fax through its newsletter, and I found a copy of it in ABREA's archives. Giannasi's letter addressed some of the issues considered in this chapter. It highlighted the importance of establishing transnational collaboration to empower the locally organized mobilizations. In particular, the letter mentioned the connections linking Casale Monferrato and Osasco. Considering their similar history of exploitation and contamination, she expressed the wish that the Italian and Brazilian activists could combine their efforts to achieve justice. Moreover, there was an explicit reference to the conflicts and difficulties faced by activists, asbestos-contaminated workers and their families in Brazil. In particular, she invited biomedical doctors who had investigated the community of contaminated workers and citizens in Casale Monferrato to assist with the efforts in Brazil. She suggested that the Italian health professionals might offer a training workshop to their Brazilian colleagues, who did not yet have a deep knowledge of ARDs. The lack of training was one of the causes of the underdiagnosis of ARDs in Brazil, which was (and still is) a frequent phenomenon in countries where asbestos was (and is) legal, according to investigations conducted in various settings by public health researchers (Pasetto et al. 2014; Marsili et al. 2016).

The letter was written at the time of the demolition of the Eternit plant in Osasco in 1995. The US multinational Walmart had bought the 150,000 m^2 of land formerly occupied by the industrial site, and demolition began without first having removed asbestos from the area, in the total absence of safety measures for workers and the neighbourhood's inhabitants (as stated in Giannasi's letter). As the inspector from the Ministry of Labour, she prescribed a 15-day suspension of the demolition. The US media, thanks to the social actors engaged in the US anti-asbestos movement who were in contact with the Brazilian activists, then highlighted the episode. The rise of protests in the US forced Walmart to take measures to improve the working conditions in Osasco. The visibility of the sanction in the media favoured the dialogue among former workers, local administrators, public health institutions and the Ministry of Labour. Giannasi has been one of the most engaged exponents in the anti-asbestos struggle since then.

After my fieldwork in Brazil, I spent a few days in Casale Monferrato in Italy to meet some of the local anti-asbestos activists who had participated in my study in 2012. We discussed the developments of my research with the ABREA activists, and we organized a visit to Osasco in the Piedmont region of Italy. I wanted to visit the tiny town from which Antonio Agù had emigrated at the end of the nineteenth century to found Osasco in Brazil. I was looking for traces of the historical connections I had read about, and I was keen to know if and how those bonds were being kept alive today. I found the traces I was looking for in the mayor's description of the current relationship between 'the two Osascos', including cultural exchanges and mutual visits by official delegations, as well as the names of the streets and the library sections dedicated to Brazil by the Municipality of Osasco (Italy).

My short stay in Casale Monferrato in 2016 was an occasion to reflect on the connections linking the Italian and Brazilian activism conducted by AFeVA and ABREA respectively. In particular, the road trip to Osasco (Italy) with three AFeVA members – including Bruno Pesce, who had had a key role in the local anti-asbestos mobilization – was an opportunity to share experiences and reflections with the social actors directly involved in the relationships and trajectories on which I had based my research in Brazil. On our way back to Casale Monferrato, I asked Bruno Pesce to narrate how contact with ABREA had begun. He started his narration as follows:

> Fernanda came to Casale Monferrato for the first time in 1994. We had met her one year before, in Milan, at the conference 'Bastamianto'. A delegation of Brazilian unionists from Osasco visited Casale Monferrato. At that time, the role of union organizations was very strong in our mobilization, and they had been decisive in the approval of Law number 257 by which Italy prohibited asbestos in 1992. The activists and unionists from Osasco wanted to know as much as possible about our struggle and achievements; they wanted to discuss with us the advancements in biomedical knowledge and legal actions. The results of a survey conducted in Casale Monferrato by a team of biomedical doctors and epidemiologists made clear in the 1980s that it was impossible to talk about 'controlled use of asbestos', as in the propaganda used by asbestos lobbies in Brazil. Based on that study, we organized the first penal lawsuit in the world against an asbestos-cement corporation. In the end, although there was not a favourable verdict for the victims, the lawsuit set an important precedent to be used in support of the anti-asbestos movement. Moreover, the Italian law was one of the most complete laws prohibiting asbestos in the 1990s, so it could be taken as an example to adapt similar laws in other countries, which was what actually happened. Our contact with ABREA dates back to that period. We went to Osasco in Brazil for the first time in 1996, and then again in 2000 to attend the largest international conference on the dangers of asbestos ever organized until then. Contact with the Brazilian activists, together with those organizations operating in other countries, have been important for us too. All of us have learnt and are still learning from each other.

The conference in Milan was one of the first crucial steps in the internationalization of the anti-asbestos campaign. In the early 1990s, collective social actors organizing anti-asbestos campaigns and actions in Europe began to establish connections. In 1991, the Ban Asbestos Network (BAN) was founded at the first meeting organized by Yves Frémion from the French Green Party, together with the AIEA, at the European Parliament in Strasbourg (Kazan-Allen 2003: 188). Two years later in Milan, the 'federation of international groups', as the network was defined by Patrick Herman (a French anti-asbestos activist who had contributed to the network's foundation), included the participation of activists from outside Europe. Fernanda Giannasi took part and brought the Brazilian case, emblematic of the 'politics of asbestos' (Waldman 2011), and its effects on health to the attention of an international audience. Her participation in a meeting that was defined by

Herman as 'an important moment in the construction of an international social movement against asbestos' (Kazan-Allen 2003: 188) was decisive in placing Brazilian activism within the international context of the anti-asbestos movement, and it empowered ABREA's role in negotiations with local political and administrative interlocutors. As one of the first consequences of the connections established with international social actors, a seminar was organized in São Paulo in 1994 by the union organizations CUT, the Confederação Geral do Trabalho – CGT [General Labour Confederation] and the Força Sindical [Union Force], in collaboration with FUNDACENTRO. The seminar, entitled 'Asbestos: Controlled Use or Banishment?', was an important occasion for debate and training among biomedical professionals, technicians and activists from various contexts gathered in a country that was one of the major global players in the toxic market of asbestos. On that occasion, the participants signed the 'Declaration of São Paulo'. Based on the declaration, the 'worldwide information network' was established and extended into regional networks (Kazan-Allen 2003: 188). Fernanda Giannasi was nominated as the coordinator of the 'Rede Virtual-Cidadã pelo Banimento do Amianto na América Latina' [Virtual Civil Network for Asbestos Prohibition in Latin America], defined as a 'virtual citizenship network' (Kazan-Allen 2003: 188). At the seminar in São Paulo, three hundred delegates heard presentations and participated in roundtables focused on three main themes:

(1) chrysotile – the carcinogenic properties of chrysotile were analysed, and calls for less scientific denial and more epidemiological data were made;

(2) asbestos victims – urgent action was called for to obtain compensation and medical treatment for asbestos victims;

(3) global action – the struggle to achieve safety at work and a global ban on asbestos could only be achieved with international cooperation. (Kazan-Allen 2003: 188)

Engagement with the transnational anti-asbestos movement led to the organization of another important event in Brazil in 2000, this time in Osasco. The International Ban Asbestos Secretariat – IBAS, established in 1999 by BAN members in agreement with other activists, gave crucial support to the organization. The report contains the following:

> Working closely with members of BAN and national groups such as ABREA in Brazil, IBAS has also emerged as a potent means of facilitating international activities.

> One of the first products of this collaboration was the 'The Global Asbestos Congress – Past, Present and Future', a landmark event held in Brazil in September 2000. One hundred international and more than three hundred Brazilian delegates gathered in Osasco for three days of plenary, workshops and roundtable sessions. The significance of the conference was reinforced by the participation of the International Labour Organization, international and national trade unions, victim-support groups and occupational and environmental health associations. (Kazan-Allen 2003: 190)

At the end of the Congress, the 'Declaration of Osasco' for the global prohibition of asbestos was approved by the delegations of associations and institutions from thirty-two countries (Giannasi 2017).

In my first days of fieldwork, before arranging formal interviews, I used to spend the afternoons with ABREA activists. One day, when I was at the ABREA office with the current president, Mr Eliezer João de Souza, he took a white photograph album from a cupboard, handed it to me, and came and sat beside me to narrate the story of the most important international event that ABREA had ever organized in Osasco, the international seminar in 2000. Mr de Souza remembered the difficulties related to organizing it – eight months to arrange and collect the necessary funding to invite activists from more than thirty countries. I quote from my fieldnotes:

> Eliezer talked about the seminar as a paramount event. He pointed out the various 'characters' portrayed in the photographs to me. I recognized some of them, people I had seen in Rome and Casale Monferrato, but many others I had never met. I recognized Eliezer and Fernanda, fifteen years younger, with glowing skin and no wrinkles on their faces, Eliezer with black hair and beard. Eliezer pointed out a pathologist who used to do the autopsies on workers [and ABREA members] who had died of ARDs. He said that the autopsies were very important, because they made it possible to obtain a reliable certificate of the presence of an ARD, and, at the same time, the doctor could improve his knowledge and experience.

The narrative of the event intertwined with Mr de Souza's story of his own AR illness and suffering. A few days before the conference, he had undergone the surgical removal of a lung nodule, which everyone, including the doctors who were caring for him, suspected could be malignant, but fortunately was not.

In 2003, Fernanda Giannasi organized the workshop 'Another Asbestos-Free World Is Possible' at the 'World Social Forum' in Porto Alegre (Rio Grande do Sul, Brazil). On that occasion, thousands of activists including environmentalists, health professionals and unionists signed a petition for asbestos prohibition in Brazil (Kazan-Allen 2003). The petition was addressed to the recently elected president of the Workers' Party (PT), Luiz Inácio 'Lula' da Silva, who since the 1980s had been leading workers' struggles as secretary of the Metalworkers Union of São Bernardo do Campo and Diadema, two of the most industrialized Brazilian cities and, like Osasco, situated in São Paulo state.

In October 2016, an international conference entitled 'International Congress: A Socio-juridical Approach' was held in Campinas (São Paulo). I had the opportunity to participate and to present my work there. The conference was funded using the fines paid by companies that had substituted or committed to substitute asbestos minerals in their production. The companies had signed the 'Termos de Ajustamento de Conduta' – TACS [Agreements of Conduct Adjustments] with the Public Ministry of Labour (MPT), on which the financial compensation for damages caused to society by asbestos manufacturing were based (Giannasi 2017). With the participation of Brazilian and foreign judges (the Italian delegation was the most numerous), prosecutors, doctors, public health experts, lawyers and trade unionists, the congress addressed the legal proceedings underway in Brazil, the Italian lawsuit against the Eternit corporation, the latest data on global asbestos production, and biomedical research on ARDs in general, and MM in particular. The legislative situation in Brazil, characterized by the specific peculiarities and contradictions of Brazil as the third asbestos producer in the world, was widely discussed.

The first 'National Meeting of Relatives and Victims of Asbestos' followed the congress. For the first time, over three hundred anti-asbestos activists, including former workers and AR sufferers from various Brazilian states, gathered in a national assembly. After the meeting, the participating delegations approved the 'Carta de Campinas' [Campinas document], in which they reaffirmed the objectives of anti-asbestos mobilization that had been declared in 2000 in Osasco, as well as setting out new strategies and addressing new topics.

I would now like to draw attention to some of the twelve points listed in the document that concern issues particularly related to the practices of anti-asbestos activism that I investigated during my fieldwork. I quote:

> Promoting solidarity among anti-asbestos activists, organizing new groups of victims, and supporting other organizations in the struggle for asbestos prohibition and justice for the victims;
>
> Disseminating in our regions to the population at large, and to the relatives and victims of asbestos in particular, information about asbestos,

> including the latest legal decisions, biomedical research and treatment, new legislations and other topics of interest;
>
> Visiting those affected by the tragedy provoked by asbestos (patients and their relatives), and providing them with all the necessary solidarity;
>
> Engaging with social networks to be periodically updated, as well as actively participating in WhatsApp groups (among others), allowing the rapid exchange of information and the organization of mobilization and activities in the name of asbestos prohibition and justice for victims. (Giannasi 2017: 11–16)

These points refer to aspects such as the role of communication and the encounter with others, both of which played a fundamental role in the practices of care and struggle promoted by ABREA and health-based activism in general (Polletta 1998a, 1998b; Fassin 2006; Cappelletto 2009).

Participation in international events, and contact and mutual support with foreign organizations, empowered ABREA's anti-asbestos activism (cf. Appadurai 2013). At a national level, this empowerment led to the foundation of other associations, and to dialogue with new groups and movements dealing with themes related to health, environment and labour. On another level, anti-asbestos activists' dialogue and collaboration with health professionals, politicians and administrators allowed ABREA to enter the negotiation processes through which new rights are acquired, knowledge is elaborated and asbestos prohibition has been declared in Brazil as an autonomous sociopolitical actor. In all of this, Fernanda Giannasi played a crucial role by broadening ABREA's network and giving a national and international resonance to its actions.

Conclusion

In this chapter, I have reflected on the role of ABREA in negotiating rights and elaborating knowledge through continuous dialogue since the 1990s with interlocutors from a variety of contexts: political and local administrative settings, public health centres, judicial arenas and the transnational movement for the global prohibition of asbestos.

In the anti-asbestos grassroots movement, it has been fundamental to give voice to the sufferers and to make the effects of disasters impacting on their lives more visible and communicable through the words of languages that rely on authority, visibility, legitimacy and a broad field of action, in the same way as biomedical knowledge, media, law, and transnational grassroots movements do.

The dialogue and relationships established over twenty years of mobilization channelled the workers' experiential knowledge of asbestos dangers into legitimate pathways of knowledge and actions. Simultaneously, engagement in activism moulded the experiences of suffering of those impacted by the toxic market of asbestos, and transformed the context in which the sufferers lived and acted.

Based on a 'collective memory' (Halbwachs 1987) and an 'embodied past' (Fassin 2008), anti-asbestos activists retraced the disaster processes they were suffering from, both as individuals and as members of a community. On the one hand, activism provided the sufferers with the lens to recognize and read the traces of the processes of disasters on their bodies as proof of injustice and exploitation. On the other hand, the raised allegations found legitimacy in the embodied knowledge of the exposed workers and in the memories of the survivors of the disasters.

If, in line with Scheper-Hughes (1994), the body is 'the most immediate, most proximate terrain where social truths are forged and social contradictions played out, as well as the locus of personal resistance, creativity and struggle', as I believe it is, then the 'afflicted, naturally subversive' body (ibid.: 232) amplifies the possibilities pertaining to (and the contradictions existing within) a 'normative' body. Taking advantage of this potential of critique, the anti-asbestos activists I met were practising forms of citizenship based on the acknowledgement of a condition that anthropologists have from time to time qualified as 'biosocial' (Rabinow 1992), 'biological' (Petryna 2002), and 'therapeutic' (Nguyen et al. 2007; Nguyen 2008).

Notes

1. I refer to Bourdieu and Wacquant's definition of 'social capital' in considering the relationships woven by ABREA with collective and individual social actors operating in Osasco: 'Social capital is the sum of the resources, actual or virtual, that accrue to an individual or group by virtue of possessing a durable network of more or less institutionalized relationships of mutual acquaintance and recognition' (Bourdieu and Wacquant 1992: 119). I considered it more appropriate to my study to refer to Bourdieu and Wacquant's definition of social capital than to that of Putnam (1993).
2. The movement in the name of environmental justice emerged in the United States in the 1980s and 1990s, when civil protests and biomedical surveys led to the awareness that 'people of colour and low-income have borne greater environmental and health risks than the society at large in their neighbourhoods, workplaces and playgrounds' (Bullard

and Johnson 2000: 555). Included in the struggles within this movement are protests against environmental racism that refer to 'any environmental policy, practice, or directive that differentially affects or disadvantages (whether intended or unintended) individuals, groups or communities, based on race or colour' (ibid.: 559). In this book, I refer to the equation between environmentalism and social justice expressed by Bullard and Johnson. In the Brazilian academy, the concept of environmental justice began to circulate in the early 2000s, first in the area of environmental sociology, and then in public health (Milanez et al. 2013: 15). A short definition of environmental justice is 'the guarantee of equal rights for all people (regardless of their social class, colour, gender, etc.) to live in a safe and not overly polluted environment' (Acselrad, Herculano and Pádua 2004).

5

Engaging Global Health, Anti-asbestos Activism and Ethnography

> Health is a product of many social, political and economic forces and institutions outside of health that produce risks for health and illness
>
> —Richard Hofrichter, 'The Politics of Health Inequalities'

What is health? How do you define and tackle global health disasters? How do you recognize the impact of global processes of social injustice within the local experiences of suffering? How do you investigate the connections between local and global, private and public, individual and collective in the bodily experiences of health disasters? These questions guided my research and posed challenges that I engaged with during my fieldwork; they were also useful when trying to make sense of what I had listened to, observed and felt during my encounters with the anti-asbestos activists and those suffering from the impact on their lives of exposure to asbestos in Brazil, and previously in Italy.

The practices of anti-asbestos activism and its struggle for the global prohibition of asbestos can be considered as part of a larger discourse on global health issues and policies. Global health is 'a collection of problems rather than a discipline', and it pivots around the 'quest for equity', according to Paul Farmer's definition (Farmer 2013: xiii). The anthropologist who grounded the concept of 'structural violence' in his personal experience of being a physician 'at the service of the destitute sick' (Farmer 2005) points to the 'just and equitable distribution of the risk of suffering and of the tools to lessen or prevent it' as crucial aspects in practising, thinking about and reimagining global health (Farmer 2013: xiii).

This final chapter is about the practices of grassroots health-based activism, work and research undertaken by those committed to a transnational movement mobilizing for the recognition of invisible health disasters, and turning ideals of social justice into concrete improvements in the everyday lives of those involved in asbestos-related (AR) suffering. In global health disasters provoked by the toxic market of asbestos, the risks of suffering are unequally distributed and have been (and still are) silenced by precise discourses and practices favoured by asbestos lobbies worldwide (cf. Braun 2008; Waldman 2011; Jobin 2013; Petrillo 2015). Asbestos contamination involves the affected and afflicted social actors in a spiral of suffering, regardless of their socio-economic status, or transcending physical proximity to polluting sites, or personal involvement in occupational activities with asbestos. However, existing literature and epidemiological surveys (to which I add the ethnographic data from my fieldwork in Italy and Brazil) show that the communities most vulnerable to AR health dangers are those with workers at toxic industrial sites, and residents in neighbouring areas (Magnani et al. 1987; Musti et al. 2009; Goldberg and Luce 2009; Park et al. 2011; Pasetto et al. 2014; Zona et al. 2016; INAIL 2018). A similar differential of risk and suffering, combined with the excess of preventable and avoidable deaths and diseases, are all symptoms of the so-called 'pathologies of power' (Farmer 2005) afflicting the most vulnerable members of our singular, globalized and interconnected world, which is becoming increasingly unequal. Inequality is a fundamental determinant of health (Hofrichter 2003a; Farmer et al. 2013), and I recall Fassin's definition of public health as 'not an impartial government technology, [but] an integral part of social and political history' (Fassin 2007: 129).

In line with Beauchamp, global health can be considered in terms of a 'health movement' (Beauchamp 2003) in which distinct social actors, including health professionals, vulnerable communities and stakeholders from civil society, all play fundamental, though differentiated, roles in negotiating knowledge and health rights. In this regard, the activism carried out by ABREA in Osasco, with its actions performed across Brazil and internationally, was part of a transnational health movement while still being grounded in local experiences of suffering, care and struggle. Researching these experiences offered stimulating reasons to question and rethink definitions, practices and policies of health and care, at both a local and global level. It also helped in understanding the processes by which health disasters occur and may persist, unperceived by the affected communities and invisible in political agendas.

I situate anti-asbestos activism in the health movement that is global health and, in this chapter, I will draw attention to the actions of anti-asbestos activists, health professionals and researchers who conceive of their engagement in activism and research as a moral commitment.

Firstly, I will present cases from my fieldwork that are illustrative of the contributions made by professionals who, by engaging in interdisciplinary collaborations and an effective exchange of knowledge with the exposed communities, operated in the service of the public good.

Secondly, I will refer to practices of activism considered as moral practices of care. I will discuss the meanings attributed by the activists to their own engagement in actions with a sociopolitical relevance.

Lastly, I will reflect on the necessity of a morally committed anthropology (Fassin 2012, 2014b) to approach and understand the global health issues that I personally investigated through a multi-sited and global ethnography (Marcus 1995; Burawoy et al. 2000) across two continents during ten years of personal commitment to the study of AR disasters and grassroots activism. By combining a 'study of everyday life with the study of processes that transcend national boundaries' (Burawoy et al. 2000), ethnographic fieldwork gave me the opportunity to get a privileged insight into the processes in which I inevitably partook as a researcher and supporter of the anti-asbestos movement (Mazzeo 2014). A similar in-depth approach contributed to grounding the transnational dynamics of AR disasters in the life stories of the social actors I met, and to grasping the interconnections between local and global in the experiences and representations of AR disasters and grassroots activism.

Anti-asbestos Activism and the Search for Justice

Both individual and population health are intertwined with the practices, morals and discourses promoted by the perverse logic of capitalism worldwide, which considers men, women, young adults and children as merely exploitable and disposable resources, and favours their isolation and competitiveness. On a daily basis, anti-asbestos activists struggle against such logic, and, by performing practices of care and activism locally, mobilize in the name of social and environmental justice.

Referring to Nancy Fraser's definition, justice is essentially coincident with 'the social arrangements that permit all to participate as peers in social life. Overcoming injustice means dismantling institutionalized obstacles that prevent some people from participating on a par with others as full partners in social interaction' (Fraser 2007: 20). Through their engagement in activism, the anti-asbestos activists I met during my multi-sited ethnography across Italy and Brazil, while locally experiencing the health disasters provoked by the toxic market of asbestos, were entering the negotiation processes related to knowledge and rights that had a direct impact on their lives.

Taking into account the interconnectedness and complexity of the globalized world in which we all live (and in which health disasters occur), it is particularly opportune to refer to Fraser's three-dimensional theory of justice (Fraser 2007). To her previously elaborated two-dimensional definition of justice as a dynamic and processual system moulded by claims for economic redistribution and cultural recognition, Fraser adds a third, specifically political, dimension of representation that incorporates both elements. The representational element is political because it concerns inclusion or exclusion from fair distribution and mutual recognition. While Fraser refers to representation in terms of 'social belonging' (ibid.), I would prefer to use the term 'biosocial belonging' in referring to the representation sought by and shaping anti-asbestos activism (see Rabinow 1992; Petryna 2002).

Fraser considers the inadequacy of discourses on justice that reiterate (but do not question) the supremacy of modern territorial states and that consider the citizens of these states as the uniquely legitimate recipients of justice achievements. A similar limitation would condemn to a 'non-person status in front of justice' (Fraser 2007) an increasing number of victims of the 'pathogenic effects of inequity' (Farmer 2005) affecting vulnerable social actors regardless of their nationality, although with a 'preferential option for the poor' of the world (Hofrichter 2003a).

> Thanks to heightened awareness of globalization, many observe that the social processes shaping their lives routinely overflow territorial borders. They note, for example, that decisions taken in one territorial state often impact the lives of those outside it, as do the actions of transnational corporations, international currency speculators, and large institutional investors. Many also note the growing salience of supranational and international organizations, both governmental and non-governmental, and of transnational public opinion, which flows with supreme disregard for borders through global mass media and cybertechnology. The result is a new sense of vulnerability to transnational forces. (Fraser 2007: 18)

Quoting Castells (1996: 440–60), Fraser argues that similar transnational forces determining injustice throughout our interconnected world belong not to 'the space of places' but rather to 'the space of flows' (Fraser 2007: 25). Again, I find it particularly appropriate to refer to Fraser's contributions in reflecting on the particular nature of anti-asbestos activism.

> What turns a collection of people into fellow subjects of justice is not geographical proximity, but their imbrication in a common structural or institutional framework that sets the ground rules governing their social interaction, thereby shaping their respective life possibilities, in patterns of advantage and disadvantage. (Fraser 2007: 25)

Anti-asbestos activists are 'fellow subjects of justice', or better 'fellow subjects of the struggle in the name of justice', while being, at the same time, 'fellow victims' of disasters provoked by the same cause – the toxic market of asbestos. As Hofrichter notes, 'social justice is not a thing but rather an ongoing series of relationships that permeate everyday life. Social justice concerns the systematic treatment of people as members of a definable group' (Hofrichter 2003b: 12).

Men and women taking action, suffering and dying because of the impact of exposure to asbestos on their existence form a transnational movement in the name of objectives of social justice such as access to knowledge, health rights and compensation. Survivors of AR disasters recognize themselves as members of a community made up of activists who are victims and simultaneously become aware of the processes of structural violence that in disparate sociopolitical settings have been perpetrated on both the environment and vulnerable social actors such as themselves. Mobilizing in the name of social justice means opposing, diverting and changing the discourses and practices through which the known and unknown perpetrators of this violence legitimately act.

Moral Commitments in Global Public Health and Anti-asbestos Activism

> A major obstacle to achieving equality in health status is a belief in its impossibility, based on a deeper belief that progressive social change is impossible. It is not. The contemporary system of political power is the result of struggle, not a natural order. (Hofrichter 2003b: 38)

By mobilizing in the name of social justice, anti-asbestos activists prompted the moral engagement of interlocutors whose participation would empower their struggle for health. These interlocutors were found among academics, biomedical professionals, engineers, lawyers and researchers from international institutions who had the knowledge (and power) to tackle and prevent health disasters, and to make the principle of health (and justice) effective for all. I found numerous points of contact between the moral frame of anti-asbestos activism and global public health as analysed and discussed by Suri et al. (2013). The authors reflect on the moral values that may shape global health policies and practices.

It is necessary to 'unpack [the] motivations and morals' (Kleinman and Hanna 2011 in Suri et al. 2013: 247) to which global health practitioners refer, because

> global health work is extremely difficult. It requires a hard look at preventable suffering and death, global inequalities of disturbing proportions, and many other failures of modernity; these problems lack simple solutions ... Critical self-reflection – honestly examining one's values, motivations, accomplishments, failures – can help practitioners face the anguish and moral crisis that are often inherent in global health work without resorting to cynicism or despair. (Suri et al. 2013: 247)

I considered the influence of Liberation Theology (LT) on the organization of the struggles and practices of resistance spreading across Latin America at the end of the 1970s and in the early 1980s. LT had influenced the specific sociocultural fabric of Osasco from which ABREA activism emerged. By comparing a human rights frame with an approach inspired by LT principles to global health, Suri et al. (2013) highlight the potential of critique brought by LT in trying to understand and tackle the effects of inequality on health.

> LT draws attention to the large-scale social forces that pattern risk among populations, rich and poor; it thus offers an implicit critique of, and complement to, human rights theory, which has often obscured the structural roots of violence, poverty, disease and inequality. (Ibid.: 282)

The human rights discourse that considers health as a human right presents meaningful affinities with the objectives pursued by anti-asbestos activism (e.g. the right of all human beings to health, life and work in safe environments). However, in my analysis, I interpreted the practices undertaken to reach similar goals by predominantly referring to LT principles and social justice. I would adopt a human rights frame only critically and cautiously. I agree with Marxist critics who argue that public health issues should be tackled by focusing on species-beings based on the fact that 'individuals are inexorable members of a community', whereas 'human rights discourse is grounded in political liberalism focused on protecting individuals as they are separate from society' (Suri et al. 2013: 274). Nevertheless, in line with Suri et al., I recognize that the 'belief that health is a human right offers a powerful rationale for global health equity: everyone should have access to decent health services by virtue of being human' (ibid.: 263). There is a revolutionary potential in the statement above, which I read as a call to action. 'Reimagining health as a human right, and implementing an ambitious equity agenda capable of realizing that vision, could strengthen other development priorities too' (ibid.: 273).

I draw particular attention to the influence of contributions referring to social justice theory, both on the strategies of struggle undertaken by the anti-asbestos activists I met, and on the morals shaping the understanding of global health problems.

> The particular macro-level pathways by which health inequities link to specific exposures are intricate. Establishing with any quantifiable certainty how given social contexts interact with multidimensional biological and psychological pathways to cause disease remains a challenge. These pathways are often linked to the way in which production and investment decisions, labour market policies, neighbourhood and workplace conditions, racism and sexism interact with individual histories. Essentially, social injustices become embodied in the individuals as disease. (Hofrichter 2003b: 4)

The role of biomedical and social scientists who have combined a vocation for their profession with a moral commitment to public health in general and the anti-asbestos movement in particular has been crucial (see the contributions and reflections from the settings I know best, Italy and Brazil). In Casale Monferrato (Italy), anti-asbestos mobilization gained legitimacy from the results of the first epidemiological surveys conducted among citizens and workers in the early 1980s (Magnani et al. 1987). Seminal work was conducted by a team of biomedical doctors from local public hospitals who examined the clinical reports of patients diagnosed with malignant mesothelioma (MM) in Casale Monferrato between 1973 and 1983 (Mossano 2010). The shocking results – fifty out of the seventy cases were related to environmental, non-occupational exposure to asbestos – triggered a second study called 'Progetto Cemento Amianto' [Asbestos-Cement Project], conducted by a larger team including oncologists, epidemiologists, lung specialists, and occupational physicians (ibid.). Among them were the epidemiologists Benedetto Terracini and Corrado Magnani, whose works have become internationally renowned reference points in understanding AR health hazards (Magnani et al. 1987; Terracini 2005, 2006; Terracini, Pedra and Otero 2015; Terracini and Mirabelli 2016; Marsili et al. 2016).

In Brazil, the investigation conducted by the lung specialist Jefferson Benedito Pires de Freitas (Freitas 2001) on pleural diseases among asbestos workers has had relevant repercussions on the outcomes of numerous recently filed lawsuits. These lawsuits concern asbestos-contaminated workers diagnosed with pleural plaques, an AR pathology. Before the results of Freitas's study became known in Brazil, pleural plaques were not considered a disabling disease, so that exposed workers were denied the right to compensation. This is just an example of the contribution of the work of biomedical and health professionals operating in Brazil, whose studies I have referred to throughout my research (Giannasi and Thébaud-Mony 1997; Algranti et al. 2001; de Castro, Giannasi and Novello 2003; Raile 2008; D'Acri et al. 2009; Novello and de Castro 2010; Raile and Markowitz 2011).

In the transnational health movement in favour of the global prohibition of asbestos, health professionals and international research institutes have offered remarkable contributions. I agree with Beauchamp, who argues:

> Challenging medical [and I would add, economic] dominance could go a long way toward reclaiming health as a public concern and an issue of social justice. Challenging these centres of power in order to incarnate the priority of human life requires not only a new ethic but also a supporting base of power. I believe that while professional prestige is an important attribute in the modern-day public policy process, public health is ultimately better understood as a broad social movement. (Beauchamp 2003: 278)

In the global public debate and health policies on asbestos issues, certain actions and certain studies stand out. I would note here the 'Collegium Ramazzini Statements' (Collegium Ramazzini 1999, 2010, 2015), the investigations conducted by Arthur Frank (LaDou et al. 2010; Frank 2013; Frank and Joshi 2014) and Barry Castleman (Castleman and Navarro 1987; Castleman 1979, 1983, 2003, 2005, 2016), as well as the actions and studies promoted by public and occupational health research institutes such as the Italian Istituto Superiore di Sanità – ISS [Superior Health Institute] (Zona et al. 2016), the Brazilian FUNDACENTRO (FUNDACENTRO 2015), and Fundação Oswaldo Cruz – FIOCRUZ [Oswaldo Cruz Foundation] (FIOCRUZ 2008).

A similar transnational and transdisciplinary engagement is necessary to ensure a just redistribution of risk and suffering. This redistribution should derive from an acknowledgement of the particular responsibilities of powerful actors, groups and institutions. Because their actions have so much more impact than the actions of individuals, they have a greater responsibility for the costs of death and disability that result.

Moral Practices of Care and Activism

The short quotes below are from interviews conducted with anti-asbestos activists I met in the three sites where I have so far conducted fieldwork:

> 'I do it to help others – because from my wife's experience, I learned so much that it would be unjust not to share the knowledge I developed'. (Bari, Italy, April 2012)
>
> 'I do it because it reminds me of my father'. (Casale Monferrato, Italy, May–June 2012)
>
> 'Every time I can, I go to the association to meet my friends'. (Casale Monferrato, Italy, May–June 2012)
>
> 'At my age, I would never have imagined that I could live such a wonderful experience'. (Casale Monferrato, Italy, May–June 2012)
>
> 'I joined ABREA because my husband deserves it; I do it for him'. (Osasco, Brazil, June 2015)
>
> 'I am not able to explain what I felt when I heard my husband's name pronounced in so many accents by all those activists … I knew that in that moment he was being gratified'. (Osasco, Brazil, June 2015)
>
> 'We share a sad experience, but a word pronounced by a friend can console'. (Osasco, Brazil, May 2015)
>
> 'I talk to you honestly and with all my sincerity. Our struggle is not for myself, for my friends who have already died, nor for those who are sick. Our struggle is for the next generations, because for those of us who are contaminated, there is no way – we are going to die soon… the disease can appear even tomorrow. Asbestos is in our bodies, we are all at risk, asbestos cannot be removed from us'. (Osasco, Brazil, March 2015)

Although my focus in this book has been on anti-asbestos activism in Osasco (Brazil), narratives gathered during my fieldwork in Italy help to make clear the global dimension of AR disasters and of the health-based grassroots activism I have witnessed over the last ten years. While trying to grasp the moral reasoning behind a person's decision to engage in activism, I have often asked myself 'in what terms do anti-asbestos activists make their experiences of suffering and activism meaningful?' I have searched for answers by establishing a dialogue with those authors whose contributions have framed and inspired my research: Arthur Kleinman, Didier Fassin and Nancy Scheper-Hughes. The anti-asbestos activists I met were engaged in a larger movement by which they were reclaiming health, both as a public concern and as an issue of social justice. Moved by personal motives, they acted in the micro-political arena of their everyday life of suffering and struggle by enacting gradual and pervasive revolutions, while also criticizing and taking action against the perverse logic of the capitalist system and its attendant violence. Their 'afflicted bodies' were an embodied, radical and subversive critique of the status quo (Scheper-Hughes 1994), and their new *habitus* (Bourdieu 1977) of sufferers and activists showed that experiences such as illness, grieving and ageing could be lived and made meaningful in a variety of ways differing from, and challenging, those that society might expect from vulnerable social actors (Pandolfi 2003). By contesting deeply rooted forms of knowledge and power, anti-asbestos activists aimed at and actually achieved important goals of social justice. In their everyday experience of suffering, these goals consisted of access to health rights and increased opportunities of care. Their mobilization produced effects that were publicly recognized. For instance, in Brazil, it achieved the approval of laws prohibiting asbestos in eight states of the federative republic that, in 2011, still represented the third largest producer of asbestos in the world, according to the Departamento Nacional de Produção Mineral – DNPM [National Department of Mineral Production] (Ministério da Saúde 2016). In their everyday experiences of illness and grief, ageing and disability, 'sufferer-activists' lived a revolution. The relationships they had constructed represented a critique and resistance to the ruthless individualism celebrated and nurtured by capitalism.

Hofrichter refers to a 'modal suffering' afflicting the vulnerable of the world. This suffering is provoked by structural violence systematically and rationally perpetrated; the afflictions 'are not caused by accidents of force majeure, they are the consequences, direct or indirect, of human agency' (Hofrichter 2003b: 40). The basic practices of resistance and the objectives of anti-asbestos mobilization lay in opposing the 'fatalism of death', emphasized by the individualism imbuing capitalistic society and favouring awareness of the processes provoking one's own suffering, disease and death. In the struggle for health, considered as an issue of social justice, anti-asbestos activists pointedly accused those responsible (i.e. worldwide asbestos lobbies) for the socio-political and economic dynamics producing the disasters from which they were suffering. Action to break the silence and tear the veil of invisibility suffocating their voices was fundamental in stopping the dynamics that threatened to consume their bodies and dissolve their social (affective) bonds. The anti-asbestos activists from Bari and Casale Monferrato in Italy and Osasco in Brazil were struggling everyday to achieve the change they wanted to assure for the lives of future generations. At the same time, they were painfully embodying the irreversible changes provoked by the impact of AR disasters on their own lives.

Engagement in activism provided the sufferers with the tools to relate private and intimate experiences, such as those of AR illness and grieving, to historical processes and economic dynamics. This represented a 'necessary step to reformulate and make salient the conditions for health, and [to] politicize its meaning more thoroughly in order to reveal that what appears to be objective and neutral [and private, *added by author*] is in fact subjective and political' (Hofrichter 2003b: 40).

> The supporters of global health equity do not need to hold official positions of power to make a significant impact. Students, health workers, lawyers, people living with HIV [and other diseases, *added by author*] and other grassroots activists have changed global health policy through effective advocacy; their tactics are available to anyone with a passion for equity. (Basilico et al. 2013: 347)

Conducting ethnographic research with anti-asbestos activists in Italy and Brazil, I found what Basilico et al. affirmed in the above quote to be true. The sufferers and activists I met were deploying all the tools that Basilico et al. listed as being the most useful and accessible tools available to global health activists. They were 'engaging in critical self-reflection, finding good partners, knowing the issues, starting a dialogue with policymakers, highlighting key issues, organizing public demonstrations, building a coalition and being the change'. (Basilico et al. 2013: 347–49).

In our world, individualism transfers total responsibility for actions, successes and failures to individuals. In this regard, I recall the accusations of plant managers addressed to workers of following reprehensible behaviour such as smoking or being non-compliant with the correct use of the protection equipment provided by the firm. In the narratives elaborated by the corporations, such behaviour triggered the onset of respiratory problems and represented a threat even more dangerous than exposure to asbestos.

> By transforming public issues into private matters of lifestyle, self-empowerment and assertiveness, individualism precludes organized efforts to spur social changes. It fits perfectly with a declining welfare state and also influences responses to health inequities. From this perspective, each individual is self-interested and possesses a fixed, competitive human nature … Individualism presumes that individuals exist in parallel with society instead of being formed by society. (Hofrichter 2003b: 28)

On the contrary, 'a key principle of the public health ethic is the focus on the identification and control of the hazards of this world, rather than a focus on the behavioural defects of those individuals damaged by these hazards' (Beauchamp 2003: 273).

ABREA activism may be considered as a revolutionary form of health activism. Its main tool of struggle was reacting to sovereign individualism by favouring the establishment of new (bio)social and affective relationships. Moreover, the activists' struggles were aimed at demystifying fatalistic explanations of workers' deaths and diseases, and, in so doing, were overtly set against the fatalistic approach to death nurtured by capitalistic discourses.

Engaging Ethnography and Global Public Health

> Responsibility cannot be acquired intellectually, but only through experience. (Freire 2005: 212)

The 'imperative of responsibility' (Jonas 1985) largely motivates anti-asbestos activists in their daily struggle, and should also be felt by those who have knowledge (and power), and operate in the conditions to act in favour of global public health. A moral commitment is more urgent than ever, and 'inaction is not a real option, but rather an illusion – one maintained with difficulty in even the tallest ivory towers or most gated retreats' (Farmer 2013: xxiii).

Scholars from various disciplines have debated how to understand and tackle global health disasters. Rooted in the encounter with 'the other', ethnographic research presents an incomparable, intimate insight into the impact of processes that would otherwise remain evanescent. Hahn and Inhorn (2009) suggest starting with the aspects that anthropological and biomedical approaches to public health problems have in common, rather than emphasizing their differences. This approach would overcome the frictions and resistance impeding the elaboration and implementation of effective public health strategies.

I am aware of the challenges of defining a common space for collaborative action and dialogue between anthropology and biomedical sciences. However, in line with Inhorn (1995), I believe that the 'perceived divergences' between anthropology and biomedical sciences can be turned into a terrain of convergence and cooperation for a more critical and holistic understanding of health problems, as contributions from medical anthropology and cultural epidemiology have shown. Global health requires transdisciplinary dialogue.

> Combining anthropology, sociology, history, political economy and other 'resocializing disciplines' with fields such as epidemiology, demography, clinical practice, molecular biology and economics allows us to build a coherent new field that might better be termed 'global health equity'. It is this multidisciplinary approach [that] leads us from the large-scale to the local, and from the social to the molecular, [and that] permits us to take a properly biosocial approach to what are, without exception, biosocial problems. (Farmer 2013: xiv)

In the multidisciplinary approach needed to understand and face global health issues such as AR disasters, the contribution of anthropology is crucial: 'Explaining the distribution of suffering requires many minds and resources. Case studies of individuals reveal suffering, they tell us what happens to one or many people; but to explain suffering, one must embed individual biography in the larger matrix of culture, history, and political economy' (Hofrichter 2003b: 41).

In this regard, anthropological approaches and methods add a significant contribution to critical reflection on global health and to addressing global health issues, including those recognized as disasters and those that remain invisible because of precise dynamics and human actions. One of the most valuable and original contributions that anthropology has to offer to the multidisciplinary dialogue on global public health comes precisely from the range of ethnographic fieldwork and analysis, its reflexive attitude and its ability to raise thorny issues and to question taken-for-granted assumptions.

The dynamics characterizing the disasters caused by the toxic market of asbestos offer notable input for critical thinking about the processes by which scientific paradigms and epidemiological data are elaborated, and the extent to which their communication (or lack of it) has effects on public health. I would like to draw attention to aspects concerning AR disasters that not only challenge taken-for-granted assumptions on health, but are also emblematic of the necessity of approaching global public health issues from a critical perspective. For instance, as Amartya Sen noted, joblessness is a crucial determinant of health since 'poverty might keep individuals from accessing health services because [for instance] they have no means of transport to a hospital or because the opportunity cost of leaving their family is too high' (Sen 2000, cited in Suri et al. 2013: 258–59). However, as in the case of AR disasters, work often represents a major source of danger and of threat to life.

In a brilliant analysis of the contribution of anthropology to global health, Pigg (2013) adopts the concept of invisibility to refer to anthropologists' methodological and theoretical tools for questioning taken-for-granted practices and discourses, and identifying invisible problems.

> An ethnography of global health listens in the spaces that are rendered invisible (or at least off to the side) by the very practices most valued as 'getting things done'. Methodologically, an ethnographer of global health has to be agnostic, asking first, 'what is going on?' before asking whether or why it is good or bad (in what ways and for whom). The relationship that activities convened for global health problem-solving set up between the visible/valued/known and the invisible/ignored/uncertain is especially diagnostic. The concept of invisibility can be useful because it is inherently perspectival and situational: that which is overlooked, camouflaged, hidden, not known, or not particularly noticed still exists … We need to keep in mind that invisible work, marginalized perspectives, forgotten realities and indeterminacy are very much part of the empirical social realities being built by global health activities. We have ways of theorizing such processes. They are not unanalysable. (Pigg 2013: 133)

In this regard, the invisible health disasters provoked by the toxic market of asbestos may be considered as paradigmatic of the processes that define how a global health disaster occurs and is defined, how to address it, and how to prevent it.

> Whereas global public health policy looks to ethnography solely as a source of information, pertinent to its goals, ethnographers see their task quite differently, holding that the purpose of patient ethnography is to listen and to be in situ, a practice that opens up a space for the questioning of received certainties through a responsiveness to multiple viewpoints and contested perspectives. We call this critical reflexivity …
>
> The anthropology of global health proceeds from the premise that there may be important things happening in the social arenas created by global health activities other than those already accounted for by the medical and public health frameworks that define problems and structure solutions. The improvisational praxis of ethnographic attentiveness is especially suited to discovering what these other important things might be. (Pigg 2013: 127–28)

As an anthropologist, I respond positively to the call 'for the primacy of the ethical and a more morally engaged anthropology' (Scheper-Hughes 1995), but I am not an activist, and have never considered myself to be one. Despite the fact that the ABREA members in Osasco used to call me *'a companheira nossa'* (our comrade), I hardly recognize myself as the 'anthropologist-*companheira*' as the medical anthropologist Nancy Scheper-Hughes referred to the role she assumed while doing research in north-eastern Brazil in the 1980s (Scheper-Hughes 1992, 1995).

I did not become a member of any of the non-governmental organizations that I accompanied over the years of my multi-sited ethnography, although I am constantly in touch with their members and became close friends with some of them. I participated in numerous activities and awareness campaigns, although my role never shifted from researcher to activist. I let myself be 'affected by the events' (Foucault 1997) and encounters I experienced, but I do not claim – nor do I have the naivety– to equate the public and social contribution that might derive from my study to the actions resulting from the daily commitment of anti-asbestos activists. I do, however, recognize and hope to increase the sociopolitical repercussions that my ethnographic investigation may have in support of the movement. I recognize my role as a 'moral actor', and the anthropological experience as a form of 'moral commitment to the world' (Fassin 2007: 202–3).

I approached and conceived of my work according to Scheper-Hughes's definition of 'witnessing' as a form of militancy, linking anthropology to moral philosophy:

> Witnessing, the anthropologist as *companheira*, is in the active voice, and it positions the anthropologist inside human events as a responsive, reflexive and morally committed being, one who will 'take sides' and make judgements, though this flies in the face of the anthropological non-engagement with either ethics or politics. Of course, non-involvement was, in itself, an 'ethical' and moral position. (Scheper-Hughes 1995: 418)

Inspired by an 'ethical orientation to the other' as demanded by anthropology (Scheper-Hughes 1995: 418), this book is grounded in the narratives and memories my interlocutors in the field shared, narrated and elaborated with me during the encounters, interviews and experiences we lived together. By pursuing the public use of the knowledge emerging from my research, my wish and commitment is to situate those memories and their narration within an anthropological debate, inside and outside of academia.

A Reflexive Note

> The inequality of lives, biological and political, local and global, is perhaps the greatest violence with which anthropologists are confronted in the field, as they daily prove the truly existential and vital distance that separates them from the men and women whose histories and lives they encounter. (Fassin 2007: 270)

On my way back home after interviews with research participants, which had often lasted five or six hours, I usually had an espresso and *pão de queijo* (cheese bread) in the café where I used to stop to cheer myself up before tackling the 1-to-2-hour crowded commuter train from Osasco to São Paulo.

I used to take the train to Pinheiros, one of the largest train and metro stations in São Paulo, with a constant flow of people frantically moving across the capital from one side to another. Commuting on public transport between São Paulo and Osasco influenced my perception of the space I was crossing as a boundless pulsating living creature, whose movements and limits were out of my control and comprehension. I had the feeling that I had no other option but to be part of that movement.

Numerous huts made of bricks, wooden boards and Eternit roofing flew uninterruptedly by the window along the tracks connecting Osasco and São Paulo. Small details of those precarious homes captured my attention; I could see the dignity of the lives led in those poor conditions. All around was filth, waste materials and squalor, with no visible sign of beauty other than the majestic, gnarled trees whose roots seemed to claim the mistreated earth by re-emerging on the surface. I had the impression that the fresh smell of the clean clothes hung out to dry in that toxic environment might actually reach my nose. The curtains on the windows and the gleaming aluminium doors gave me a pleasant feeling of care and dignity. It was as if people were trying to make a space for shelter, protection and a little peace – somewhere to call 'home' – built in the midst of the frenzied movement crossing the megalopolis.

During my stay in Osasco and São Paulo, I had ambivalent feelings towards the environment surrounding me. I felt a strong sense of repulsion and distance, but also of attraction and closeness. That pulsating interweaving of lights, bodies and lives, each traced by unique experiences, dreams and nightmares, scared and overwhelmed me, but at the same time filled me with a thrilling love and curiosity for life. At times I felt unbearably lonely, but more often I felt that I was not alone. I had the feeling that we all were participating as vulnerable, minute pawns in the same movement, despite all the differences between us.

One morning, I conducted an interview that, unlike the others, ended after a few hours and did not include having lunch with my research partners. On that occasion, my interlocutor, the widow of an ABREA member, had family commitments and, apologizing, told me that she could not invite me for lunch, even though she would have liked to. So, by around 12:30, I was free. There was a clear sky, the light was warm and the temperature pleasant. In a quiet residential area, my interlocutor's house was near Aquilino dos Santos – Vítima do Amianto [Asbestos Victim] Square, dedicated to the first victim of asbestos to have died immediately after the foundation of ABREA in

1995 (I refer to this square in Chapter 3). Taking advantage of being free and having no other commitments in the afternoon, I stopped to take photographs of the square, dwelling on some details and enjoying the shade of the wonderfully majestic trees. There were no people in the streets. It was a weekday and at that time most of the inhabitants of that neighbourhood were probably at work. At one point, I saw two barefooted boys running fast in my direction. My first reaction was to put the camera in my bag, thinking that I could be robbed. I continued to walk slowly in the same direction as the two young boys. I saw one of them climbing onto the roof of a house. I thought they wanted to break into it. I kept moving forward. One boy was on the roof by now, while the other was on the road, a few steps away from me. He looked up at his friend. I also looked in the same direction. The boy on the roof was retrieving a kite caught in the power lines. The two youngsters were smiling and exchanging jokes. I also smiled for a moment, more out of relief than empathy. Actually, I felt ashamed for having thought that the two young boys might be thieves, and for having been afraid of them – two children! I felt ashamed for not having been able to control the conditioning that the society I was living in exercised over me, for not having been able to distance myself from the prejudices that circulated in the everyday world in which I was immersed. I cried with the awareness that I would never have had a similar reaction in a different context, such as my home in Europe, in which I would not have instinctively considered two young boys as possible thieves, simply for their liveliness, their running in the street, and the colour of their skin. I cried because I felt shame and a deep sense of guilt for the way I had viewed the two young boys from a white, Western, European perspective. At that moment, I realized how much my life experiences in Brazil had led to an instinctive perception of an ordinary situation that was so deeply (albeit unconsciously) influenced by a hegemonic perspective elaborated across centuries of exploitation and domination of millions of people – a perspective that in Brazil is rooted in the Portuguese colonization from the sixteenth century onwards (Ribeiro 2006; Botelho and Schwarcz 2009; Schwarcz and Starling 2015).

I was suddenly faced with what I, as an anthropology student, had learnt from books about the impossibility of completely eliminating the conditioning of culture and history when approaching and encountering *the other* (de Martino 1948).

From the first days of my fieldwork, I realized that I was in a context dramatically marked by a history of brutality committed by local and foreign perpetrators throughout centuries of 'violence in war and peace' (Scheper-Hughes and Bourgois 2004). There, a vast number of men, women, children and elderly people might take part in the same, endless movement of bodies, ideas, aspirations and actions, but only from a condition of chronic vulnerability with crucial and structural differences from the vulnerability that I might have felt (and often did feel) living and moving side by side with them.

Several times, I have been asked why I chose Brazil to conduct my doctoral research on anti-asbestos activism, and why I decided to focus on a struggle that to my European interlocutors evidently appeared marginal and less interesting, perhaps less exotic, than other social movements spreading in Brazil that could have been considered to be more urgent. Living in São Paulo for almost one year, I recognized the relevance and necessity of the actions promoted and organized by other social movements (see Holston 2008). I refer, for instance, to the mobilizations of public-school students and teachers studying and working in precarious conditions, and to the movements against the genocide of the black, poor and peripheral population. Indeed I had friends and fellow students engaged in feminist groups and movements against the discrimination towards minority communities. I lived in São Paulo and Osasco. Every day I witnessed the profound socio-economic disparities that violently constrained a vast number of people, young and old, in conditions of poverty, despair, and 'non-person' status (see Biehl 2005). Thus, I might have been tempted to ask myself: why am I here? Does it make sense to focus my study, energy and time on investigating the practices and experiences of processes of this asbestos disaster, whose impact might be less dangerous than many other atrocious conditions to which millions of people are exposed daily throughout their entire lives?

Similar thoughts came to mind when feelings of powerlessness and sadness overwhelmed me, especially during my lonely daily journeys between São Paulo and Osasco. This happened particularly while coming back home at night through working-class neighbourhoods bordered by shanty towns that had lost their vivid shining daytime colours, when the darkness pervaded everything, me included.

I noticed that when somebody asked me how my research and life experience in Brazil was going, my answer revealed a schizophrenic combination of feelings and memories of encounters, places and circumstances, beauty and horror, which frequently left me speechless. Often, I told my interlocutors that what upset me most was the violence I felt and came to know in my daily life. This violence consisted not only of homicides, shootings and robberies (*assaltos*), which I was informed about on a daily basis, but rather it was an almost palpable feeling of terror and anguish. Usually, my interlocutors found it difficult to understand what I wanted to convey; they were surprised, and told me that they could only imagine a similar climate in places afflicted by war.

The landmark work of Loïc Wacquant on the criminalization of poverty (Wacquant 1993, 1994, 1999, 2008) reflected on the 'omnipresence of violence' and 'climate of terror' as particular aspects that made the 'dictatorship over the poor' in Brazil, as well as in other settings, cruelly effective. Wacquant coined the term 'Brazilianization' to describe the 'protracted process of societal fission and ramification of inequalities and insecurities of the metropoles of Europe and North America' (Wacquant 1994). Focusing on the 'climate of terror' which is palpable in Brazil, Wacquant wrote:

> Since 1989, lethal crime has been Brazil's leading cause of mortality, with homicide earning the title of 'great villain of public health' for the 1980s, during which decade the national rate doubled to pass 20 per 100,000 people – twice the U.S. peak of the early 1990s and about fifteen times the level of the societies of Western Europe. The incidence of murders in Rio de Janeiro, São Paulo and Recife now exceeds 60 per 100,000, a rate approaching those for the most violent metropoles in the Americas in recent years (New Orleans, Detroit and Washington in the North, and Caracas, Lima and Medellin in the South, sported rates above 80 in the early 1990s), and far higher than anything Brazilian urbanites had previously experienced. (Wacquant 2008: 59)

The 'close spatial propinquity of rich and poor in Brazilian urban settings' (Wacquant 2008) by no means attenuated the existing disparities; it exacerbated them, making them concretely visible, with the frenzied construction of 'fortress cities' instead (Low 1997).

> Middle-class streets and upper-class residences have been turned into fortified enclaves secured by iron gates, intercoms, attack dogs and armed guards in watchbooths or manning roadblocks after dark, while 'gated communities', cordoned off from the city by high walls and advanced surveillance technology, have mushroomed and become a coveted ingredient of elite status (Caldeira 1996). A huge private security industry has grown to provide proximate protection to apartment buildings, businesses and social clubs, as well as to wealthy individuals and their families. (Wacquant 2008: 59)

Undoubtedly and significantly, breathing that 'climate of terror' in my daily life – and finding myself unable to make use of public spaces in the way I was used to – affected my fieldwork experience as well as my understanding of the practices of 'care-activism' (Mazzeo 2018c) undertaken by ABREA members. Immersed in a context marked by violence and suffering perpetrated by human actions motivated by specific logics and parts of processes begun centuries before, I was gripped by a sense of despair that made me question my hypotheses and interpretations. Could I really consider the knowledge emerging from the suffering endured by the activists and triggered by the impact of AR disasters on their lives in terms of power? Did it make sense? Did the vocabulary that an engagement in activism provided, a vocabulary for understanding the symptoms of ARDs as traces of injustice, represent tools for bringing about change? Despite being relevant, what might the impact of the changes promoted and goals achieved by the activists be, in relation to a context so deeply corrupted, devastated and fragmented? By tackling these upsetting questions and trying neither to fall into anguish nor to get lost, I looked for direction and solace in what I retrospectively read as the answers the sufferers and activists I met offered me, often without being explicitly asked. The ability to grasp, at least partly, those answers was based on analysis of the countless informal conversations I had had with my gatekeepers and Brazilian friends.

One conversation was particularly incisive during the process through which I elaborated my interpretation and perception of the field. I quote a small part of it:

> Agata, I do not want to get used to the brutality that surrounds me. This violence and misery must continue to trouble and upset me. Only if I do not get used to all this can I be at peace with myself. If you become indifferent, it is the end. I must continue to behave according to what I think it is normal and just. I cannot resign myself to such violence and consider the suffering around me normal.

This conversation was crucial for me in grasping the revolutionary repercussions of anti-asbestos mobilization from an emic perspective. A severe critique was embodied and revolutionary practices and counter-hegemonic discourses were elaborated by those who had been affected by the impact of AR disasters on their lives. A similar subversive force emerging from a suffering condition that was as private as it was social had then been channelled into a grassroots movement, making the invisible disasters provoked by the toxic market of asbestos communicable and recognizable through the collective narratives elaborated through the 'words' of political, legal and biomedical language.

The 'power of the suffering bodies' (Mazzeo 2017a, 2017b, 2018a, 2018b, 2018c) conveyed in the pathways of activism that the sufferers themselves had marked out was changing a system that had previously seemed immutable and firm in its certainty, sustained by the fears and threats that this system itself had established.

Figure 5.1 Osasco, São Paulo, Brazil, 2015. Photograph by the author.

Conclusion

In this chapter, I have situated anti-asbestos activism within the global public health arena as a broad health social movement addressing equity and social justice. As discussed, individual and collective health are deeply intertwined with social, economic, political and cultural processes and dynamics. Asbestos-related disasters offer paradigmatic and dramatic examples of similar entanglements, while the anti-asbestos movement and the practices of activism performed locally shed light on alternative paths of care, and trigger a reflection on the necessity of multidisciplinary dialogue and action in tackling global health issues. I have referred to the position taken by international public health research institutes about the 'controlled use of asbestos'. This consideration calls into question the political and ethical role of institutionalized forms of knowledge (and power), and attendant professional practitioners. Finally, I have concluded with a reflection on the contributions that anthropology as the 'most resocializing discipline' (Farmer et al. 2013) may offer for understanding and acting in the globally interconnected but increasingly unequal world in which we all live.

Practising what Scheper-Hughes (1995) calls an engaged – militant – ethnography offers unique opportunities for acting and investigating, in depth, the transnational socio-political, economic and cultural processes informing global health disasters. It provides the opportunities for exploring the politics, understanding, experiences and knowledge of people affected by such disasters. How do they embody these transnational processes, and how do they make them meaningful locally in the situational specificity of their own lives? The contribution of anthropology is crucial in raising thorny questions, in tearing the veil of invisibility that hides silent disasters, and in challenging taken-for-granted assumptions. Above all, the anthropological view on global health issues (Biehl 2011) and the ethnographer's 'mindful participation' (Pigg 2013) are essential in grasping the invisible disasters suffered in everyday lives by millions of 'nobodies' (Galeano 1989) and in listening to their voices. This does not mean making the anthropologist's voice an echo of the men and women encountered in the field, but rather it is a response to anthropology's demand for an ethical commitment to 'the other' (Scheper-Hughes 1995). A similar commitment should represent the basis of all scientific research involving human beings and the environment, and it is essential in tackling global health disasters, both visible and invisible.

Conclusion

> *Deixamos algo de nós para trás ao deixar um lugar. Permanecemos lá, apesar de termos partido. E há coisa em nós que só reencontraremos ao voltar. Viajamos ao nosso encontro, quando vamos a um lugar, onde vivemos parte de nossa vida. Por mais breve que tenha sido.*
>
> [We leave some of us behind when we leave a place. We remain there, although we left. And there is something in us that we will only find again when we get back. We travel towards the encounter with ourselves, when we go to a place where we lived a part of our life, as brief as it might have been.]
>
> —Pascal Mercier, *Trem Noturno para Lisboa*

Below is an extract from the notes I wrote in October 2016, when visiting Osasco one year after the end of my fieldwork:

> Morning – bus, train. Vila Lobos-Jaguaré, Presidente Altino, Osasco all stations… people are going to work. I arrive in Osasco at 8.40 A.M. Antonio Agù Street is not alive with people at this hour. The *cachorro quente* [hot dog] kiosks are not crowded.
>
> It is grey and cold. I wear my jacket and a scarf, but after all the going up and down in the city, I am sweating. I did not remember how tiring it could be to do all this climbing to reach the ABREA office in Santo Antonio Street. There, there are more steep steps to climb.
>
> As soon as I enter the entrance hall of the building, I hear Eliezer's loud, shrill voice. I smile. It is lovely to meet him again and to find myself here, where I feel as if I have come home.

This book contains what I felt, thought, noticed, discussed, read and observed during my encounters in the field while researching the anti-asbestos activism in Osasco, Brazil, in 2014 and 2015. The data presented here emerged from my interlocutors' narratives and my reflections elaborated during lonely journeys, on countless occasions when I felt disoriented and lost, and my certainties teetered. On the one hand, this book is the written expression of solitary work of analysis and writing conducted in Italy, during which I felt powerless and repeatedly relived my anger, indignation and sorrow about the silent AR disasters, injustices and acts of 'violence in war and peace' (Scheper-Hughes and Bourgois 2004) that I had witnessed in Brazil. On the other hand, the information in this book is moulded by the connections I identified and established during over ten years of multi-situated ethnography (begun in Italy), my travel from Bari (my hometown) to Casale Monferrato (Italy) and then Osasco (Brazil), and by the displacement between Europe and Latin America. The movements I retrace in this book are the movements of bodies and struggles, capital and disasters – including myself – as I simultaneously acted as a researcher and a research instrument with my body, background, hypotheses and expectations.

Throughout this book, I have tried not to fall into a solipsistic monologue, but rather to offer input for dialogue and to raise questions for reflection. The decision to include extended quotes from my fieldnotes and my interlocutors' narratives was motivated by a methodological rigour in which I have made my voice and position evident and clear in relation to the study participants. Furthermore, I have acknowledged their role in the elaboration of my knowledge of the AR disasters and grassroots activism contained in this monograph.

The anti-asbestos activists I met made a 'militant' use of the past inscribed in their bodies that has continued to affect their present (Mazzeo 2017b). The acts of memory they performed individually and collectively were practices of activism to the extent that the past–present they remembered and narrated became the proof of the injustices from which they were still suffering.

I would sincerely like there to be public, social use of the relational knowledge emerging from my encounters with anti-asbestos activists as a basis for engaging in further dialogue within anthropology, and between anthropology and other disciplines, addressing public health and issues of social justice. I borrow the following words from Scheper-Hughes (1995: 419):

> In the act of writing culture, what emerges is always a highly subjective, partial and fragmentary but also deeply personal record of human lives based on eyewitness accounts and testimony … If 'observation' links anthropology to the natural sciences, 'witnessing' links anthropology to moral philosophy.

In line with Scheper-Hughes, I consider myself to be a witness, and I want my study to have social resonance in favour of the transnational movement for the global prohibition of asbestos.

The quantitative transposition into anonymous cases and numbers neutralizes the potentialities of critique of the afflicted (and dying) body, and often ignores the politics at play in the determination of suffering. The experiences of suffering and the practices of activism discussed in this book shed light on the politics in our innermost self, on the social dimension of cancer, the economics of risk and the negotiable dimension of scientific truths. Thus, this ethnography offers an occasion to reflect on and reimagine what institutionalized forms of knowledge (and power) consider to be a global health issue, how they tackle it, and how their concern about the issue reveals itself.

Anthropology has to be ethically and politically committed to recognizing and letting others see the invisible and unrecognized disasters afflicting the 'nobodies' (Galeano 1989) of our world. There is a moral commitment to take action based on the tools and skills that define anthropology as 'one of the most socializing disciplines', and whose contribution in the definition of global public health policies and practices is crucial (Farmer et al. 2013).

I firmly believe in the importance of anthropology in identifying problems and collaborating with less socializing disciplines in creating and carrying out studies and projects regarding public health issues, such as the epidemiological mapping of a disaster or the communication of risks concerning health hazards threatening vulnerable communities. Rooted in Osasco's historical and cultural tradition and sociopolitical context, ABREA's struggle made the suffering of hundreds of contaminated workers and their families the basis for a sociopolitical engagement that has produced revolutionary changes on multiple levels. Living and understanding the disaster through the language and morals of activism has produced multiple revolutions in the individual experiences of illness, risk and grieving. In the local context, based on biosocial – i.e. political and affective – relationships, AR sufferers, and anti-asbestos activists have formed a community, and established an emotional and practical support network assuring care for the afflicted survivors. Moreover, ABREA has been able to enter legal and biomedical knowledge-making processes and their respective institutions (e.g. hospitals, health research institutes and courts) with the power to negotiate rights as a collective and respectable social actor. In the national context, the connections established by ABREA with other anti-asbestos organizations have empowered the anti-asbestos movement in Brazil, and led to significant achievements. In an international context, I mention ABREA's role in the movement for the global prohibition of asbestos, and the dialogue it has conducted for more than twenty years with the AFeVA in Casale Monferrato, Italy, where I conducted my previous study.

AR disasters and anti-asbestos activism are paradigmatic of manifold crucial issues afflicting our world – those that should not happen and those that should be supported. This book's contribution to knowledge is not restricted to AR processes of disasters and activism, but rather it aims to broaden reflection and shed light on other invisible disasters, suffering experiences and practices of everyday struggle. I refer, for instance, to the role of other health/environment-based movements in the name of social and environmental justice, and to the processes determining a population's vulnerability to specific health hazards and disasters provoked by industrial activities using toxic substances.

In concluding this work, it would be ethically and theoretically impossible for me to consider my involvement in this study as over, or the investigation of the field(s) as saturated. Instead of an end, I see an occasion for renewing a personal commitment to the transnational and transdisciplinary movement that is public health.

The Current State of the Asbestos Ban in Brazil

In November 2017, the Brazilian Supremo Tribunal Federal – STF [Federal Supreme Court] prohibited the exploration, production, commercialization or transportation of chrysotile asbestos and of all products containing it over the whole national territory. This represents an extraordinary achievement for the anti-asbestos movement, and its significance goes way beyond the national context because of the role played by Brazil in the global market of asbestos. Soon afterwards, asbestos stakeholders began a hectic lobbying campaign to continue extracting and exporting asbestos in the name of safeguarding the jobs of hundreds of workers.

While I was finishing writing this book, the Brazilian 'Eternit S.A.' publicly announced that it would recommence extraction activities (since ceased in 2019) at the Cana Brava quarry of Minaçu (Goiás), in order to reclaim and export 24,000 tonnes of asbestos (Lemes 2020). This would be possible under Law 20,514 – passed in July 2019 by the state of Goiás – which allowed the extraction of chrysotile asbestos for exportation purposes only. On 12 February 2020, the Associação Nacional dos Procuradores do Trabalho – ANPT [National Association of Labour Attorneys] harshly condemned Eternit's decision, and urged the STF to consider the Goiás law as unconstitutional, as it is in open contravention of the national prohibition on asbestos (Lemes 2020).

If the extraction activities recommence, asbestos will be exported, especially to the Asian market, in particular India and Indonesia, which were the major buyers of Brazilian asbestos before the ban (Kazan-Allen 2019b). In April 2019, delegates from the Asian Ban Asbestos movement, including activists from Japan, India and Indonesia, joined ABREA's annual national meeting and awareness campaign, organized each year on the occasion of the events organized in April, the month internationally dedicated to occupational health. During the mission in Brazil, with the support of ABREA members, the Asian delegation travelled to Brasilia and had the opportunity to talk to court justices, federal prosecutors specialized in environmental cases, civil servants, legal experts, politicians and unionists. The delegation also held public protests against the export of asbestos from Brazil to Asian countries (ibid.).

The joint mobilization of Asian and Brazilian activists is an example of the transnational dimension of a grassroots movement aiming at the global prohibition of asbestos. Local and national NGOs become empowered by mutual support and recognition from social actors engaged in activities pursuing similar objectives, though occurring in distinct sociocultural contexts (Appadurai 2013). As the ethnographic and historical study of the trajectories connecting the processes of disaster and activism that occurred in Casale Monferrato in Italy and Osasco in Brazil has shown in this book, a transnational activist network, combined with a transdisciplinary investigation, including the embodied knowledge of the impacted communities, seems to be essential in tackling global health disasters and pursuing objectives of social justice.

Glossary

Caixa d'agua	water reservoir
Conscientização	the process of developing a critical thinking
Cruzeiro	old Brazilian currency
Falta de ar	shortness of breath
Pó/Polvere	dust (i.e. asbestos)
Real/Reais	Brazilian currency
Roça	rural area

References

ACEO (Associação Comercial e Empresarial de Osasco). 2003/2006. *Visão Empresarial da História de Osasco* [Entrepreneur view of Osasco's history]. Osasco: Editora ACEO.

Acselrad, H., S. Herculano and J.A. Pádua (eds). 2004. *Justiça Ambiental e Cidadania* [Environmental justice and citizenship]. Rio de Janeiro: Relume Dumará.

Algranti, E. 2014. 'Comments on the Introduction of the Paper Overview of the Biochemical and Genetic Processes in Malignant Mesothelioma', *Jornal Brasileiro de Pneumologia* 40(5): 584–85.

Algranti, E., et al. 2001. 'Non-malignant Asbestos-Related Diseases in Brazilian Asbestos Cement Workers', *American Journal of Industrial Medicine* 40: 240–54.

———. 2019. 'Prevention of Asbestos Exposure in Latin America within a Global Public Health Perspective', *Annals of Global Health* 85(1): 49, 1–15.

Allen, D., and L. Kazan-Allen (eds). 2012. *Eternit and the Great Asbestos Trial*. London: Justasec Print Services Ltd.

Almeida, C. 2016. 'Eternit é Condenada a Pagar mais de R$ 400 Milhões a Ex-Funcionários [Eternit is sentenced to pay more than 400 million reais to former employees], *O Globo Economia*, 26 February. Retrieved 24 March 2017 from http://oglobo.globo.com/economia/eternit-condenada-pagar-mais-de-400-milhoes-ex-funcionarios-18766483.

Altopiedi, R. 2011. *Un Caso di Criminalità d'Impresa: L'Eternit di Casale Monferrato* [A case of company criminality: L'Eternit of Casale Monferrato]. Turin: L'Harmattan.

Altopiedi, R., and S. Panelli. 2012. 'Il Grande Processo' [The great trial], Theme Issue 'Dossier Eternit', *Quaderni di Storia Contemporanea* 51: 17–67.

Amancio J.B., M. Bonciani and S.D. Urquiza. 1988. 'Avaliação Radiológica de Trabalhadores da Indústria de Fibrocimento do Estado de São Paulo' [Radiological evaluation of workers in the asbestos-cement industry of São Paulo state], *Revista Brasileira de Saúde Ocupacional* 16: 51–55.

Antunes, R., and M. Ridenti. 2007. 'Operários e Estudantes contra a Ditadura: 1968 no Brasil' [Workers and students against the dictatorship: 1968 in Brazil], *Mediações* 12(2): 78–89.

Appadurai, A. 1996. *Modernity at Large: Cultural Dimensions of Globalization*. Minneapolis: University of Minnesota Press.

———. 2000. 'Grassroots Globalization and the Research Imagination', *Public Culture* 12(1): 1–19.
———. 2013. *The Future as Cultural Fact: Essays on the Global Condition*. New York: Verso.
Assis L.V., and M.C. Isoldi. 2014. 'Overview of the Biochemical and Genetic Processes in Malignant Mesothelioma', *Jornal Brasileiro de Pneumologia* 40(4): 429–42.
Assmann, A. 2002. *Ricordare: Forme e Mutamenti della Memoria Culturale* [Remembering: Forms and changes of cultural memory]. Bologna: Società Editrice il Mulino.
Athanasiou, A., P. Hantzaroula and Y. Yannakopoulos. 2008. 'Towards a New Epistemology: "The Affective Turn"', *Historein* 8: 5–16.
Barbé, D. 1983. *A Graça e o Poder: As Comunidades Eclesiais de Base no Brasil* [The grace and the power: The base ecclesial communities in Brazil]. São Paulo: Paulinas.
Barca, S. 2012. 'On Working-Class Environmentalism: A Historical and Transnational Overview', *Interface: A Journal for and about Social Movements* 4(2): 61–80.
Barthes, R. 1980. *La Camera Chiara: Nota sulla Fotografia* [Camera Lucida: Reflections on photography]. Translated by R. Guidieri. Turin: Einaudi.
Basilico, M., et al. (eds). 2013. 'A Movement for Global Health Equity? A Closing Reflection', in P. Farmer et al. (eds), *Reimagining Global Health: An Introduction*. Berkeley: University of California Press, pp. 340–53.
Bauer, C. 2010. 'Brasil, 1968. Estudantes, Operários e Guerrilheros Escrevem a História a Contrapelo' [Brazil, 1968. Students, Workers, and *Guerrilheros* Write the History *a Contrapelo*], *Contexto Radial* 12: 7–21.
Beauchamp, D.E. 2003. 'Public Health as Social Justice', in R. Hofrichter (ed.), *Health and Social Justice: Politics, Ideology, and Inequity in the Distribution of Disease*. San Francisco: Jossey-Bass, pp. 267–83.
Beck, U. 1992. *Risk Society: Towards a New Modernity*. London: Sage.
Benadusi, M., C. Brambilla and B. Riccio (eds). 2011. *Disasters, Development and Humanitarian Aid: New Challenges for Anthropology*. Rimini: Guaraldi.
Benson, P., and S. Kirsch. 2010. 'Capitalism and the Politics of Resignation', *Current Anthropology* 51(4): 459–86.
Berlinguer, G., S.F. Teixeira and G.W.S. Campos. 1988. *Reforma Sanitária na Itália e no Brasil* [Health reform in Italy and Brazil]. São Paulo: Cebes/Hucitec.
Bernardo, T. 1998. *Memória em Branco e Negro: Olhares sobre São Paulo* [Memory in black and white: Glances on São Paulo]. São Paulo: Editora Unesp.
Berryman, P. 1987. *Liberation Theology: The Essential Facts about the Revolutionary Movement in Latin America and Beyond*. London: I.B. Tauris.
Biehl, J. 2005. *Vita: Life in a Zone of Social Abandonment*. Berkeley: University of California Press.
———. 2011. 'Antropologia no Campo da Saúde Global' [Anthropology in the global health field], *Horizontes Antropológicos* 17(35): 257–96.
Biehl, J., and P. Locke. 2010. 'Deleuze and the Anthropology of Becoming', *Current Anthropology* 51(3): 317–51.
Blume, S. 2017. 'In Search of Experiential Knowledge', *The European Journal of Social Science Research* 30(1): 91–103.

Boholm, A. 2003. 'The Cultural Nature of Risk: Can There Be an Anthropology of Uncertainty?', *Ethnos* 68(2): 159–78.
Botelho, A., and L.M. Schwarcz. 2009. *Um Enigma Chamado Brasil: 29 Intérpretes e um País* [An enigma called Brazil: 29 interpreters and a country]. São Paulo: Companhia das Letras.
Bourdieu, P. 1977. *Outline of a Theory of Practice*. Cambridge: Cambridge University Press.
———. 1991. *Language and Symbolic Power*. Oxford: Polity Press.
Bourdieu, P., and M.C. Bourdieu. 2004. 'The Peasant and Photography', *Ethnography* 5(4): 601–16.
Bourdieu, P., and L.J. Wacquant. 1992. *An Invitation to Reflexive Sociology*. Chicago: University of Chicago Press.
Braun, L. 2008. 'Structuring Silence: Asbestos and Biomedical Research in Britain and South Africa', *Race & Class* 50(1): 59–78.
Braun, L., and S. Kisting. 2006. 'Asbestos-Related Disease in South Africa: The Social Production of an Invisible Epidemic', *American Journal of Public Health* 96(8): 2–12.
Brodeur, P. 1985. *Outrageous Misconduct: The Asbestos Industry on Trial*. New York: Pantheon Books.
Brown, P., and S. Zavestoski. 2004. 'Social Movements in Health: An Introduction', *Sociology of Health & Illness* 26(6): 679–94.
Brown, P., et al. 2004. 'Embodied Health Movements: Uncharted Territory in Social Movement Research', *Sociology of Health and Illness* 26(1): 1–31.
Bullard, R.D., and G.S. Johnson. 2000. 'Environmental Justice: Grassroots Activism and Its Impact on Public Policy Decision Making', *Journal of Social Issues* 56(3): 555–78.
Burawoy, M. 1979. 'The Anthropology of Industrial Work', *Annual Review of Anthropology* 8: 231–66.
Burawoy, M., et al. (eds). 2000. *Global Ethnography: Forces, Connections, and Imaginations in a Postmodern World*. Berkeley: University of California Press.
Cable, S., and M. Benson. 1993. 'Environmental Injustice and the Emergence of Grass-Roots Environmental Organizations', *Social Problems* 40(4): 464–77.
Caldeira, T.P.R. 1996. 'Fortified Enclaves: The New Urban Segregation', *Public Culture* 8(2): 303–28.
Calvino, I. 1954. 'La Fabbrica nella Montagna' [The factory in the mountain], *L'Unità*, 28 February.
Cappelletto, F. 2009. 'Vivere l'Etnografia: Osservazioni sul Rapporto Medico-Paziente' [Living the ethnography: Observations on the doctor–patient relationship], in F. Cappelletto (ed.), *Vivere l'Etnografia* [Living the ethnography]. Firenze: SEID, pp. 199–225.
Cappelletto, F., and E. Merler. 2003. 'Perceptions of Health Hazards in the Narratives of Italian Migrant Workers at an Australian Asbestos Mine (1943–1966)', *Social Science & Medicine* 56: 1047–59.
Castells, M. 1996. *The Power of Identity*. Oxford: Blackwell.
Castleman, B.I. 1979. 'The Export of Hazardous Factories to Developing Nations', *International Journal of Health Services* 9(4): 569–606.
———. 1983. 'The Double Standard in Industrial Hazards', *International Journal of Health Services* 13(1): 5–14.

———. 2003. 'Controlled Use of Asbestos', *International Journal of Occupational and Environmental Health* 3(9): 294–98.

———. 2005. Asbestos: Medical and Legal Aspects. Fifth Edition. New York: Aspen Publishers.

———. 2016. 'The Export of Hazardous Industries in 2015', *Environmental Health* 15(8): 1–6.

Castleman, B.I., and V. Navarro. 1987. 'International Mobility of Hazardous Products, Industries, and Wastes', *International Journal of Health Services* 17(4): 617–33.

Chiozzi, P. 1993. *Manuale di Antropologia Visuale* [Handbook of visual anthropology]. Milan: UNICOPLI.

Ciccozzi, A. 2013. *Parola di Scienza: Il terremoto dell'Aquila e la Commissione Grandi Rischi. Un'Analisi Antropologica* [Word of Science: The Earthquake of L'Aquila and the Great Risks Commission. An Anthropological Analysis]. Rome: DeriveApprodi.

Clifford, J., and G.E. Marcus. 1986. *Writing Culture: The Poetics and Politics of Ethnography*. Berkeley: University of California Press.

Collegium Ramazzini. 1999. 'Call for an International Ban on Asbestos'. Sixth Collegium Ramazzini Statement. Retrieved 23 March 2017 from http://collegiumramazzini.org/download/6_SixthCRStatement(1999).pdf.

———. 2010. 'Asbestos Is Still With Us: Repeat Call for a Universal Ban'. Fifteenth Collegium Ramazzini Statement. Retrieved 23 March 2017 from http://collegiumramazzini.org/download/15_FifteenthCRStatement(2010).pdf.

———. 2015. 'The Global Health Dimensions of Asbestos and Asbestos-Related Diseases'. Eighteenth Collegium Ramazzini Statement. Retrieved 23 March 2017 from http://www.collegiumramazzini.org/download/18_EighteenthCRStatement(2015).pdf.

Collino de Oliveira, N., and A.L. Marquetti Rocha Negrelli. 1992. *Osasco e Sua História* [Osasco and its history]. Osasco: CG Editora.

Costa, J.L.R. 1983. 'Estudo da Asbestose no Município de Leme-SP' [Study of asbestosis in the municipality of Leme-SP]. Master's thesis. Campinas: UNICAMP.

Crenshaw, K. 1989. 'Demarginalizing the Intersection of Race and Sex: A Black Feminist Critique of Antidiscrimination Doctrine, Feminist Theory and Antiracist Politics', *University of Chicago Legal Forum* 1(8): 139–67.

Csordas, T.J. 1990. 'Embodiment as a Paradigm for Anthropology', *Ethos* 18(1): 5–47.

Cullinan, P., et al. 2017. 'Occupational Lung Diseases: From Old and Novel Exposures to Effective Preventive Strategies', *The Lancet Respiratory Medicine* 5(5): 445–55.

D'Acri, V., M.B. Marques dos Santos and K.R. de Souza. 2010. 'A Indústria Têxtil de Amianto e de Cimento-Amianto e a Luta dos Trabalhadores pela Saúde no Rio de Janeiro' [The asbetsos textile and asbestos-cement industry and the workers' struggle for health in Rio de Janeiro], in M.I. Souza Bravo, V. D'Acri and J. Bilate Martins (eds), *Movimentos Sociais, Saúde e Trabalho* [Social movements, health and labour]. Rio de Janeiro: ENSP/FIOCRUZ, pp. 135–58.

D'Acri, V., et al. 2009. 'Formação de Trabalhadores e Pesquisa na Construção do Movimento de Ação Solidária de Luta pela Saúde: O Caso da Associação Brasileira de Expostos ao Amianto do Rio de Janeiro (ABREA/RJ)' [Workers' education and research in the construction of the solidarity action movement for the struggle for health: The case of the Brazilian Association of Asbestos-Exposed Persons (ABREA/RJ)], *Saúde e Sociedade* 18(1): 154–63.

da Cruz Paiva, O., and S. Moura. 2008. *Hospedaria de Imigrantes de São Paulo* [Shelter of immigrants of São Paulo]. São Paulo: Paz e Terra.

Das, V. 1995. *Critical Events: An Anthropological Perspective on Contemporary India*. Oxford: Oxford University Press.

Da Silva Camargo, T. 2001. 'Bodily Memory and the Politics of Remembrance: The Aftermath of Goiânia Radiological Disaster'. Special Issue 'Understanding Disasters and Catastrophes: An Anthropological Perspective', *High Plains Applied Anthropologist* 21(1): 40–52.

———. 2010. 'Eventos Críticos: Sobreviventes, Narrativas, Testemunhos e Silêncios' [Critical events: Survivors, narratives, witnesses and silences]. Paper presented at the 27th Reunião Brasileira de Antropologia, 1–4 August, Belém (Pará, Brasil).

Dawson, A. 2007. 'The Origins and Character of the Base Ecclesial Community: A Brazilian Perspective', in C. Rowland (ed.), *The Cambridge Companion to Liberation Theology*. Cambridge: Cambridge University Press, pp. 139–58.

de Castro, H.A., F. Giannasi and C. Novello. 2003. 'A Luta pelo Banimento do Amianto nas Américas: Uma Questão de Saúde Pública' [The struggle for the prohibition of asbestos in the Americas: A public health issue], *Ciência e Saúde Coletiva* 8(4): 903–11.

de Castro Andrade, R. 1998. 'Trabalho e Sindicalismo: Memória do 30 anos do Movimento de Osasco' [Work and unionism: Memory of the 30 years of the Osasco's movement], *Tempo Social. Revista de Sociologia da USP* 10(2): 37–49.

de Jesus, P.S. 2006. 'A Cidade de Osasco: JOC (Juventude Operária Cátolica), ACO (Ação Cátolica Operária), JUC (Juventude Universitária Cátolica) no Movimento Operário (1960–1970)' [The city of Osasco: JOC (Catholic Worker Youth), ACO (Catholic Worker Action), JUC (Catholic University Youth) in the Worker Movement (1960–1970)], *Projeto História* 33: 365–73.

Deleuze, G. 1988. *Spinoza: Practical Philosophy*. Translated by R. Hurley. San Francisco: City Lights Books.

Della Porta, D., et al. 2006. *Globalization from Below: Transnational Activists and Protest Networks*. Minneapolis: University of Minnesota Press.

de Martino, E. 1948. *Il Mondo Magico: Prolegomeni a una Storia del Magismo* [The magic world: Prolegomena to a history of Magism]. Turin: Einaudi.

De Oliveira D'Arede, C. 2009. 'O Tempo das Águas e dos Ventos: Significações do Asbesto Atribuídas às Viúvas e Ex-Trabalhadores da Mina de São Félix, em Bom Jesus da Serra, Bahia' [The time of waters and winds: The meanings of asbestos given to the widows and former workers at the mine of São Felix in Bom Jesus da Serra, Bahia]. Master's thesis. Faculdade de Medicina, Universidade Federal da Bahia.

de Oliveira Rovai, M.G. 2009. 'Narrativas Femininas sobre o Heroísmo masculino: as Fronteiras do Gênero' [Female narratives on the male heroism:

The gender boundaries], Atos do Congresso Internacional de História, 9–11 September, Maringá (Paraná, Brasil).
———. 2014. 'A Memória na Luta contra o Trauma: Significados da Greve de Osasco em 1968 nas Narrativas de Trabalhadores' [The memory in the struggle against trauma: Meanings of Osasco's strike of 1968 in the workers' narratives], *Revista Mundos do Trabalho* 6(11): 41–56.
Derrida, J. 2004. 'Je suis en Guerre Contre Moi-Même' [I am at war against myself], *Le Monde*, 19 August. Retrieved 19 September 2016 from http://www.lemonde.fr/archives/article/2004/08/18/jacques-derrida-je-suis-en-guerre-contre-moi-meme_375883_1819218.html.
Di Giulio, G.M., et al. 2015. 'Percepção de Risco: um Campo de Interesse para a Interface Ambiente, Saúde e Sustentabilidade' [Risk perception: A field of interest for the interface between environment, health and sustainability], *Saúde e Sociedade* 24(4): 1217–31.
Douglas, M. 1991. *Come Percepiamo il Rischio: Antropologia del Rischio* [How we perceive the risk: Anthropology of risk]. Milan: Feltrinelli.
Douglas, M., M. Thompson and M. Verweij. 2003. 'Is Time Running Out? The Case of Global Warming', *Daedalus* 132(2): 98–107.
Douglas, M., and A. Wildavsky. 1982. *Risk and Culture: An Essay on the Selection of Technological and Environmental Dangers*. Berkeley: University of California Press.
Elias, N. 1999. *La Solitudine del Morente* [The loneliness of the dying]. Bologna: Il Mulino.
Epstein, A.L. 1958. *Politics in an Urban African Community*. Manchester: Manchester University Press.
Farmer, P. 1996. 'On Suffering and Structural Violence: A View from Below', *Daedalus* 125(1): 261–83.
———. 2005. *Pathologies of Power: Health, Human Rights, and the War on the Poor*. Berkeley: University of California Press.
———. 2013. 'Preface', in P. Farmer et al. (eds), *Reimagining Global Health: An Introduction*. Berkeley: University of California Press, pp. xiii–xxiii.
Farmer, P., et al. (eds). 2013. *Reimagining Global Health: An Introduction*. Berkeley: University of California Press.
Fassin, D. 2006. 'Un Ethos Compassionevole: La Sofferenza come Linguaggio, l'Ascolto come Politica' [A compassionate ethos: The suffering as language, listening as politics], in U. Fabietti (ed.), *Antropologia*. Milan: Ledizioni, pp. 93–109.
———. 2007. *When Bodies Remember: Experiences and Politics of AIDS in South Africa*. Berkeley: University of California Press.
———. 2008. 'The Embodied Past', *Social Anthropology/Anthropologie Sociale* 16(3): 312–28.
———. 2011. 'The Trace: Violence, Truth, and the Politics of the Body', Special Issue 'The Body and the State: How the State Controls and Protects the Body', *Social Research: An International Quarterly* 78(2): 281–98.
——— (ed.). 2012. *A Companion to Moral Anthropology*. Malden, MA: Wiley-Blackwell.
———. 2014a. *Ripoliticizzare il Mondo: Studi Antropologici sulla Vita, il Corpo e la Morale* [Repoliticizing the world: Anthropological studies on life, the body and the moral]. Verona: Ombre Corte.

———. 2014b. 'The Ethical Turn in Anthropology: Promises and Uncertainties', *HAU: Journal of Ethnographic Theory* 4(1): 429–35.
Fassin, D., and R. Rechtman. 2009. *The Empire of Trauma: An Inquiry into the Condition of Victimhood*. Oxford: Princeton University Press.
Ferraro, S. 2015. 'Una Medicina Sociale dell'Amianto: Per un Visibile Segreto e un'Invisibile Verità su Isochimica' [A social medicine of asbestos: For a visible secret and an invisible truth on Isochimica], in A. Petrillo (ed.), *Il Silenzio della Polvere: Capitale, Verità e Morte in una Storia Meridionale di Amianto* [The silence of the dust: Capital, truth and death in a southern story of asbestos]. Milan-Udine: Mimesis Edizioni, pp. 123–59.
FIOCRUZ (Fundação Oswaldo Cruz). 2008. 'Fiocruz Pesquisa os Riscos do Amianto para o Trabalhador' [Fiocruz investigates the asbestos risks for workers]. Retrieved 25 March 2017 from https://portal.fiocruz.br/pt-br/node/2185.
Fonseca, C. 2010. 'O Anonimato e o Texto Antropológico: Dilemas Éticos e Políticos da Etnografia em Casa' [The anonimity and the anthropological text: Ethical and political dilemmas in ethnography at home], in P. Schuch, M.S. Vieira and R. Peters (eds), *Experiências, Dilemas e Desafios do Fazer Etnográfico Contemporâneo* [Experiences, dilemmas and challanges in contemporary ethnography]. Porto Alegre: Universidade Federal de Rio Grande do Sul, pp. 205–27.
Fortun, K. 2001. *Advocacy after Bhopal: Environmentalism, Disaster, New Global Orders*. Chicago: University of Chicago Press.
Foucault, M. 1997. *Ethics: Subjectivity and Truth: Essential Works of Foucault 1954–1984*. Edited by P. Rabinow. New York: The New Press.
———. 2005. *Sicurezza, Territorio, Popolazione: Corso al Collége de France (1977–1978)* [Security, territory, population: Lectures at the Collège de France, 1977–1978]. Milan: Feltrinelli.
Frank, A.L. 2013. 'Why Countries Ban Asbestos: Some Alternative Thoughts', *International Journal of Occupational and Environmental Health* 19(2): 136.
Frank, A.L., and T.K. Joshi. 2014. 'The Global Spread of Asbestos', *Annals of Global Health* 80: 257–62.
Frankenberg, R.J. 1992. 'Preface', in S. Scott et al. (eds), *Private Risks and Public Dangers*. Aldershot: Avebury, pp. xv–xix.
Fraser, N. 1968. 'From Redistribution to Recognition? Dilemmas of Justice in a Post-Socialist Society', *New Left Review* 93: 68–93.
———. 2007. 'Re-framing Justice in a Globalizing World', in T. Lovell (ed.), *(Mis)Recognition, Social Inequality and Social Justice: Nancy Fraser and Pierre Bourdieu*. New York: Routledge, pp. 17–35.
Freire, P. 1967. *Educação como Prática da Liberdade* [Education as practice of freedom]. São Paulo: Cortez.
———. 1970. *Pedagogia do oprimido* [Pedagogy of the oppressed]. Rio de Janeiro: Zahar.
———. 1980. *Conscientização* [Conscientization]. São Paulo: Moraes.
———. 2005. *Pedagogy of the Oppressed. 30th Anniversary Edition*. Translated by M. Bergman Ramos. New York: Continuum.
Freitas, J.B.P. 2001. 'Doença Pleural em Trabalhadores da Indústria do Cimento-Amianto' [Pleural disease in asbestos-cement industry workers]. Master's thesis. São Paulo: FS/USP.

Freyre, G. 1933. *Casa-Grande e Senzala*. Rio de Janeiro: Maia e Schmidt.

FUNDACENTRO (Fundação Jorge Duprat Figueiredo de Segurança e Medicina do Trabalho). 2015. 'Servidores da Fundacentro se Posicionam contra Portaria sobre Uso Seguro do Amianto' [FUNDACENTRO's employees stand against the law on safe use of asbestos]. Retrieved 25 March 2017 from http://www.fundacentro.gov.br/noticias/detalhe-da-noticia/2015/10/servidores-da-fundacentro-se-posicionam-contra-portaria-sobre-uso-seguro-do-amianto.

Galeano, E. 1989. *El Libro de los Abrazos* [The book of embraces]. Madrid: Siglo XXI Editores.

Geertz, C. 1973. 'Thick Description: Toward an Interpretive Theory of Culture', in C. Geertz (ed.), *The Interpretation of Cultures: Selected Essays*. New York: Basic Books, pp. 3–30.

Giannasi, F. 2012. 'Eternit in Brazil', in D. Allen and L. Kazan-Allen (eds), *Eternit and the Great Asbestos Trial*. London: Justasec Print Services Ltd, pp. 65–71.

———. 2017. 'Amianto Mata' [Asbestos kills], *Trabalho & Saúde* 42: 11–16.

Giannasi, F., and A. Thébaud-Mony. 1997. 'Occupational Exposures to Asbestos in Brazil', *International Journal of Occupational and Environmental Health* 3: 150–57.

Giannotti, V. 2007. *A História das Lutas dos Trabalhadores no Brasil* [The history of workers' struggles in Brazil]. Rio de Janeiro: Mauad X.

Gluckman, M. 1960. 'Tribalism in Modern British Central Africa', *Cahiers d'Études Africaines* 1: 55–70.

Gohn, M.G. 1997. *Teorias dos Movimentos Sociais: Paradigmas Clássicos e Contemporâneos* [Theories of social movements: Classic and contemporary paradigms]. São Paulo: Loyola.

Goldberg, M., and D. Luce. 2009. 'The Health Impact of Nonoccupational Exposure to Asbestos: What Do We Know?', *European Journal of Cancer Prevention* 18(6): 489–503.

Good, B.J. 1994. *Medicine, Rationality and Experience: An Anthropological Perspective*. Cambridge: Cambridge University Press.

———. 1999. *Narrare la Malattia: Lo Sguardo Antropologico sul Rapporto Medico-Paziente* [Narrating the illness: The anthropological glance on the doctor–patient relationship]. Turin: Edizioni di Comunità.

Goodwin, J., J.M. Jasper and F. Polletta. 2000. 'The Return of the Repressed: The Fall and Rise of Emotions in Social Movement Theory', *Mobilization: An International Quarterly* 5(1): 65–83.

——— (eds). 2001. *Passionate Politics: Emotions and Social Movements*. Chicago: University of Chicago Press.

Gordon, D. 1991. 'Culture, Cancer and Communication in Italy', in B. Pfleiderer and G. Bibeau (eds), *Anthropologies of Medicine: A Colloquium on West European and North American Perspectives*. Heidelberg: Vieweg, pp. 137–56.

Gould, D.B. 2009. *Moving Politics: Emotion and ACT UP's Fight Against AIDS*. Chicago: University of Chicago Press.

Gramsci, A. 1975. *Quaderni del Carcere* [The prison notebooks]. Turin: Einaudi.

Gregg, M., and G.J. Seigworth (eds). 2010. *The Affect Theory Reader*. London: Duke University Press.

Grenfell, M., and F. Lebaron (eds). 2014. *Bourdieu and Data Analysis: Methodological Principles and Practice*. Bern: Peter Lang.

Gutiérrez, G. 1972. *Teologia de la Liberación* [Theology of liberation]. Salamanca: Sígueme.

———. 2007. *The Task and Content of Liberation Theology* (translated by Judith Condor), in C. Rowland (ed.), *The Cambridge Companion to Liberation Theology*. Cambridge: Cambridge University Press, pp. 19–38.

Hahn, R.A., and M.C. Inhorn. 2009. *Anthropology and Public Health: Bridging Differences in Culture and Society*. New York: Oxford University Press.

Halbwachs, M. 1987. *La Memoria Collettiva* [The collective memory]. Milan: Unicopli.

Hobson, B. 2003. *Recognition Struggles and Social Movements: Cultural Claims, Contested Identities, Power and Agency*. Cambridge: Cambridge University Press.

Hoffman, S.M., and A. Oliver-Smith (eds). 2002. *Catastrophe & Culture: The Anthropology of Disaster*. Santa Fe, NM: School of American Research Press.

Hofrichter, R. 1993. *Toxic Struggles: The Theory and Practice of Environmental Justice*. Philadelphia, PA: New Society Publishers.

——— (ed.). 2003a. *Health and Social Justice: Politics, Ideology and Inequity in the Distribution of Disease*. San Francisco: Jossey-Bass.

———. 2003b. 'The Politics of Health Inequalities: Contested Terrain', in R. Hofrichter (ed.), *Health and Social Justice: Politics, Ideology and Inequity in the Distribution of Disease*. San Francisco: Jossey-Bass, pp. 1–56.

Holston, J. 2008. *Insurgent Citizenship: Disjunctions of Democracy and Modernity in Brazil*. Princeton, NJ: Princeton University Press.

IARC (International Agency for Research on Cancer). 2012. 'Asbestos (chrysotile, mosite, crocidolite, tremolite, actinolite and anthophyllite)', in IARC (ed.), *Metals, Arsenic, Dusts, and Fibres: A Review of Human Carcinogens (Monograph on the Evaluation of Carcinogenic Risks to Humans, 100C)*. Lyon: IARC, pp. 219–309.

INAIL (Istituto Nazionale Assicurazione Infortuni sul Lavoro). 2018. *Il Registro Nazionale dei Mesoteliomi: VI Rapporto* [The national register of Mesotheliomas: VI report]. Milan: Tipolitografia Inail.

Inhorn, M.C. 1995. 'Medical Anthropology and Epidemiology: Divergences or Convergences?', *Social Science and Medicine* 40(3): 285–90.

Iocca, G. 2011. *Casale Monferrato: La Polvere che Uccide. Voci dalla Chernobyl Italiana* [Casale Monferrato: The dust that kills. Voices from the Italian Chernobyl]. Rome: Ediesse.

Jasper, J.M. 1998. 'The Emotions of Protest: Affective and Reactive Emotions in and around Social Movements', *Sociological Forum* 13(3): 397–424.

Jobin, P. 2013. 'The Criminalization of Industrial Disease: Epidemiology in a Japanese Asbestos Lawsuit', in R. Peckham (ed.), *Disease and Crime: A History of Social Pathologies and the New Politics of Health*. London: Routledge, pp. 129–50.

Johnston, R., and A.J. McIvor. 2000. *Lethal Work: A History of the Asbestos Tragedy in Scotland*. Edinburgh: John Donald.

Jonas, H. 1985. *The Imperative of Responsibility: In search of an Ethics for the Technological Age*. Chicago: University of Chicago Press.

Kazan-Allen, L. 2003. 'The Asbestos War', *International Journal of Occupational and Environmental Health* 9(3): 173–93.
———. 2019a. 'Current Asbestos Bans', retrieved 29 February 2020 from http://ibasecretariat.org/alpha_ban_list.php.
———. 2019b. 'Report from Asian Ban Asbestos Mission to Brazil, April 2019', retrieved 29 February 2020 from http://www.ibasecretariat.org/lka-status-report-from-asian-ban-asbestos-mission-to-brazil-apr-24-2019.php.
Klawiter, M. 2004. 'Breast Cancer in Two Regimes: The Impact of Social Movements on Illness Experience', *Sociology of Health & Illness* 26(6): 845–74.
———. 2008. *The Biopolitics of Breast Cancer: Changing Cultures of Disease and Activism*. Minneapolis: University of Minnesota Press.
Kleinman, A. 1980. *Patients and Healers in the Context of Culture: An Exploration of the Borderland between Anthropology, Medicine, and Psychiatry*. Berkeley: University of California Press.
———. 1995. *Writing at the Margin: Discourse between Anthropology and Medicine*. Berkeley: University of California Press.
———. 1997 '"Everything That Really Matters": Social Suffering, Subjectivity, and the Remaking of Human Experience in a Disordering World', *The Harvard Theological Review* 90(3): 315–35.
———. 1999. 'Moral Experience and Ethical Reflection: Can Ethnography Reconcile Them? A Quandary for the New Bioethics', *Daedalus* 128(4): 69–97.
———. 2006. *What Really Matters: Living a Moral Life Amidst Uncertainty and Danger*. New York: Oxford University Press.
———. 2009. 'Caregiving: The Odyssey of Becoming More Human', *The Lancet* 373: 292–93.
———. 2012. 'Caregiving as Moral Experience', *The Lancet* 380(3): 1550–51.
Kleinman, A., V. Das and M. Lock (eds). 1997. *Social Suffering*. Berkeley: University of California Press.
Kleinman, A., and B. Hanna. 2011. 'Religious Values and Global Health', in D.K. Swearer and S. Lloyd McGarry (eds), *Ecologies of Human Flourishing*. Cambridge: Harvard University Press.
Kleinman, A., and J. Kleinman. 1991. 'Suffering and its Professional Transformation: Toward an Ethnography of Interpersonal Experience', *Culture, Medicine and Psychiatry* 15(3): 275–301.
Kleinman, S., and M.A. Copp. 1993. *Emotions and Fieldwork*. Newbury Park: Sage Publications.
Koensler, A., and A. Rossi (eds). 2012. *Comprendere il Dissenso: Etnografia e Antropologia dei Movimenti Sociali* [Understanding the dissent: Ethnography and anthropology of social movements]. Perugia: Morlacchi Editore.
Krieger, N. 2003. 'Theories for Social Epidemiology in the 21st Century', in R. Hofrichter (ed.), *Health and Social Justice: Politics, Ideology, and Inequity in the Distribution of Disease*. San Francisco: Jossey-Bass, pp. 428–50.
Kuhn, T.S. 1963. *The Structure of Scientific Revolutions*. Chicago: University of Chicago Press.
LaDou, J., et al. 2010. 'The Case for a Global Ban on Asbestos', *Environmental Health Perspective* 118: 897–901.
Leavitt, J. 1996. 'Meaning and Feeling in the Anthropology of Emotions', *American Ethnologist* 23(3): 514–39.

Lemes, C. 2020, 'Advogados Condenam Eternit por Voltar a Processar Amianto: "Gravíssimo; Acinte às Decisões do STF". E agora, Ministro Alexandre de Moraes?' [Lawyers condemn eternit for returning to process asbestos: 'Very serious; it doesn't comply with STF decisions'. And now, Minister Alexandre de Moraes?], *Viomundo*, 13 February. Retrieved 29 February 2020 from https://www.viomundo.com.br/denuncias/advogados-condenam-eternit-por-voltar-a-processar-amianto-gravissimo-acinte-as-decisoes-do-stf-e-agora-ministro-alexandre-de-moraes.html.

Ligi, G. 2009. *Antropologia dei Disastri* [Anthropology of disasters]. Rome/Bari: Laterza.

———. 2011a. 'Valori Culturali del Paesaggio e Antropologia dei Disastri' [Cultural values of the landscape and anthropology of disasters], *La Ricerca Folklorica* 64: 119–29.

———. 2011b. 'Emotions and Knowledge in the Anthropology of Disasters', in M. Benadusi, C. Brambilla and B. Riccio (eds), *Disasters, Development and Humanitarian Aid: New Challenges for Anthropology*. Rimini: Guaraldi, pp. 47–64.

Lispector, C. 1999. *A Descoberta do Mundo* [The discovery of the world]. Rio de Janeiro: Rocco.

Lock, M. 1993. 'Cultivating the Body: Anthropology and Epistemologies of Bodily Practice and Knowledge', *Annual Review of Anthropology* 22: 133–55.

Lock, M., and N. Scheper-Hughes. 1990. 'A Critical-Interpretive Approach in Medical Anthropology: Rituals and Routines of Discipline and Dissent', *Medical Anthropology: Contemporary Theory and Method* 3: 47–73.

Low, S.M. 1997. 'Urban Fear: Building the Fortress City', *City & Society* 9(1): 53–71.

Lupton, D. 1999. *Risk and Sociocultural Theory: New Directions and Perspectives*. Cambridge: Cambridge University Press.

Lutz, C., and G.M. White. 1986. 'The Anthropology of Emotions', *Annual Review of Anthropology* 15: 405–36.

Mack, A. 2011. 'Introduction', Special Issue 'The Body and the State: How the State Controls and Protects the Body', *Social Research: An International Quarterly* 78(2): xvii–xviii.

Magnani, C., et al. 1987. 'Mortalità per Tumori ed Altre Malattie del Sistema Respiratorio tra i Lavoratori del Cemento-Amianto a Casale Monferrato: Uno Studio di Coorte Storico' [Mortality for tumours and other respiratory system diseases among asbestos-cement workers in Casale Monferrato: A historical cohort study], *La Medicina del Lavoro* 78: 411–53.

Marcus, G.E. 1995. 'Ethnography in/of the World System: The Emergence of Multi-sited Ethnography', *Annual Review of Anthropology* 24: 95–117.

Marquetti Rocha Negrelli, A.L., and N. Collino de Oliveira. 2003. *Osasco e Seus Imigrantes: Uma Volta ao Passado* [Osasco and its immigrants: Back to the past]. Osasco: Scortecci Editora.

Marsili, D., et al. 2016. 'Prevention of Asbestos-Related Disease in Countries Currently Using Asbestos', *International Journal of Environmental Research and Public Health* 13(494): 1–19.

Martins Rodrigues, L. 1974. *Trabalhadores, Sindicatos e Industrialização* [Workers, unions and industrialization]. São Paulo: Editora Brasilense.

Massumi, B. 2002. *Parables for the Virtual: Movement, Affect, Sensation*. Durham, NC: Duke University Press Books.
Mauss, M. 1973. 'Techniques of the Body', *Economy and Society* 2(1): 70–88.
Mayer, P. 1961. *Townsmen or Tribesmen*. Cape Town: Oxford University Press for the Rhodes University Institute of Social and Economic Research.
Mazzeo, A. 2014. 'Contaminazione, Coinvolgimento, Impegno: Riflessioni su una ricerca di antropologia medica in contesti urbani affetti da disastri ambientali e sociali provocati dalla lavorazione del cemento-amianto in Italia' [Contamination, engagement, commitment: Reflections on a medical anthropological study in urban contexts affected by environmental and social disasters caused by asbestos-cement manufacturing in Italy], in A.L. Palmisano (ed.), *Antropologia Applicata* [Applied anthropology]. San Cesario di Lecce: Pensa Editore, pp. 217–50.
———. 2017a. 'Disastri Invisibili e Pratiche di Attivismo' [Invisible disasters and practices of activism], Special Issue 'Salute e Ambiente: Etnografie Italiane' [Health and environment: Italian ethnographies], *Antropologia* 4(1): 203–19.
———. 2017b. 'Movements and Militant Memory'. Doctoral dissertation. University of Bologna and University of São Paulo.
———. 2018a. 'The Temporalities of Asbestos Mining and Community Activism', *The Extractive Industries and Society: An International Journal* 5: 223–29.
———. 2018b. 'L'impatto dell'esposizione all'amianto su comunità di lavoratori e residenti in Italia e Brasile' [The impact of asbestos exposure on workers and residents' communities in Italy and Brazil], in C. Minoia and P. Comba (eds), *Amianto: Un Fantasma del Passato o una Storia Infinita?* [Asbestos: A ghost from the past or an endless story?]. Cermenate: New Press Edizioni, pp. 467–81.
———. 2018c. '"Care-Activism" in Asbestos Contaminated Communities', in I. Quaranta, M. Minelli and S. Fortin (eds), *Assemblages, Transformations, and the Politics of Care*. Bologna: Bononia University Press, pp. 93–111.
———. 2019. 'Narrating and Remembering as Practices of Care, Community and Commitment in Asbestos Contaminated Contexts', *Annali dell'Istituto Superiore di Sanità* 55(1): 94–99.
McCulloch, J. 2006. 'Saving the Asbestos Industry, 1960 to 2006', *Public Health Report* 121(5): 609–14.
Mead, M. 1972. *Blackberry Winter: My Earlier Years*. New York: William Morrow and Company.
Mercier, P. 2015. *Trem Noturno para Lisboa* [Night train to Lisbon]. Rio de Janeiro: BestBolso.
Merleau-Ponty, M. 1945. *Phénoménologie de la Perception* [Phenomenology of perception]. Paris: Gallimard.
Michaels, D. 2008. *Doubt Is Their Product: How Industry's Assault on Science Threatens Your Health*. Oxford: Oxford University Press.
Milanez, B., et al. (eds). 2013. 'Injustiça Ambiental, Mineração e Siderurgia' [Environmental injustice, mining industry and siderurgy], in M.F. Porto, T. Pacheco and J.P. Leroy (eds), *Injustiça Ambiental e Saúde no Brasil: O Mapa dos Conflitos* [Environmental injustice and health in Brazil: The map of conflicts]. Rio de Janeiro: Editora Fiocruz, pp. 175–206.

Ministério da Saúde. 2016. 'Doenças Relacionadas ao Asbesto na Saúde do Trabalhador, Brasil, 2007–2013' [Asbestos-related diseases in occupational health, Brazil, 2007–2013], *Boletim Epidemiológico* 47(4): 1–8.

Mitchell, J.C. 1960. *Tribalism and the Plural Society: Inaugural Lecture at the University College of Rhodesia and Nyasaland*. London: Oxford University Press.

Mol, A. 2008. *The Logic of Care: Health and the Problem of Patient Choice*. New York: Routledge.

Mossano, S. 2010. *Malapolvere: Una Città si Ribella ai Signori dell'Amianto* [Bad dust: A city rises against the lords of asbestos]. Casale Monferrato: Edizioni Sonda.

MTC (Movimento de Trabalhadores Cristãos) (ed.). 2001. *Jesus: Sua Terra, Seu Povo, Sua Proposta* [Jesus: His land, His people, His proposal]. 8th edition. Rio de Janeiro: REPROARTE Gráfica.

Musti, M., et al. 2009. 'The Relationship between Malignant Mesothelioma and an Asbestos-Cement Plant Environmental Risk: A Spatial Case-Control Study in the City of Bari (Italy)', *International Archives of Occupational and Environmental Health* 82(4): 489–97.

Negri, A., and G. Cocco. 2006. *Global: Biopotere e Lotte in America Latina* [Global: Biopower and struggles in Latin America]. Rome: Manifestolibri.

Negri, A., and M. Hardt. 1999. 'Value and Affect', *Boundary* 2(26): 77–88.

Nguyen, V.K. 2008. 'Antiretroviral Globalism, Biopolitics, and Therapeutic Citizenship', in A. Ong and S.J. Collier (eds), *Global Assemblages*. Oxford: Blackwell, pp. 124–44.

Nguyen V.K., et al. 2007. 'Adherence as Therapeutic Citizenship: Impact of the History of Access to Antiretroviral Drugs on Adherence to Treatment', *AIDS* 21(5): S31–S35.

Nixon, R. 2011. *Slow Violence and the Environmentalism of the Poor*. Cambridge, MA: Harvard University Press.

Nogueira D.P., et al. 1975. 'Asbestose no Brasil: Um Risco Ignorado' [Asbestosis in Brazil: An ignored risk], *Revista de Saúde Publica* 9: 427–32.

Novello, C. 2012. *O Amianto e o Passivo Ambiental da Mineração no Brasil: O Mal do Século XX* [Asbestos and environmental liabilities of the mining industry in Brazil: The evil of the twentieth century]. Doctoral dissertation. Rio de Janeiro: ENSP/FIOCRUZ.

Novello, C. and H.A. de Castro 2010. *O Amianto no Brasil: Controle Sociale na Vigilância* [The Asbestos in Brazil: Social Control in the Vigilance], in M. I. Souza Bravo, V. D'Acri, and J. Bilate Martins (eds.), *Movimentos Sociais, Saúde e Trabalho* [Social Movements, Health, and Labour]. Rio de Janeiro: ENSP/FIOCRUZ, pp. 209-27.

Oreskes, N., and E.M. Conway. 2010. *Merchants of Doubt: How a Handful of Scientists Obscured the Truth on Issues from Tobacco Smoke to Global Warming*. New York: Bloomsbury.

Paim, J.S. 2008. *Reforma Sanitária Brasileira: Contribuições para a Compreensão Crítica* [Brazilian health reform: Contribution for a critical understanding]. Rio de Janeiro: FIOCRUZ.

Pandolfi, M. 2003. 'Le Arene Politiche del Corpo' [The political arenas of the body], *Antropologia* 3(3): 141–54.

Park, E.K., et al. 2011. 'Global Magnitude of Reported and Unreported Mesothelioma', *Environmental Health Perspective* 119: 514–18.

Parkhill, K.A., et al. 2010. 'From the Familiar to the Extraordinary: Local Residents' Perceptions of Risk when Living with Nuclear Power in the UK', *Transactions of the Institute of British Geographers* 35(1): 39–58.

Pasetto, R., et al. 2014. 'Occupational Burden of Asbestos-Related Cancer in Argentina, Brazil, Colombia and Mexico', *Annals of Global Health* 80: 263–68.

Pellegrini, M. 2014. 'Violência: Brasil Mata 82 Jovens por Dia' [Violence: Brazil kills 82 young people per day], *CartaCapital*, 4 December. Retrieved 22 March 2017 from https://www.cartacapital.com.br/sociedade/violencia-brasil-mata-82-jovens-por-dia-5716.html.

Petrillo, A. (ed.). 2015. *Il Silenzio della Polvere: Capitale, Verità e Morte in una Storia Meridionale di Amianto* [The silence of the dust: Capital, truth and death in a southern story of asbestos]. Milan: Mimesis Edizioni.

Petryna, A. 2002. *Life Exposed: Biological Citizens after Chernobyl*. Princeton, NJ: Princeton University Press.

Piasere, L. 2002. *L'Etnografo Imperfetto: Esperienza e Cognizione in Antropologia* [The imperfect ethnographer: Experience and cognition in anthropology]. Rome: Laterza.

Pigg, S.L. 2013. 'On Sitting and Doing: Ethnography as Action in Global Health', *Social Science & Medicine* 99: 127–34.

Pignatari Werner, H. 1981. *Raízes do Movimento Operário em Osasco* [Roots of the workers' movement in Osasco]. São Paulo: Cortez.

Pizza, G. 2007. *Antropologia Medica: Saperi, Pratiche e Politiche del Corpo* [Medical anthropology: Knowledges, practices, and politics of the body]. Rome: Carocci.

Polletta, F. 1998a. 'Contending Stories: Narrative in Social Movements', *Qualitative Sociology* 21(4): 419–46.

———. 1998b. '"It Was Like A Fever…": Narrative and Identity in Social Protest', *Social Problems* 45(2): 137–59.

Polletta, F., and J.M. Jasper. 2001. 'Collective Identity and Social Movements', *Annual Review of Sociology* 27: 283–305.

Polo, M. 1496. *Delle Meravigliose Cose del Mondo* [The book of the marvels of the world]. Venice: Giovanni Battista Sessa.

Porto, M.F., T. Pacheco and J.P. Leroy (eds). 2013. *Injustiça Ambiental e Saúde no Brasil: O Mapa de Conflitos* [Environmental injustice and health in Brazil: The map of conflicts]. Rio de Janeiro: Editora FIOCRUZ.

Prüss-Ustün, A., et al. 2011. 'Knowns and Unknowns on Burden of Disease due to Chemicals: A Systematic Review', *Environmental Health* 10(9): 1–15.

Pussetti, C. 2005. 'Introduzione' [Introduction]. Special Issue 'Discorsi sull'Emozione' [Discourses on Emotion], *Antropologia* 5(6): 5–14.

Putnam, R.D. 1993. 'The Prosperous Community: Social Capital and Public Life', *American Prospective* 13: 35–42.

Quaranta, I. 1999. 'Costruzione e Negoziazione Sociale di una Sindrome: Un'Indagine Antropologica sul Contenzioso intorno alla Chronic Fatigue Sindrome (CFS) nel Regno Unito' [Construction and social negotiation of a syndrome: An anthropological investigation on the controversy about the Chronic Fatigue Syndrome (CFS) in the United Kingdom], *AM Rivista della Società Italiana di Antropologia Medica* 7–8: 129–72.

——— (ed.). 2006a. *Antropologia Medica: I Testi Fondamentali* [Medical anthropology: The fundamental texts]. Milan: Cortina Editore.

———. 2006b. *Corpo, Potere e Malattia: Antropologia e AIDS nei Grassfields del Camerun* [Body, power and disease: Anthropology and AIDS in the grassfields of Cameroon]. Rome: Meltemi.

———. 2006c. 'Introduzione' [Introduction]. Special Issue 'Sofferenza Sociale' [Social suffering], *Antropologia* 6(8): 5–15.

———. 2012a. 'From the Communication of Information to the Production of Meaning as a Strategy for Promoting the Right to Health', *RECIIS* 6(2): 1–15.

———. 2012b. 'La Malattia e l'Incorporazione Individuale dei Processi Sociali: Il Contributo dell'Antropologia' [The disease and the individual embodiement of social processes: The contribution of anthropology], in V. Lagioia (ed.), *Storie di Invisibili, Marginali ed Esclusi* [Stories of invisible, marginal and excluded]. Bologna: Bononia University Press, pp. 263–74.

Rabinow, P. 1992. 'Studies in the Anthropology of Reason', *Anthropology Today* 8(5): 7–10.

Raile, V. 2008. 'Asbesto y Medio Ambiente No Ocupacional. Presentación de Datos Preliminares de Alteraciones Radiológicas en Cónyuges de Ex Trabajadores de uma Industria de Fibrocemento del Municipio de Osasco' [Asbestos and non-occupational environment: Presentation of preliminary data of radiological alterations in the wives of former workers in an asbestos-cement plant in the municipality of Osasco], *Ciencia & Trabajo* 10(28): 57–62.

Raile, V., and S.B. Markowitz. 2011. 'Enfermedades Pulmonares No Malignas entre Obreros del Cemento-Asbesto en Brasil: un Estudio de Prevalencia' [Non-malignant lung disabilities among asbestos-cement workers in Brazil: A prevalence study], *Ciencia & Trabalho* 13(40): 65–71.

Rawls, J. 1971. *A Theory of Social Justice*. Cambridge, MA: Belknap.

Renn, O. 2008. *Risk Governance: Coping with Uncertainty in a Complex World*. London: Earthscan.

Ribeiro, D. 2006. *O Povo Brasileiro: A Formação e o Sentido do Brasil* [The Brazilian people: The formation and meaning of Brazil]. São Paulo: Companhia das Letras.

Ribeiro Corossacz, V. 2004. *Il Corpo della Nazione: Classificazione Razziale e Gestione Sociale della Riproduzione in Brasile* [The body of the nation: Racial classification and social management of reproduction in Brazil]. Rome: CISU.

———. 2005. *Razzismo, Meticciato, Democrazia Razziale: Le Politiche della Razza in Brasile* [Racism, mixed race, racial democracy: The politics of race in Brazil]. Soveria Mannelli: Rubbettino.

Rosaldo, M. 1984. 'Toward an Anthropology of Self and Feeling', in A.R. LeVine and A.R. Shweder (eds), *Culture Theory: Essays on Mind, Self and Emotion*. Cambridge: Cambridge University Press, pp. 135–57.

Rose, N. 2007. *The Politics of Life Itself: Biomedicine, Power, and Subjectivity in the Twenty-First Century*. Princeton, NJ: Princeton University Press.

Roselli, M. 2010. *La Mentira del Amianto: Fortunas y Delitos* [The lie of asbestos: Good fortunes and murders]. Malaga: Ediciones del Genal.

Rossi, A., and L. D'Angelo. 2012. *Antropologia, Risorse Naturali e Conflitti Ambientali* [Anthropology, natural resources, and environmental conflicts]. Milan: Mimesis.
Rossi, G. 2008. *La Lana della Salamandra: La Vera Storia della Strage dell'Amianto a Casale Monferrato* [The salamander's wool: The true story of the massacre of asbestos in Casale Monferrato]. Rome: Ediesse.
———. 2012. *Amianto: Processo alle Fabbriche della Morte* [Asbestos: Trial to the factories of death]. Milan: Melampo.
Rowland, C. (ed.). 2007. *The Cambridge Companion to Liberation Theology*. Cambridge: Cambridge University Press.
Saitta, P. 2013. *Quota Zero. Messina dopo il Terremoto: La Ricostruzione Infinita* [Quota Zero. Messina after the earthquake: The endless reconstruction]. Rome: Donzelli.
Sanazar, H. 2000. *Osasco, Sua História, Sua Gente* [Osasco, its history, its people]. Osasco: Gráfica Benfica.
Santos, M. 1993. *A Urbanização Brasileira* [The Brazilian urbanization]. São Paulo: HUCITEC.
Scarry, E. 1985. *The Body in Pain: The Making and Unmaking of the World*. New York: Oxford University Press.
Scheper-Hughes, N. 1992. *Death without Weeping: The Violence of Everyday Life in Brazil*. Berkeley: University of California Press.
———. 1994. 'Embodied Knowledge: Thinking with the Body in Critical Medical Anthropology', in R. Borofsky (ed.), *Assessing Cultural Anthropology*. New York: MacGraw-Hill, pp. 229–42.
———. 1995. 'The Primacy of the Ethical: Propositions for a Militant Anthropology', *Current Anthropology* 36(3): 409–40.
———. 1997. 'Demography Without Numbers', in D.I. Ketzer and T. Fricke (eds), *Anthropological Demography: Toward a New Synthesis*. Chicago: University of Chicago Press, pp. 201–22.
Scheper-Hughes, N., and P. Bourgois (eds). 2004. *Violence in War and Peace: An Anthology*. Oxford: Blackwell.
Scheper-Hughes, N., and M. Lock. 1987. 'The Mindful Body: A Prolegomenon to Future Work in Medical Anthropology', *Medical Anthropology Quarterly* 1(1): 6–41.
Schwarcz, L.M., and H.M. Starling (eds). 2015. *Brasil: Uma Biografia* [Brazil: A biography]. São Paulo: Companhia das Letras.
Selikoff I.J., J. Churg and E.C. Hammond. 1964. 'Asbestos Exposure and Neoplasia', *JAMA Journal of American Medical Association* 188(1): 22–26.
———. 1965. 'Relation between Exposure to Asbestos and Mesothelioma', *New England Journal of Medicine* 272(11): 560–65.
Semeraro, G. 2007. 'Da Libertação à Hegemonia: Freire e Gramsci no Processo de Democratização do Brasil' [From liberation to hegemony: Freire and Gramsci in the process of democratization of Brazil], *Revista de Sociologia Política* 29: 95–104.
Sen, A. 2000. *Development as Freedom*. New York: Anchor Books.
Shouse, E. 2005. 'Feeling, Emotion, Affect', *M/C Journal* 8(6).
Slovic, P. 2010. 'The Psychology of Risk', *Saúde e Sociedade* 19(4): 731–47.

Sontag, S. 1990. *On Photography*. New York: Anchor.

Souza Bravo, M.I., V. D'Acri and J. Bilate Martins (eds). 2010. *Movimentos Sociais, Saúde e Trabalho* [Social movements, health and labour]. Rio de Janeiro: ENSP/FIOCRUZ.

Spradley, J.P. 1979. *The Ethnographic Interview*. New York: Holt, Rinehart and Winston.

Suri, A., et al. 2013. 'Values and Global Health', in P. Farmer et al. (eds), *Reimagining Global Health: An Introduction*. Berkeley: University of California Press, pp. 245–86.

Tassan, M. 2012. 'Le Riserve Estrattiviste in Brasile: La Cogestione delle Risorse Forestali in una Prospettiva Socioambientalista' [The exctractivist reservoirs in Brazil: The co-management of forestal resources in a socioenvironmentalist perspective], in A. Rossi and L. D'Angelo (eds), *Antropologia, Risorse Naturali e Conflitti Ambientali* [Anthropology, natural resources, and environmental conflicts]. Milan: Mimesis, pp. 129–54.

Taussig, M.T. 1980. 'Reification and the Consciousness of the Patient', *Social Science & Medicine* 12: 85–93.

Terracini, B. 2005. 'Development of Environmental Epidemiology in Latin America: Scope, Methodological Issues, Priorities', *International Journal of Epidemiology* 34: 485–87.

———. 2006. 'Additional Features of the Worldwide Double Standards in the Prevention of Asbestos-Related Diseases', *Annali dell'Istituto Superiore di Sanità* 42(2): 174–77.

Terracini, B., and D. Mirabelli. 2016. 'Asbestos and Product Defence Science', *International Journal of Epidemiology* 45(3): 614–18.

Terracini, B., F. Pedra and U. Otero. 2015. 'Asbestos-Related Cancers in Brazil', *Cadernos de Saúde Pública* 31(5): 903–5.

Throop, C.J. 2012. 'Moral Sentiments', in D. Fassin (ed.), *A Companion to Moral Anthropology*. Malden, MA: Wiley-Blackwell, pp. 150–68.

Tsing, A.L. 2005. *Friction: An Ethnography of Global Connections*. Princeton, NJ: Princeton University Press.

US Geological Survey. 2017. 'Mineral Commodity Summaries', retrieved 21 March 2017 from https://minerals.usgs.gov/minerals/pubs/commodity/asbestos/.

Wacquant, L. 1993. 'Urban Outcasts: Stigma and Division in the Black American Ghetto and the French Urban Periphery', *International Journal of Urban and Regional Research* 17(3): 366–83.

———. 1994. 'Retorno do Recalcado: Violência Urbana, "Raça" e Dualizaçâo em Três Sociedades Avançadas' [The return of the repressed: Urban violence, 'race', and dualization in three advanced societies], *Revista Brasileira de Ciências Sociais* 24: 16–30.

———. 1999. 'Urban Marginality in the Coming Millennium', *Urban Studies* 36(10): 1639–47.

———. 2008. 'The Militarization of Urban Marginality: Lessons from the Brazilian Metropolis', *International Political Sociology* 2: 56–74.

Waldman, L. 2007. 'Evaluating Science and Risk: Living with and Dying from Asbestos', *IDS Bulletin* 38(5): 36–49.

———. 2009. '"Show Me The Evidence": Mobilisation, Citizenship and Risk in Indian Asbestos Issues', *IDS Working Papers* 329: 1–48.

———. 2011. *The Politics of Asbestos: Understanding of Risk, Disease and Protest*. London: Earthscan.

WHO (World Health Organization). 2018. 'Asbestos: Elimination of Asbestos-Related Diseases', Fact Sheet, 15 February.

Wikan, U. 1992. 'Beyond the Words: The Power of Resonance', *American Ethnologist* 19(3): 460–82.

Wilkinson, I., and A. Kleinman. 2016. *A Passion for Society: How We Think about Human Suffering*. Berkeley: University of California Press.

Zampolin Coelho, M.I., and H.M. Moreti. 2005. *Osasco: História e Identidade* [Osasco: History and identity]. Osasco: Fito.

Zhang, E.Y. 2012. 'Mourning', in D. Fassin (ed.), *A Companion to Moral Anthropology*. Malden, MA: Wiley-Blackwell, pp. 264–82.

Zoller, H.M. 2005. 'Health Activism: Communication Theory and Action for Social Change', *Communication Theory* 4: 341–64.

Zona, A., et al. (eds). 2016. 'SENTIERI – Epidemiological Study of Residents in National Priority Contaminated Sites: Incidence of Mesothelioma', *Epidemiologia e Prevenzione* 40(5): 1–116.

Index

affect(s), 13, 14, 17, 22, 72
Agù, Antonio, 3, 6, 50–51, 61, 127
Algranti, Eduardo, 116
Amiantus S.A. (firm), 32
anarchism, 60–61
  anarchosyndicalism, 60
Angela, 1
Appadurai, Arjun, 113–14, 119
Área de Saúde Ocupacional (ASO), Universidade de Campinas (UNICAMP) [Occupational Health Department, University of Campinas], 110
asbestos
  ban, 160
  chrysotile, 29, 31, 48n1, 115, 117, 129, 160
  contamination, 2, 6, 16, 23, 32, 40, 45, 95, 136
  'controlled use of', 108, 114–16, 128–29, 155
  prohibition, 6, 17, 41, 48n1–2, 70, 106–08, 116–19, 125, 130–32, 135, 142, 158–59, 161
asbestos exposure, 2, 11, 24, 28, 37, 41–43, 45, 47, 59, 65, 75, 86, 99, 108, 113, 115, 122, 124
  domestic exposure, 2, 38–39, 59
  environmental exposure, 1, 13, 20, 74, 141
  occupational exposure, 13, 38, 85, 108–09, 113–14, 121
asbestosis, 12, 21, 42, 45–46, 67, 83–86, 104, 110, 112–15
Associação Nacional dos Procuradores do Trabalho (ANPT) [National Association of Labour Attorneys], 160
Associação Recreativa dos Colaboradores Eternit (ARCE) [Recreational Association of Eternit Collaborators], 118
Associazione Familiari e Vittime Amianto (AFeVA) [Asbestos Victims and Relatives Association], 2, 4, 126–27, 160
Associazione Italiana Esposti Amianto (AIEA) [Italian Association of Persons Exposed to Asbestos], 126, 128
Avellino (city), 10
awareness campaigns, 9, 18, 23, 81–82, 87, 98, 100, 112, 117, 123, 126, 149, 161

Baer, Jean, 32
Bagnoli (city), 25n1
Balangero (mine), 30–31
Ban Asbestos Network (BAN), 128
Barbé, Domingos, 68–69. *See also* worker-priests
Bari (city), 1–2, 45, 94, 143–44, 158
Barros Filho (neighbourhood), 82
Base Ecclesial Communities (BECs), 63, 68–70
Basilico, Matthew, 145
'Bastamianto' (seminar), 126, 128
Beatriz, 90–98
Beauchamp, Dan E., 136, 142
Belgian Cimenteries & Briqueteries Réunies S.A. (firm), 32
biosocial bonds, 95

biosocial connections, 66
biosocial relationships, 159
biosocial condition, 13, 120–21, 133
Bobicasa (firm), 33
body, 12
bodily experiences, 6, 15, 135
bodily practices, 12
bodily struggle, 14, 18
bodily suffering, 105–6
suffering body, 13–14, 23, 103, 105–6, 154
Boletim Epidemiológico, 39
Bologna (city), 2
Bom Jesus da Serra (town), 18, 31
Bourdieu, Pierre, 15–16
and Loïc Wacquant, 15, 133n1
Bras (station), 86
Brasilia (city), 161
Brasilit S.A. (firm), 31, 66
Braun, Lundy, 10
and Sophia Kisting, 10
Bullard, Robert D., 134n2
and Glenn S. Johnson, 134n2
Butler, Judith, 101

Calvino, Italo, 30–31
Campania (region), 10
Campinas (city), 39, 131
Cana Brava (mine), 31–32, 160
cancer (experience), 1, 12, 77–78, 81, 86, 94, 98, 104, 159
capitalism, 137, 144
Cappelletto, Francesca, 104
and Enzo Merler, 48
'care-activism', 88, 153
Carlos, 81–82, 90–98
Carrefour (shopping centre), 36
'Carta de Campinas', 131
carta de chamada, 54, 73n5. *See also* emigration
Casale Monferrato (city), 2–5, 9, 23, 25n1, 26–28, 30, 37, 40, 45, 50, 74, 79–80, 88, 94–96, 116, 125–28, 130, 141, 143–44, 158, 160–61
Castel Verde (ship), 54. *See also* emigration
Castells, Manuel, 138
Castleman, Barry, 142
catastrophe, 12, 15, 39. *See also* disaster
Cavagnolo (town), 25n1
Central Única dos Trabalhadores (CUT) [General Confederation of Workers], 126, 129
Centro de Referência em Saúde do Trabalhador – CEREST (Reference Centre for Occupational Health], 109–10, 118
Chernobyl (disaster), 10
Chico, 85–90, 98–99, 121
child labour, 53, 62
citizenship, 9, 13, 49, 95, 113–14, 121–22, 129, 133
Coassolo (town), 30
Cobrasma (firm), 7
coffee plantations, 50, 61, 63
Collegium Ramazzini Statements, 142
colonization, 63, 76, 151
compensation, 66–67, 86, 120, 122–24, 129, 131, 139, 142
Confederação Geral do Trabalho (CGT) [General Labour Confederation], 129
Confederação Nacional dos Trabalhadores na Indústria (CNTI) [National Confederation of Industrial Workers], 117
conscientização [elaboration of critical thinking], 8, 64–65
Cooperativa dos Vidreiros. *See under* Vidraria Santa Marina
Corio (town), 30
Crenshaw, Kimberle, 25n5
Cullinan, Paul, 39

danger, 11, 27–28, 42, 47, 147
asbestos dangers, 2, 8, 33, 37, 41–42, 45, 47–48, 57, 82, 87, 104, 108, 112, 115, 119, 123, 128, 133, 136
Da Silva, Luiz Inacio 'Lula', 131
De Cartier de Marchienne, Louis, 25n1, 40

'Declaration of Osasco', 130. *See also* asbestos prohibition
'Declaration of São Paulo', 129. *See also* asbestos prohibition
death, 12, 21, 27, 46, 82, 97–98, 101–2, 104, 122, 140, 144, 146
democratization, 69, 108, 111
Derrida, Jacques, 101–2
De Souza, Eliezer João, 35, 67, 100, 116, 125, 130, 157
Diadema (city), 131
disaster(s), 3, 5, 9–16, 18, 23, 27–29, 44, 46–47, 75–76, 80, 94–95, 98–99, 102–6, 109, 133, 152, 159, 161
  disaster experience(s), 13, 15, 28, 104, 106
  disaster survivors, 26
  environmental disaster manslaughter, 3, 25n1, 88
  epidemic disaster(s), 27, 46
  global health disasters(s), 5, 9, 26, 28, 39, 46, 75, 113, 135–36, 146, 148, 156, 161
  health disaster(s), 5, 24, 113, 135–36, 138, 140, 148
discrimination, 16, 152. *See also* racism
disease, 12–13, 16, 27, 46, 77, 82, 84, 88, 93, 98–99
  undiagnosed disease, 86, 109, 115
disparities, 152–53
displacement, 68, 152
Duralit Bolivie (firm), 33

'Earth Summit' (1992), 125
Eingetragene Genossenschaft Portland (firm), 32
Elisabete, 55
embodiment, 15–16
emigration
  across Brazil, 52
  from Europe to Brazil, 3–4, 54, 62, 73n5, 127
emotions, 13, 22
  emotional attachment, 45
  emotional bonds, 118
  emotional constraints, 21
  emotional difficulties, 112
  emotional support, 88, 94, 159
  emotional understanding, 20, 82
Emsens (family), 33
engagement, 2, 15, 21, 46, 70, 93, 98–99, 105, 122, 124, 129, 133, 137–39, 142, 145, 154
  civil engagement, 49, 65, 68
  emotional engagement, 15
  sociopolitical engagement, 6, 14, 159
environmental racism, 126, 134n2
epidemiology, 40, 108, 146
  cultural epidemiology, 146
  epidemiological data, 12, 40, 113, 129, 147
  epidemiological evidence, 11, 13, 74, 104, 108–9, 111, 113
  epidemiological surveillance, 77
  epidemiological survey(s), 113, 115–16, 136, 141
Época (magazine), 125
equity, 17, 69, 135, 141, 145, 147, 155
Eternit
  AG Berlin (firm), 33
  AG Niederurnen (firm), 32–33
  'bis' (trial), 25n1
  Colombia (firm), 33
  do Brasil Cimento e Amianto S.A. (firm), 4, 7, 31
  Ecuatoriana (firm), 33
  S.A. Brasil (firm), 31, 33, 41, 160
  SpA Genoa (firm), 33
  'trial', 3–5, 25n1, 40, 88
  Venezuela (firm), 33
ethnography, 19, 23–24, 40, 71–73, 104, 135, 137, 146, 148, 156, 159
  historiography and, 72–73
  multi-sited ethnography, 3, 28, 30, 74, 138, 148, 158
Eureka Mexico (firm), 33
European Parliament, 128
Everite Ltd. Johannesburg (firm), 33
exploitation, 8, 53, 62, 70, 76, 106, 126, 133, 151

falta de ar [shortness of breath], 45, 75, 78, 81, 83, 86

Farmer, Paul, 16, 135
Fassin, Didier, 16, 40, 71–72, 107, 111, 136, 143
fazenda [farm], 31
Fibronit (firm), 2
First World War, 50
Florianópolis (city), 18
focus groups, 19
Fonseca, Claudia, 23
Força Sindical [Union Force], 129
Ford (firm), 7
Frank, Arthur, 142
Fraser, Nancy, 137–39
Freire, Paulo, 7, 64, 116
Fundação Jorge Duprat Figueiredo de Segurança e Medicina do Trabalho (FUNDACENTRO) [Jorge Duprat Figueiredo Foundation of Safety and Occupational Health], 66, 109–10, 118, 129, 142
Fundação Oswaldo Cruz (FIOCRUZ) [Oswaldo Cruz Foundation], 142

genocide (black genocide), 152. *See also* racism, discrimination
Giannasi, Fernanda, 125–32
Goiânia (city), 18
Gramsci, Antonio, 65
Grief, 13, 24, 69, 75, 144
  grieving, 12, 102, 144–45, 159
Grupo Interinstitucional de Estudo de Trabalhadores Expostos ao Asbesto (GIETEA) [Interinstitutional Study Group of Asbestos-Exposed Workers], 110, 114–15
Gutiérrez, Gustavo, 63

Hahn, Robert A., 146
  and Marcia C. Inhorn, 146
Hatschek, Ludwig, 30
health
  global health, 40, 135–37, 140–41, 145–48, 155–56, 159
  health-based activism, 1, 6, 18, 24, 132, 136
  health hazards, 5, 11, 28, 40–41, 43, 46, 113, 141, 159–60
  health inequities, 141, 145
  occupational health, 6, 66, 77, 100, 108–10, 117, 124, 142, 161
  public health, 2, 4, 9, 13, 18, 37, 39, 46, 59, 84, 104, 107–12, 119, 124, 127, 131–32, 134, 136, 141–42, 145–48, 153, 155, 158–60
hegemony, 64. *See also* Gramsci
Herman, Patrick, 128–29
Hoffmann, Susanna, 12
  and Anthony Oliver-Smith, 12
Hofrichter, Richard, 25n2, 139, 144
Hondulit (firm), 33

Iacoviello, Francesco Mauro (prosecutor), 26
Ilha da Madeira (island), 54
Indústria de Artefatos de Ferro Cimaf (firm), 7
Indústria Eléctrica Brown Boveri S.A. (firm), 7
industrialization, 49, 52, 60, 62–63, 71
inequality, 5, 16, 136, 140, 149
Inhorn, Marcia C., 146
injustice, 5, 16, 69, 97–98, 101, 107, 114, 119, 133, 135, 138, 154
Instituto do Coração-InCor/Hospital das Clínicas, Faculdade de Medicina, Universidade de São Paulo (HCFMUSP) [Cardiology Institute/'Das Clínicas' Hospital, Faculty of Medicine, University of São Paulo], 110
International Ban Asbestos Secretariat (IBAS), 129
intersectionality, 25n5. *See also* Crenshaw
Irene, 80–82, 98
Isochimica (firm), 10
Istituto Superiore di Sanità [Superior Institute of Health], 110, 142

João, 76–78, 98, 114–15
justice, 26–28, 59, 97, 101, 121, 123, 126, 131–32, 137–40

environmental justice, 25n2, 133n2, 137, 160
social justice, 6, 13, 24, 25n2, 25n5, 63, 65, 69, 74, 119, 126, 134, 136, 139–42, 144, 155, 158, 161

Kilometre 16 (neighbourhood), 50
Kilometre 18 (neighbourhood), 85
kit-morte [death-kit], 86–87
Kleinman, Arthur, 104–5, 143
knowledge
biomedical knowledge, 12–13, 41, 111, 128, 132, 159
embodied knowledge, 133, 161
emotional knowledge, 22
experiential knowledge, 46–47, 106, 133
relational knowledge, 22, 158
theoretical knowledge, 47

L'Unità (newspaper), 30
Leandro, 35, 55–56, 113
'Lei Áurea' [Golden Law]. *See under* Lei Imperial
'Lei do Ventre Livre' [Law of Free Belly], 73n1. *See also* slavery
'Lei Imperial' [Imperial Law], 73n1. *See also* slavery
Leticia, 76–78, 98, 114–15
Liberation Theology (LT), 7, 62–63, 69, 116, 140
Ligi, Gianluca, 10
Lima Leivas, Luciano, 5
Lonaflex (firm), 66
Londrina (city), 18
Ltda Divisão Brasilit (firm), 31
Lucas, 53–55
lung(s), 1, 10, 21, 29, 31, 45–46, 77–78, 81, 83, 86–88, 92–93, 108–10, 114–16
lung cancer, 39, 42, 76, 79, 112, 114
lung nodule, 130
lung specialist(s), 18, 112, 141
Luz (station), 57–58
Lyon (city), 41

Magnani, Corrado, 141
malignant mesothelioma (MM), 1, 12, 27, 75, 80, 83, 141
Manchester, School of, 73n4
Marcia, 80
Martins, Marcos, 116, 118–19, 125
Medellín (conference), 70
memory, 12, 14–15, 23, 27, 62, 72, 84, 99, 101–2, 105–6, 107, 113, 121, 158
'collective memory', 100, 109, 133
militant memory, 114, 121
narrative memory, 105
Merleau-Ponty, Maurice, 107
Milan (city), 126, 128
military dictatorship, 7–8, 63–65, 68–69
Minaçu (mine), 31–32, 160
mining
industry, 31–32
village, 10
Ministério Publico do Trabalho (MPT) [Public Ministry of Labour], 5, 66, 123, 131
Ministry of Labour, 109, 127
Morumbi (neighbourhood), 36
mourning, 26, 82, 101
movement(s)
anti-asbestos movement, 5, 18, 40, 96, 105, 119, 127–29, 137, 141, 155, 160
'embodied health social movements', 13
environment-based movement, 160
grassroots movement, 4–6, 13, 15, 46, 97, 117–18, 132, 154, 161
health-based movement, 160
student movement, 8
transnational movement, 6, 71, 132, 136 139, 158
Museo da Imigração [Museum of Immigration], 73n5

Neuss, Congress of, 40–41
Nicalit Nicaragua (firm), 33

Oliver-Smith, Anthony, 10

'os autonomistas' (party), 6
Osram (firm), 7

Paris (city), 96
Parkhill, Karen A., 47
participant observation, 19, 104
Partido dos Trabalhadores (PT) [Workers' Party], 116, 120, 131
Paula, 37–38, 57–59
Pedro, 82–84, 98
Pesce, Bruno, 127–28
phenomenological approach, 12, 14, 22, 47, 73
photography, 22
Piedmont (region), 2–3, 30, 50–51, 127
Pigg, Stacy Leigh, 19, 147
Pinheiros (station), 150
Pires de Freitas, Jefferson Benedito, 141
pleural plaques, 21, 42, 45, 83, 85–86, 104, 110, 112, 114–15, 142
Pliny, The Elder, 30
Poções (city), 18, 31
Polo, Marco, 29
Pont-à-Mousson (firm), 31
Porto Alegre (city), 130
poverty, 7, 16, 52–53, 63–64, 68, 76, 140, 147, 152–53
Praça Aquilino dos Santos – Vítima do Amianto [Asbestos Victim Square], 100, 103, 150
Praça da Sé [Sé Square], 73n2, 85
Praça do Samba [Samba Square], 85
Presidente Altino (station), 157
pulmonary emphysema, 115
Putnam, Robert D., 133n1

Quebec (province), 31

racism, 16, 73n6, 141
Recife (city), 153
recognition, 2, 9–10, 14, 23, 98, 107, 114, 119–20, 136, 138, 161
Rede Nacional de Atenção Integral à Saúde do Trabalhador (RENAST), Regional Osasco [National Network of Comprehensive Care of Occupational Health, Osasco Region], 110
Rede Virtual-Cidadã pelo Banimento do Amianto na América Latina [Virtual Civil Network for Asbestos Prohibition in Latin America], 129
resistance, 7–8, 13–14, 17–18, 63–64, 68, 106, 108, 133, 140, 144
Rheintalische Cementfabrik Rüthi AG (firm), 32
Ribeiro Corossacz, Valeria, 73n6
Ricalit (firm), 33
Ricardo, 37–38, 57–59
rights
  health rights, 120, 136, 139, 144
  social rights, 9, 68
'Rio 1992', 126. *See also* 'Earth Summit' (1992)
Rio de Janeiro (city), 4, 18, 53, 82, 85, 109, 125, 153
risk
  awareness, 28, 46–47
  category, 11, 42, 46–47
  communication, 33, 46
  denial, 28
  double standard management of, 5
  perception, 38, 46, 48
Roberto, 80–81, 94–96, 98
roça [rural area], 52, 54–56, 67, 71, 80, 95
Rome (city), 4–5, 26–27, 46, 110, 130
Rossoni, Edmondo, 61. *See also* anarchism
Rowland, Christopher, 63
Rubiera (city), 25n1

Saint Gobain do Brasil (firm), 31
Salazar regime, 54
Salvador (city), 18
Sangallese valley of Reno, 32
Santista (firm), 36
Santo André (city), 18
Santos (seaport), 54
Santos, Milton, 52

São Bernardo do Campo (city), 131
São Caetano (city), 18, 66
São Felix (mine), 31–32
Saudi Arabian Amiantit Co. Ltd. Dammam (firm), 33
Scheper-Hughes, Nancy, 133, 143, 148–49, 156, 158
Schmidheiny
  Ernst, 32
  family, 32–3
  Jacob, 32
  Stephan, 5, 25n1, 26, 40–42
Second World War, 7
  post-Second World War, 4
Sen, Amartya, 147
Sensaud de Lavaud, Barão, 50
shanty towns, 63, 70, 152
Sistema Único de Saúde (SUS) [Unified Health System], 111
slave trade. *See under* slavery
slavery, 50, 60–61, 63, 73n1
'social capital', 108, 133n1
socialism, 61
  socialist ideals, 60–61
Societé Associé d'Industries Amianteciment (SAIAC) [Associated Society of Asbestos-Cement Industries], 33, 41
Sorocabana (station), 50
Strabo, 29
Strasbourg (city), 128
Straub, Herman, 41
strike(s), 8, 49, 60–62, 64, 68
'sufferer-activists', 23, 25n5, 75, 104, 114, 144
suffering (experience), 15, 74, 103, 106, 160
Supremo Tribunal Federal (STF) [Federal Supreme Court], 32, 160–61
Suri, Arjun, 140

Tecno Plásticos (firm), 33
Teodoro Sampaio (station), 85
Teodoro, 34–36, 100
Terracini, Benedetto, 141
Tubovinil (firm), 33
Turin, Court of, 25n1, 26

underdiagnosis, 39, 94, 127
union, 8, 60–62, 69, 124
  metallurgic union, 6, 8
  metalworkers union, 131
  union organizations, 42, 60, 128–29
University of São Paulo (USP), 22, 64, 90, 110
urbanization, 49, 52–53, 62–63, 71

Vargas Era, 52
Vidraria Santa Marina, 61–62
Vila Lobos-Jaguaré (station), 157
Vila Nova (neighbourhood), 100
Vila Yolanda (neighbourhood), 67–68
violence, 5, 16, 27, 46, 97–98, 101, 118, 140, 144, 149, 151–54, 158
  structural violence, 16, 135, 139, 144
vulnerability, 10, 45, 64–65, 89, 109, 122, 138, 152, 160

Wacquant, Loïc, 153
Waldman, Linda, 10
Walmart (shopping centre), 36, 127
Wilkinson, Iain, 105
  and Arthur Kleinman, 105
Wittenoom (mine), 48
worker-priests, 62–64, 67–69, 70–71
working-class
  working-class awareness, 60–61
  working-class identity, 62
  working-class neighbourhood(s), 63, 67–68, 152
  working-class struggles, 7, 60, 62, 126
workplace(s), 6, 29, 39, 44–45, 76, 109, 126, 133n2, 141
'World Social Forum', 130

Zampolin Coelho, Maria Inêz, 53
  and Helio Marcos Moreti, 53
Zhang, Everett Yuehong, 101

CPSIA information can be obtained
at www.ICGtesting.com
Printed in the USA
LVHW051732280121
677758LV00006B/162

9 781789 209310